HARVARD THEOLOGICAL REVIEW
HARVARD DISSERTATIONS IN RELIGION

edited by
Caroline Bynum
and
George Rupp

Number 5

POPULATION GROWTH AND JUSTICE:
AN EXAMINATION OF MORAL ISSUES
RAISED BY RAPID POPULATION GROWTH

by
Ronald Michael Green

SCHOLARS PRESS
Missoula, Montana

POPULATION GROWTH AND JUSTICE:
AN EXAMINATION OF MORAL ISSUES
RAISED BY RAPID POPULATION GROWTH

by

Ronald Michael Green

Published by
SCHOLARS PRESS
for
Harvard Theological Review

Distributed by

SCHOLARS PRESS
University of Montana
Missoula, Montana 59812

POPULATION GROWTH AND JUSTICE: AN EXAMINATION OF MORAL ISSUES RAISED BY RAPID POPULATION GROWTH

by

Ronald Michael Green

Library of Congress Cataloging in Publication Data

Green, Ronald Michael.
  Population growth and justice.

  (Harvard dissertations in religion ; no. 5)
  Originally presented as the author's thesis, Harvard.
  Bibliography: p.
  1. Population—Moral and religious aspects.
2. Birth control—Religious aspects. I. Title.
II. Series.
HQ766.2.G73 1975   261.8'3   76-44233
ISBN 0-89130-099-6

Printed in the United States of America

Edwards Brothers, Inc.
Ann Arbor, Michigan 48104

TABLE OF CONTENTS

To my beloved wife,

Mary Jean

ACKNOWLEDGEMENTS

I wish to express my gratitude to the Danforth Foundation,and, in particular, to the staff of the Kent Fellowship program for the assistance they have given me over the course of my graduate career. Throughout what has become a long association, members of the Foundation have been an unfailing source of cooperation and support.

I owe a great debt of thanks to Professor James Luther Adams. His passionate concern for social justice, combined with a commitment to disciplined moral reflection, furnish a model to which my own work seeks to conform. A similar debt is owed to Professor John Rawls. His lectures were a high point of my academic career and served to illuminate the rational basis for what, until then, had been only deeply held opinion.

Finally, I must thank Professor Arthur J. Dyck. His criticisms of drafts of the thesis and his comments served constantly to guide my work. If I can say that this thesis has been an educational experience, Professor Dyck is largely responsible for that.

Hanover, New Hampshire
July 16, 1975

Introduction

Rapid population growth is widely considered one of the major threats to human well-being today. In an era when new reasons for worry abound and when each new problem receives transitory renown, population growth has continually commanded a measure of attention. In view of this, one would think that the nature of the population problem would be well understood. While disagreement over the gravity of the problem might be expected, and while different courses to its solution might be advanced, one would at least expect there to be some consensus over the basic question of why population growth is a source of moral concern. But in fact this is not the case. Among those who are convinced of the existence of a population problem there is broad disagreement concerning the nature of the evils threatened by population growth. In some cases, apparent agreement on the seriousness of the population problem dissolves when it is asked why population growth is of concern. Values cherished by those holding one view of the problem may be of marginal interest to those with a different view.

This disagreement over the nature of the problem is sharpened by those thinkers who deny that there is any such thing as a population problem at all.. This view has been taken for some time by many Roman Catholic and Marxist theorists, and it is shared today by some "New Left" and minority group spokesmen. Occasionally, this viewpoint has been interpreted simply as a denial of the present seriousness of the popula-tion problem. But in fact, this denial seems to cut more deeply than that. In saying that there is no such thing as a population problem, some Catholics and Marxists have questioned whether rapid population growth should be thought of as a cause of evils at all. And they have even suggested that population growth may be a beneficial phenomenon.

1

The purpose of this thesis is to sort out this dispute. My aim is to learn why population growth has been viewed as a threat to cherished values, and whether it ought to be considered so. In other words, I am after a fundamental understanding of the nature of what has been called the population problem. I am not concerned with the question of how serious this problem is, since I wish to determine whether there is a problem at all. Nor am I primarily interested in proposing policies for handling population growth. Of course, to the degree that any clarification of a moral problem aids in its solution, my efforts have policy implications. And I shall not hesitate to spell these out. But my focus from beginning to end is on the nature of what is called the population problem. I seek to determine whether and why rapid population growth poses a moral problem.

The thesis itself is divided into two parts. In the first and shorter part, I proceed inductively, examining various efforts to answer the questions of whether and why population growth poses a moral problem. Initially, I explore those views which affirm the existence of a population problem, and I seek to distinguish the values which growth is believed to threaten. Following this I look at the views of those who deny that population growth need be a source of moral concern. In the second part of the thesis I proceed in a more deductive fashion. Here I employ a moral theory, John Rawls's contract view of justice, to work out a fresh understanding of the moral issues raised by population growth. This second approach is necessitated by the sharp, and in some cases, ultimate disagreements on the moral significance of population growth that are revealed by my initial survey of views.

Much of the debate we will be looking at in the first part of the thesis revolves around the question of whether population growth poses or does not pose a moral problem. To understand this first part, therefore, it is useful to have in mind some conception of what it means to say that an event or pattern of behavior "poses a moral problem." In ordinary discourse, we frequently employ this phrase, yet there is little clarity concerning its meaning. The following paradigm is offered as an explanation of the phrase: to say that an event or pattern of behavior poses a moral problem is to say that it

is a significant cause of evils for moral agents; it is also to
say that it is a cause subject to the control of moral agents
and one that ought to be controlled. Thus, five conditions or
requirements must be fulfilled for something to pose a moral
problem: it must (1) significantly cause (2) evils (3) for
moral agents; it must be (4) subject to control, and it (5)
ought to be controlled. When any of these five conditions is
lacking, we do not say of a phenomenon that it poses a moral
problem. Events clearly beyond human control, for example,
such as earthquake or flood are not commonly considered to pose
a moral problem in themselves. Phenomena associated with evils
but not significantly the cause of those evils are not considered to pose a moral problem. The infectious diseases to
which drug addicts are exposed are evils and bring evils in
their train. But we do not generally say of these diseases
that they pose a moral problem. We seem to prefer to reserve
this phrase for the drug addiction which is the significant
cause of disease and other evils. Nor do we consider a
phenomenon to pose a moral problem when it does not inflict
evils on moral agents, or when it bestows goods on them.
Events in nature which destroy excess populations of insect
pests exemplify both these situations.

Disagreement on any one of these points can lead people
to differ on the final item of this paradigm, the question of
whether something ought to be subject to control. Of course,
with respect to a particular event individuals can agree on
most of these points and still differ over whether it ought to
be subject to control. Some writers have interpreted the
population debate this way, seeing the dispute over whether
there is or is not a population problem simply as one over
whether the demographic variable ought to be manipulated in
order to eliminate observable evils.[1] The difficulty in conceptualizing the dispute this way, however, is that it can lead
to neglect of some of the more fundamental differences that

---

[1]See, for example, Ralph B. Potter, "The Simple Struc-
ture of the Population Debate: The Logic of the Ecology
Movement," Documentary Study prepared for the Commission on
Population Growth and the American Future (Hastings-on-Hudson,
N.Y.: Institute of Society, Ethics and the Life Sciences,
1971), p. 4.

produce these divergent moral recommendations. In some cases, differences begin over other items in our paradigm, as when Marxist thinkers deny that population growth is in any way a significant cause of observable social evils, or when, in conjunction with Roman Catholic thinkers, they affirm population growth to be primarily a source of goods.

My effort in the first part of the thesis is to apply this paradigm to different moral estimations of population growth in an effort to learn why some consider it to pose a moral problem and some do not. I have anticipated the results of this survey by suggesting that there is disagreement on virtually every point of this paradigm. More important than this, however, is the discovery that much of this dispute originates in conflict over one central question: how the various goods and evils associated with rapid population growth are to be distributed. That growth brings about both goods and evils becomes readily clear when one considers that, if nothing else, the unrestrained fertility associated with growth is esteemed as good by many persons. The question, then, of whether growth ought to be controlled is very much a function of one's distributive preferences. Those who on moral grounds favor individuals, groups or classes that suffer evil as a result of population growth will tend to affirm that high fertility poses a moral problem, although they may differ on why this is so, depending upon the group or groups whose interests they consider morally important. On the other hand, those who are morally committed to the welfare of persons advantaged by continued high fertility will tend to deny that population growth poses a problem. They may be led to see growth as a cause of goods and they may seek to deny that obvious social evils are in any way caused by high fertility itself. Indeed, their very distributive preferences may shape their understanding of the way the pattern of goods and evils associated with a given social order is to be interpreted.

Viewed in this way the debate over the nature of the population problem and over whether there is such a thing as the population problem is a dispute over justice. It is a dispute over how basic rights and responsibilities, values and disvalues are to be distributed in a social order. And it is a dispute over which individuals or groups validly command

moral respect in cases of social conflict. As such, the resolution of this dispute depends upon a prior determination of
how a society is to be justly regulated. Such a determination
is needed to establish the basic moral context in which consideration of any specific distributive issue like population
is to take place. And the moral perspective which yields this
determination is needed to furnish the mechanism by which the
specific issue of population growth can be considered and
resolved. This further explains my resort in the second part
of the thesis to a theory of justice. Having examined the
views of those who affirm and deny the existence of a population problem, my effort there is to bring some order to the
dispute, and to do so in a way that can command assent from all
parties to the conflict. In saying this, however, I run well
ahead of myself. For the moment the task ahead is to examine
differing moral estimates of population growth and to clarify
the varying distributive preferences and moral assumptions on
which these estimates rest.

Part I

Moral Assessments of Population Growth:

Is There A 'Population Problem' and, If So, Why?

8

A. *Views Affirming that Population Poses a Moral Problem*

Views affirming that population poses a moral problem and that there is such a thing as a "population problem" abound in popular and scholarly literature. My aim in the following section is to gather together the more important of these views in order to examine their factual and moral assumptions. Each of these views rests on the belief that population growth meets the five conditions in our paradigm of what it means to say that something poses a moral problem. What most visibly distinguishes these views from one another is the evil which they believe population growth to bring about.

In the course of the population debate each of these views has sometimes been advanced as the most adequate way of understanding the population problem. It is important to note this. In some recent discussions of population growth it has become common to refer to these various emphases as "parts" of a larger population problem.[1] That may be true. But this way of approaching these views ignores the fact that those who have advanced them have frequently esteemed their perspective as the most significant way of comprehending the population problem. Unless this is understood, some of the intense argumentation associated with these views becomes meaningless and whole lines of discussion within the population debate do not make sense. The individual who views high fertility as of concern because of its impact on vital resources, for example, is likely to be agitated by quite different data than the individual concerned with the impact of population growth on aesthetic experience. Furthermore, unless each of these views is approached as the comprehensive assessment of the problem it has sometimes been taken to be, a critical process of value selection and value weighting is also obscured. The claim that there is one most appropriate way of assessing the problem of

---

[1]Bernard Berelson, for example, maintains that there are "several problems" deriving from population factors, but he reveals his own central concern by maintaining that "perhaps the main one is that of undue population growth in the developing countries." --*Family-Planning Programs; An International Survey*, ed. Bernard Berelson. (New York: Basic Books, 1969) p. 291.

population involves the belief that one or another of several values imperiled by growth is of consummate importance. Those who conceive the population problem in terms of the meaning of high fertility for the welfare of individual families, for example, may well possess different value priorities than those who are concerned with the effect of growth on economic development. In approaching these views in the way they have been advanced, as comprehensive perceptions of the problem, we thus make this process of value selection explicit.

1. The Family-Planning View

When it is not employed merely as a euphemism for contraception, the term "family planning" has come to be identified with a specific set of policies aimed at easing the population problem. This problem is commonly perceived in broad social terms--as, for example, the pressure of population on scarce resources, or high fertility's hindrance of economic development--and family planning is viewed as a means of reducing birth rates by assisting and encouraging individual couples voluntarily to limit their family size.

Though family planning has become identified with one policy for solving the population problem, the concept of family planning has also encompassed a particular view of the population problem. Indeed, at times this has been a dominant view of the problem. In the course of its use, in other words, family planning has sometimes served as as a significant answer to at least two questions raised by our paradigm: what is the evil produced by rapid population growth and upon which moral agents is that evil inflicted?

The family-planning answers to these questions direct attention to the meaning of high fertility for the individual family unit. Extrapolating from particular expressions, I can state this view as follows: Rapid population growth within any social group must be understood as reflective or symptomatic of difficulties within individual families. The social evils of high fertility, while serious in their own right, are a consequence of more basic evils within the family. Where large

families proliferate amidst poverty, illiteracy and disease,
couples may be assumed to be out of control of their sexual
capacity. Either because they have been deprived of the
knowledge or means, couples are victims of their own sexuality.

All other evils associated with high fertility flow
from this lack of control on the part of the couple. Within
the family high fertility leads to elevated infant and maternal
death rates; frequent conceptions result in excessive resort to
abortion or the advent of unwanted, and subsequently neglected
children; constant childbearing eliminates the wife's opportunity for self-development and leads to a deterioration of the
husband-wife relationship because of the economic and emotional
burdens it imposes. Outside the family, the couple's lack of
freedom to control their sexuality expresses itself in an
erosion of the quality of community life. Some of this results
from the sheer increase in numbers. But most observable social
evil is caused directly by evils within the family unit. Thus,
the strife and social deviance characteristic of many poor,
densely populated communities are largely attributed to the
family's failure to perform its function as the primary agency
of socialization and nurture. In this respect, high fertility
is above all else a problem for the family. The family is at
once the primary source and recipient of the evils produced by
population growth. Implicit within this view, moreover, is
the confidence that solving the family's problem--by facilitating married couples' free, rational choice in sexual matters--
is also likely to resolve the most pressing difficulties
generated by population growth on the social level.[2]

In some instances, this general family-planning perspective has joined with or been supplemented by other views of
the population problem. As we shall see, it has even achieved

---

[2]Expressions of this view are common in the family-planning
literature. See the bibliography, Section C. For one recent
and explicit statement of this view see Mary S. Calderone,
"What I Do DOES Matter," *Harvard Medical Alumni Bulletin*,
XLI (Spring 1967), 22f. Also her article, "Family Planning,"
in *Foundations for Christian Family Policy*, ed. E. S. Gennie
(New York: National Council of Churches of Christ in the
U.S.A., 1961), pp. 191-99.

some acceptance within Catholic and Marxist thought, where the
existence of a population problem is otherwise denied. But in
addition to this partial acceptance, the family-planning view
has had a history in its own right as a dominant mode of
appreciating the difficulties generated by high fertility.
Elements of the family-planning view are found in the work of
Malthus, although they are submerged by his primary focus on
the catastrophic social consequences of increasing population.[3]
However, during the nineteenth century, as the Malthusian preoccupation with famine faded from attention, the measure of
concern for the family already implicit in his work came to the
fore. D. V. Glass notes that after 1870 the English birth control movement became disinterested in debating the population-
resources issue. Instead, birth control came to be viewed as
"beneficial *in itself*," that is, for its direct value to the
married couple.[4] "Neo-malthusianism" thus differs from Malthus' thinking not only in stressing the legitimacy of artificial
birth control, but also in its fundamental understanding of the
population problem. The "Neo-malthusian" perspective essentially
expresses a family-planning view of the population problem.

This sort of attention to the familial consequences of
high fertility largely characterized the active birth control
movement that developed in this country and Europe during the
opening decades of this century. Birth control came to be
viewed, within a medical framework, as part of a total program
of maternal and child care. Particular attention was given to
extending contraceptive services to the poorer sections of the
community. The lower-income female, ignorant of contraception,
came to be viewed as the chief victim of unchecked fertility.
The title of a collection of letters by Margaret Sanger,

---

[3]In later editions of his *Essay on the Principle of
Population* Malthus occasionally expresses concern for the
familial or household effects of high fertility. See his
remarks in the 7th edition (1882) reprinted in *On Population*,
ed. Gertrude Himmelfarb (New York: The Modern Library, 1960),
pp. 488ff., 492.

[4]*Introduction to Malthus* (New York: John Wiley & Sons,
1953), p. 82.

Motherhood in Bondage, aptly sums up the view.[5] It was with
this orientation, moreover, that birth control was first
exported to the less-developed nations. When high fertility
within the depressed communities and sub-groups of the industrialized nations was seen as resulting from families' lack of
reproductive freedom, it was natural that population growth in
poorer nations should be viewed the same way.[6]

During the period following the Second World War, the
precipitous decline of mortality in many of these nations and
their correspondingly high fertility rates rekindled the older
Malthusian concern with the extra-familial implications of
population growth. Many of those who were concerned with the
population problem of the less-developed nations came to conceive this problem in terms of the pressure of population
against scarce vital resources, and particularly food supplies.
Nevertheless, "family planning" lingered on as a policy to
reduce birth rates, and in many cases, it continued to function,
whether consciously or unconsciously, as an understanding of
the population problem itself.

A 1967 article by Kingsley Davis entitled "Population
Policy: Will Current Programs Succeed?" marks a clear end of
the period of dominancy of the family-planning view and represents a lucid expression of the extra-familial focus that comes
to replace it.[7] Davis' aim in this article is to evaluate

---

[5]New York: Brentano's, 1928. For a brief history of
the family-planning movement in Europe and England see D. V.
Glass, "Family Limitation in Europe: A Survey of Recent
Studies," in *Research in Family Planning*, ed. Clyde V. Kiser
(Princeton, N.J.: Princeton University Press, 1962), pp.
231-61. David M. Kennedy's *Birth Control in America* (New
Haven: Yale University Press, 1970) is the best introduction
to the life and work of Margaret Sanger as well as to the
assumptions that motivated her and other members of the
American family-planning movement.

[6]R. A. Gopalaswami refers to an "orthodox school" of
Indian family-planning experts who vehemently opposed programs
aimed simply at the reduction of birth rates rather than at the
facilitation of sexual freedom and responsibility for individual
couples. See his article, "Family Planning: Outlook for Government Action in India," in *Research in Family Planning*, ed. Clyde
V. Kiser, pp. 71ff.

[7]*Science*, CLVIII (November 10, 1967), 730-39.

family-planning programs in the underdeveloped nations. He is
ostensibly concerned with questions of policy and deliberately
bypasses any discussion of the nature of the population problem (or "population crisis" as he terms it). Nevertheless,
Davis' criticism of family planning really amounts to a sub-
ordination or repudiation of some of the values and concerns
central to the family-planning view. Thus, Davis is particularly disturbed by what he calls the distinct "goal peculiari-
ties" of the family-planning movement. These goals include the
protection of the family and the facilitation of a couple's
choice in reproductive matters.[8] The problem with these goals,
in Davis' view, is that they are essentially private and
abstracted from concern with community values. Even if family
planning proves entirely successful, he maintains, social
values may be jeopardized:

> "Family *planning*" and "fertility control" suggest
> that reproduction is being regulated according to
> some rational plan. And so it is, but only from
> the standpoint of the individual couple, not from
> that of the community. What is rational in the
> light of a couple's situation may be totally
> irrational from the standpoint of a society's
> welfare.[9]

Davis here not only distinguishes between the social and
familial consequences of reproductive behavior, but he questions
the confidence of family planning advocates that a solution to
problems at the family level would necessarily eliminate the
social evils accompanying rapid population growth. Even if
couples were freed from all the unwanted and unintended consequences of their sexual relations, Davis maintains, social
problems caused by growth would remain. The congestion and
environmental problems of the industrialized nations and their
frantic efforts to keep production ahead of population illustrate
this point, Davis maintains, since it is in these nations that
family planning has been most successful.[10] Thus, family
planning may not only lead to a neglect of the larger social

---

[8]*Ibid.*, pp. 732, 734.

[9]*Ibid.*, p. 737.

[10]*Ibid.*, p. 732.

implications of high fertility, but it can obscure the fact
that family welfare and social welfare are often quite
opposed.

Driving a wedge between the family values central to
the family planning view and the social values Davis believes
threatened by generally high fertility, he finally points up
the value choice involved in adopting one view of the problem
or the other. Continued attention to the family may further
jeopardize social values. On the other hand, a commitment to
lowering fertility rates may necessitate downgrading or
eliminating some traditionally cherished family values. The
encouragement of extensive female employment outside the home
is an example. Here, says Davis, the aims of population control and family planning may be quite divergent.[11] The direction one chooses depends upon whether one considers family
autonomy and traditional family values of more pressing concern
than some of the social values imperiled by high fertility.

The immediate effect of Davis' critique was to awaken
those active in the family-planning movement to the assumptions
and implicit moral priorities with which they had been working.
Not surprisingly, few voices were raised to challenge Davis'
estimate of the population problem since, in the period following the Second World War, many proponents of family planning
for the underdeveloped nations have been concerned with the
larger social consequences of population growth. They had, in
effect, already abandoned an exclusive family-planning view of
the problem.[12]

A further result of Davis' criticism was to shift
attention to family planning, no longer as a view of the
population problem, but as a strategy or policy for population
control. In a reply to Davis, for example, Bernard Berelson
concedes that high fertility involves issues that transcend
the immediate liberty and welfare of families. But he

[11]*Ibid.*, pp. 731f.

[12]Use of the phrase "family planning and population
control" in many recent treatments of the population problem
reveals the larger concern of family-planning proponents.

challenges Davis or others to advance policies that can
achieve the agreed upon aim of fertility reduction as well.
By facilitating the free choice of couples in their reproductive
behavior, Berelson maintains, birth rates can be lowered with
the least amount of difficulty and with minimum disruption of
social and moral values.[13] Among the moral values which
Berelson has in mind are those of individual and familial
liberty in the reproductive sphere. Apart from the question of
efficacy, Berelson would champion a family-planning approach
because he sees these and other values as of at least as pressing concern as some of the extra-familial evils imposed by high
fertility. Thus, even when they take the form of a policy
recommendation, the values, priorities and perceptions that
traditionally enter into the family-planning view of the problem linger on in Berelson's position.

We should not be surprised at this. The idea of family
planning is more than a policy for handling the population
problem. It is and has been, first of all, an understanding
and interpretation of that problem. When asked why high fertility is a source of concern, proponents of family planning
have traditionally turned their initial attention to the family.
They have been concerned with the effect of uncontrolled
fertility on the family, and they have championed the reproductive freedom of husbands and wives. As a consequence, they
have also been less concerned with the extra-familial implications of growth. We should not be surprised that a criticism
like Davis' of the family-planning approach should not easily
change the position of its staunch defenders, for the discussion does not rest on a neutral ground of inquiry into which
technique is most suitable to reaching agreed upon values.
Rather, there is the question of which values and whose values
are to be defended and advanced. The family planning movement
has traditionally championed the liberty of couples to make
decisions in the sexual sphere. Those who define the population

---

[13]*Family Planning Programs*, p. 294. See also Berelson's extensive defense of family planning policies in "Beyond
Family Planning," *Science*, CLXIII (February 7, 1969), 533-43.

problem in different terms assume the existence and priority
of other values and interests than those immediately possessed
by families.

2. *Crisis Views*

Among those views which see population growth as a
threat to values and persons outside the bounds of the family
there are a set of positions which in their structure form a
common perspective. Together, we may call these the "crisis"
view of the population problem. Common to those who share this
view is the belief that high fertility is presently forcing
mankind, or very large segments of mankind, into a series of
catastrophes whose occurrence will precipitate widespread loss
of human life and an unparalleled measure of privation and
suffering. Some consider the survival of the human race or
life on earth to be in jeopardy.

This perspective clearly has its origin in the work of
Malthus. What Malthus termed the "positive checks" to population growth, the checks of famine, pestilence and war, largely
make up the range of events which today preoccupy crisis
thinkers. Malthus, of course, did not initially view population growth as a problem even though it threatened to inflict
these evils on mankind. As Thomas Sowell has noted, Malthus
at first viewed population growth as a brute fact of life and
not something controllable by men.[14] Only in his later writing,
when he came to concede the possibility of the preventive
check of "moral restraint" did Malthus presage the crisis view
of the problem.

If this perspective can be traced back to Malthus, it
has nevertheless enjoyed its greatest vigor and diffusion in
the decades since the Second World War. The rapid and externally induced declines in mortality in the underdeveloped
nations during this period set the stage for the re-emergence

---

[14]"Malthus and the Utilitarians," *Canadian Journal of
Economics and Political Science*, XXVIII (May 1962), 268-74.

of the crisis view after preceding decades of optimism about
man's ability to outproduce population growth. Since the war
a number of discussions have appeared treating the population
problem in crisis terms. Most of the best-selling contributions
to the population debate have been crisis oriented: the
writings of William Vogt, Julian Huxley, Harrison Brown, Marston
Bates, Sir Charles Darwin, Georg Borgstrom, William and Paul
Paddock, Paul Ehrlich and C. P. Snow are representative. But
in addition to the contributions of these figures, there
exists an extensive scholarly and popular literature in which
the crisis view finds expression.[15] From this literature we
can extrapolate the main lines of the crisis perspective.

The food issue appears to dominate these discussions.
While other issues, particularly the impact of growing numbers
of human beings on the earth's physical environment, have
attracted attention, it is food that has been the focal point
of debate. For many crisis writers, the growing population of
regions already unable to satisfy the minimum caloric requirements of their inhabitants threatens to plunge these regions
into famine. Some writers see famine merely as a possibility
in the near future; others argue that mass famines are an
unavoidable certainty.[16] In either case, they insist that
population limitation must begin immediately in order to forestall or at least minimize the effects of the disaster.
Efforts to cope with the food problem without immediately
halting population growth--such as by providing food aid out of
surplus stocks--are held likely only to postpone and magnify
the impending crisis.[17]

Some of the crisis-oriented writers confine their
attention to the prospect of exhausted food supplies and

---

[15] For a listing of these crisis-oriented writings see
the bibliography, Section D.

[16] Georg Borgstrom, in his *Too Many; A Study of the
Earth's Biological Limitations* (New York: Macmillan Co.,
1969), p. 319, argues that famine may be avoided. William
and Paul Paddock, in their *Famine--1975!* (Boston: Little,
Brown & Company, 1967), p. 9, insist that famines are unavoidable.

[17] Sir Julian Huxley, *The Human Crisis* (Seattle:
University of Washington Press, 1963), p. 70.

agricultural capacity. But for many of these writers, famine
is only the first event in an ever-widening series of catastrophes that threaten finally to jeopardize the survival of
all mankind. The scenarios differ in detail but follow a common
pattern: faced with the prospect of death by starvation or
disease, it is maintained, the masses in the underdeveloped
lands would be unlikely to accept their fate meekly. Severe
privation would lead to political turmoil and this might
eventuate in a series of totalitarian or militarily aggressive
regimes. These regimes, in turn, might precipitate conflicts
which could embroil the developed nations and total nuclear war
might ensue. If mankind were not exterminated in the holocaust,
no civilization as we know it would remain. Hundreds of
millions would perish and those who survive would, at best, live
on in the hand-to-mouth existence of pre-industrial culture.[18]

Apart from the extra measure of horror which nuclear
technology lends to this picture, the consequences of population growth are essentially those mentioned by Malthus:
famine, pestilence and war. Indeed, Malthus' assumptions and
his approach to the matter apparently dominate the thinking of
those who look upon rapid population growth in crisis terms.
There is, for example, the assumption of diminishing returns to
labor. While Malthus initially justified his bleak prophesies
by means of the differential progressions of food and population, he later came to see that the success of the argument
rested upon the assumption of diminishing returns to labor in
agriculture.[19] Each new pair of hands applied to the land
produces less than the pair before it until production falls
below the subsistence level. Modern crisis writers generally
follow Malthus in assuming diminishing returns to labor on
land as well as the present operation of diminishing returns
at or near the subsistence level on the farmland of many poorer
nations. These assumptions are reflected in the emphasis many

---

[18]Harrison Brown, *The Challenge of Man's Future* (New
York: The Viking Press, 1964), pp. 224f.

[19]*Principles of Political Economy* (London: W. Pickering, 1836), pp. 208-10.

of these writers place on measures and surveys of available agricultural land. Food production is viewed as a direct function of available cultivable land, and the food-crisis writers do not fail to indicate just how much of this land has already been exploited in the underdeveloped and densely populated nations.[20] Low agricultural productivity on this land is taken as a sign that diminishing returns are already operative and the exhaustion of new lands is interpreted to mean that returns beneath the subsistence level are a likely prospect in the near future.

A curious feature of many of the crisis writers' assessments of food prospects is their neglect of alternate interpretations of the agricultural conditions of the less-developed nations. Few writers, for example, openly question the assumption that additional labor applied to land in the under-developed setting cannot yield constant (or even increasing) returns. Few, as well, interpret the low agricultural productivity and poor nutrition evident in these areas as anything but evidence that returns are at or near the subsistence level. There are some exceptions to this general tendency. Occasionally a crisis writer may concede that the low productivity of the underdeveloped regions is the result of other factors, such as institutional arrangements or social practices that limit output. Thus, in one of the earliest crisis-oriented works, *Road to Survival*, William Vogt admits that agricultural productivity in many poorer nations is seriously hindered by institutions such as absentee landholding systems which depress the initiative and energy of poor farmers.[21] Nevertheless, when finally assessing the prospects of these

---

[20]Not even agricultural experts are immune to this tendency. In some of his earlier writings, Lester Brown focuses on land as the central issue. See his *Man, Land and Food*, Foreign Agricultural Economic Report II (Washington, D.C.: U.S. Department of Agriculture, 1963) and his article, "Population Growth and Per-Capita Food Output," in *Population Ethics*, ed. Francis X. Quinn (Washington, D.C.: Corpus Books, 1968), pp. 13-27. Brown seems clearly to have altered this approach in his most recent work, *Seeds of Change* (New York: Praeger Publishers, 1970).

[21]New York: William Sloane Associates, 1948, p. 155.

regions, Vogt entirely neglects to discuss the gains in productivity that might be effected by altering such institutions or practices, and he restates the prospects of the less-developed nations in terms of the limited land available to feed new mouths.[22] Fixed land divided by growing numbers of persons remains the central matter for Vogt and other crisis writers.

This treatment of food production prospects is one illustration of a characteristic common to all the crisis writers: their preoccupation with the population variable to the neglect of all other causal explanations of observable social evils. When treating malnutrition in the less developed regions, for example, these writers by-pass many of the factors contributing to food shortages that have been noted by more objective students of the problem, factors such as poor market conditions for agricultural products, farming practices that lower production, the effects of foreign food-aid programs and institutional hindrances to production.[23] It is indicative of these writers' approach, moreover, that they treated the transient food shortages of the mid-1960's as a premonition of the imminent food crisis induced by population growth.

A further illustration of this tendency to view complex situations as simple functions of population growth is the crisis writers' treatment of urbanization in both developed and under-developed nations. Commonly, these writers assume, but do not demonstrate, the existence of two causal links between the evils of contemporary urban life and population growth. First, they maintain that the increase of urban population is the source of environmental pollution in the cities, of inadequate public facilities, slum housing, widespread social

---

[22]*Ibid.*, p. 194.

[23]For a balanced interpretation of these shortages as well as of the food production prospects of the less-developed nations see Goran Ohlin, *Population Control and Economic Development* (Paris: Development Centre of the Organization for Economic Cooperation and Development, 1967), Ch. 3. Also, Willard W. Cochrane, *The World Food Problem; A Guardedly Optimistic View* (New York: Thomas Y. Crowell, 1969).

deviance and the like. Second, urban population growth is
linked unambiguously to population growth within society as a
whole.[24] Rarely is an effort made to determine whether urbanization would proceed even within a stationary or declining
population. Equally rare are sustained analyses of the breakdown of social services in many urban areas. Nevertheless,
by neglecting these matters crisis writers are able to connect
the difficulties of contemporary city life and "overpopulation."

Such neglect of other causes of social evils can be
chalked up to misunderstanding by these individuals. However,
the neglect is so systematic and persistent as to fuel the
suspicion that it results from a deliberate effort to focus
attention inescapably upon the population variable. Indeed,
when one examines the crisis literature with this suspicion in
mind, many of the arguments of these writers come to be seen as
aimed precisely at stimulating concern with the population
variable. This is the effect, for example, of the tendency to
reduce the question of food production to one of available
acreage. Once it is conceded that land is the significant
limiting factor, attention is thrust back upon population
growth, and birth limitation remains the only way of fending
off disaster.

It is true that some writers concede that productivity
can be increased by a variety of techniques on existing land
usable for agricultural purposes. But they commonly advance
other limiting factors which make this alternative of little
value. One such factor is time. Crisis is held to be so
imminent that no opportunity exists for putting these alternatives into effect.[25] Other writers employ different reasoning.
They concede that increased productivity is possible, even over

---

[24]See especially Paul Ehrlich, *The Population Bomb*
(New York: Ballantine Books, 1968), pp. 24, 26. Also Lincoln
Day, "The American Fertility Cult," in *The Population Crisis
and the Use of World Resources*, ed. Stuart Mudd (Bloomington,
Indiana: University of Indiana Press, 1964), pp. 231-38. And
Roy O. Greep, "Prevalence of People," *Perspectives in Biology
and Medicine*, XII (Spring 1969), 332.

[25]Karl Sax, *Standing Room Only; the World's Exploding
Population* (Boston: Beacon Press, 1960), p. xi.

the short run, but they insist that this increase carries a
political or social price as unacceptable in terms of human
welfare as starvation itself. Thus, Borgstrom argues that the
only way of increasing food production in the underdeveloped
countries is by imposing rigid controls over people through
a regime of forced labor. The price of avoiding starvation,
therefore, is slavery.[26]

A related argument from costs is unique to those
crisis-oriented writers concerned with the possibility of
environmental disaster. Not all biologists or ecologists view
population growth in crisis terms, and there are some who have
deliberately repudiated a crisis orientation.[27] But there are
writers for whom the impact of population on the natural
environment is of special concern and for whom it assumes
crisis proportions. These writers fear not merely a decline
in environmental quality, but the precipitous breakdown of
vital environmental systems. Ehrlich's description of "eco-
catastrophe" typifies this viewpoint.[28] Often this kind of
concern is independent of the issue of food crisis. But
frequently these different kinds of disaster are linked in
order to refute any claims that food production can be substantially increased. Thus, it is argued that the productivity
of agriculture can be increased only by the employment of
artificial aids, such as nitrate fertilizers or residual
pesticides. Eventually, however, these instrumentalities
threaten human survival by disordering vital environmental
systems. Should such aids be abandoned after being employed
to sustain growing populations, famine on an even greater
scale than before will ensue. However one tries to nourish
more persons, in other words, disaster must finally be faced.

The efforts made by crisis writers to focus attention
upon the population variable suggest that this is less a

---

[26]*Too Many*, p. 332.

[27]See, for example, Barry Commoner, *The Closing Circle*
(New York: Alfred A. Knopf, 1971).

[28]*Ramparts*, VIII (September 1969), 24-28. Also,
Lamont Cole, "Can the World Be Saved?" *New York Times Magazine*,
March 31, 1968.

scientific than an ideological position. Indeed, we can speak
of a "metaphysic of overpopulation" since the concept "overpopulation" seems to function for many of these writers more
as a means of approaching and arranging data than as the outcome of an impartial process of inquiry and investigation. It
thus becomes legitimate to ask why these writers are led to
view population growth in this way. Why are they so entranced
by the population variable and the calamities they attribute
to it? Part of the answer, of course, has to do with the fact
that most complex and distressing social evils involve the
existence of too many people for too few needed resources. In
this sense, virtually every major social evil is the result of
"overpopulation." Nevertheless, the attribution of any given
social evil to "overpopulation" may also be quite mistaken.
Excess population may have no significant causal relationship
to an evil, and reducing population may not cause an evil to go
away. If other factors are more directly related to an evil's
onslaught, its elimination may depend upon removing these
factors which are, properly speaking, its cause. Crisis
writers may thus simply be misled in their concentration on
population. They may fail to understand that not every social
evil should be owed to too many people, and they may not detect
the error in interpreting every pending catastrophe as a simple
function of growing population. Here a debt to Malthus is
evident, for it was Malthus who established the precedent of
interpreting all social evils in demographic terms. Having
elaborated a theoretical understanding according to which
population growth could produce catastrophe, Malthus insisted
on interpreting existing social evils in this light. He did
not hesitate, for example, to attribute the agricultural difficulties of England in his day to overpopulation, although he
was probably wrong in doing so.[29] This way of proceeding is

---

[29]For a discussion of Malthus' interpretation of
prevailing English agricultural conditions and for an assessment of his interpretation, see M. C. Buer, "The Historical
Setting of the Malthusian Controversy," in *London Essays in
Economics: In Honour of Edwin Cannan*, eds. T. E. Gregory and
Hugh Dalton (London: George Routledge & Sons, 1927), pp. 137-
53. Also, T. H. Marshall, "The Population of England and Wales
from the Industrial Revolution to the World War," *Economic
History Review*, V (1935), 65-78.

perhaps one item of the legacy Malthus has handed on to his
intellectual descendants.

Crisis writers, therefore, may simply be misled in
their preoccupation with overpopulation. But this is only a
partial explanation of their orientation. Their deliberate
efforts to focus on the demographic variable suggest that these
writers are eager to draw attention to population and, through
this attention, to see population growth dramatically reduced.
In this sense, the crisis perspective may be understood as a
strategy for marshalling attention and response to continued
growth. The spectre of crisis is an appropriate instrument for
this purpose since it radically simplifies the process of
value selection and ranking which any moral response requires.
Understood as the agent of impending catastrophe, high fertility
jeopardizes human life, a value of universally high priority,
and it does so on a vast scale. Presumably no rational
individual could remain indifferent to a problem of this
magnitude nor unwilling to take drastic measures and sacrifice
lesser values to its elimination.

In an article critical of much of the food-crisis
literature, the nutritionist Jean Mayer has stated that crisis
writers have used the prospect of famine in just this way to
elicit a willingness to reduce growth rates. Many of these
writers, according to Mayer, have had little contact with the
real prospects for agricultural growth in the poorer nations,
but they have focused on this issue nevertheless. These
writers, he says,

> . . . have generally been conservationists and
> social scientists rather than agricultural or
> nutritional scientists concerned--rightly--with
> the effects of the crowding which they had
> observed. At the same time, not sure that the
> public and governments would agree with them
> that there was cause for concern, and action,
> based on these grounds, they have turned to
> the threat of a worldwide shortage of food as
> an easily understood, imperative reason for a
> large scale limitation of births.[30]

---

[30]"Towards a Non-Malthusian Population Policy,"
Columbia Forum, XII (Summer 1969), 12. For a related criticism
of the crisis view see Irene B. Taeuber, "Demographic Instability: Resolution and Retrogression in Asia," in *Population*

If this interpretation of the crisis viewpoint is
correct, if this view represents less an understanding of the
problem than an effort or strategy to effect birth limitation,
then it is appropriate to ask why these crisis writers really
understand population growth to pose a moral problem. We may
assume that their intense desire to see population growth
halted is based on the belief that growth inflicts other evils
than mass catastrophe on moral agents. But what are these
evils and on which agents are they inflicted? Here the crisis
writers are remarkably uninformative. In their efforts to
present population growth as an unambiguous threat to all
human beings, crisis writers commonly fail to specify those
non-catastrophic evils generated by population growth which
concern them and they do not indicate the groups or persons
for whom they are most concerned. In this sense, the crisis
perspective is not really a view of the population problem at
all.

But this does not mean that this view is devoid of
moral implications or without importance for the welfare of
specific groups and individuals. Quite the opposite is true.
Whatever the effects of population growth, the crisis view
itself generates consequences which by their nature can
selectively disadvantage lower income groups and classes as
well as inhabitants of poorer nations. We can understand this
if we keep in mind the fact that when human survival is jeopardized virtually no limits need be placed on policies to ward
off disaster. Population policies on the extreme "regulation-
ist" or coercive end of a voluntarist-regulationist continuum
are the logical consequence of a view of the problem in crisis
terms.[31] William and Paul Paddock's advocacy of a "triage"
technique in the treatment of densely populated nations, and
Ehrlich's appeal for a morally required "callousness" in the

Growth--Threat to Peace?, ed. William E. Moran (New York:
P. J. Kennedy & Sons, 1965), p. 77.

[31]This classification of population policies is stated
in the Law Note, "Legal Analysis and Population Control: The
Problem of Coercion," *Harvard Law Review*, LXXXIV (June 1971),
1870.

reduction of growth in these areas follow logically from the
crisis understanding of the problem.[32] Since fertility is
usually highest among low income groups or nations, however,
it is these groups and nations that become subject to the
greatest amount of coercion and manipulation once these
policies are put into effect. Moreover, even when their
fertility is not distinguishably different from other groups,
it is the poor and the powerless who are most affected by such
policies, if for no other reason than that they are the groups
least able to protect themselves from coercion.

To this we might add the fact that the crisis perspective also encourages the termination of measures designed to
ease the plight of the poor and disadvantaged. Again, these
are the groups usually characterized by high fertility.
According to the crisis viewpoint, however, charitable measures
to alleviate famine or social distress can have the effect of
stimulating population growth and must, for that reason, be
discontinued. Here again Malthus' thinking sets the precedent
for this kind of argument, since he had called for the aboli-
tion of the poor laws of his day on the ground that they only
served to help the lower classes proliferate. More recently,
some crisis writers have argued that food aid must be cut off
to those nations or regions which refuse to lower their birth
rate.[33]

The net effect of the crisis view, therefore, can be to
further disadvantage those groups and individuals who are at
the bottom of the social order. Crisis writers may not
deliberately intend this result, but it follows naturally from
their position. Of course, it may be that they do intend it:
that the crisis view of the population problem is intended to

---

[32]Paddock and Paddock, *Famine--1975!*, Ch. 9; Ehrlich,
The Population Bomb, p. 165.

[33]In *Road to Survival*, p. 211, Vogt argues that the
continued shipment of American food aid should be made contingent upon the existence of national programs of voluntary birth
limitation in the recipient country. A similar point is made
by Walter E. Howard in his article, "The Population Crisis is
Here Now," *BioScience*, XIX (September 1969), 781.

inflict evils on low-income groups, or more probably, to bestow
goods upon upper-income groups and more advantaged classes.
Certainly, there is reason for believing that Malthus had this
intention in mind in advancing the principle of population.
Though he tried to present an explicit moral justification for
his distributive preferences, Malthus clearly favored middle
and upper income groups. He sought to preserve them from the
various depradations of the poor and provide the intellectual
tools for checking the assertions of the lower classes.[34]
Whether or not today's crisis writers share Malthus' intent
cannot be easily determined. Many crisis writers are possibly
unaware of the selective impact of their position. What is
important for our purposes, however, is the recognition that
this view does have certain distributive implications. Though
the crisis writers are mute on just who it is that they believe
experiences the evils generated by high fertility, the total
structure of their position generates an effective preference
or concern for groups which are nationally or internationally
at the upper end of the income and authority spectrum.

3. *Quality-of-Life Views*

When population growth is viewed as an agent of
impending disaster, it becomes natural to respond to the threat
by directly seeking to forestall disaster itself. If it is
famine that is threatened, then increased food production may
be a reasonable response. If eco-catastrophe is the threat,
an immediate cessation of polluting activities may seem
necessary. As we might expect, crisis writers have taken pains
to forestall these kinds of responses. Interested in limiting
population growth, and having used the spectre of disaster to
this end, they have not been eager to see the feared evils
instead made the object of attack. Thus the writings of crisis

---

[34]In addition to attacking the poor laws, Malthus used
the principle of population as a means of checking the lower
classes' hope for revolutionary social change. See his treatment of revolution in the 7th edition of his *Essay* in *On Population*, ed. Gertrude Himmelfarb, Bk. IV, Ch. 6, pp. 513-23.

writers are characteristically filled with arguments against
this kind of direct onslaught on the threatened evils. We have
already seen, for example, how the prospect of environmental
pollution is turned against efforts to increase food production.
    Some population writers, however, have been deeply
troubled by this exclusive attention to life and death issues.
They too have been concerned with population growth, but they
have been bothered by the way in which the crisis view makes
the existence of a population problem hinge upon whether or not
absolute catastrophe can be averted. These writers have pro-
tested that even if human survival can be assured, population
growth would still pose a moral problem. It would do so because
of its threat to one or another of the values that make human
life meaningful and enjoyable. Those who advance this perspective support what we might call the "quality-of-life view."
Like the crisis position, and unlike the family-planning
orientation, this view is concerned with values external to the
family believed threatened by high fertility. Unlike the crisis
view, however, this position looks to other values than merely
continued human existence. A statement by John D. Rockefeller
expresses this view in its most general form:

> Even if science shows us the way to feed billions
> more--as indeed it may--we would still not have
> mastered the population problem. The full
> solution depends also on society's ability to
> meet man's higher, non-material needs, to
> offer every child an opportunity to achieve in
> life more than mere existence--a chance to *live*
> as well as to survive. We are concerned with
> the quantity of life--and the rate at which that
> quantity is increasing--only because we are con-
> cerned with the quality of life.[35]

This kind of viewpoint need not be separated from the
crisis perspective. Every threat to human survival also
necessarily jeopardizes the quality of life. Nevertheless,
these views are not commonly brought together in the population
literature, at least when a writer is concerned with a single
region of the world. And this makes sense. The individual
seeking to present population growth as an agent of catastrophe

---

[35]"Toward the Enrichment of Life," in *Family Planning
Programs*, ed. Berelson, p. 4.

does not also wish to stress its effect on the quality of life.
To do so would only weaken the impact of the crisis position
and reduce its usefulness in motivating response to the problem.
Population growth either is or is not a threat to survival.
One cannot hope to impress readers with the vital urgency of the
population problem and, at the same time, make a case for attention to less serious matters. Because of this, the quality-of-
life perspective has something of an independent place within
the population debate and is frequently expressed by different
writers than those who advance the crisis view.[36]

Claims that population growth imperils the quality of
life vary considerably in their content. Like the crisis view,
the quality-of-life position actually comprises a range of
views distinguished most obviously by the value or values which
high fertility is believed to threaten. Occasionally, these
values are not clearly delineated. In the Rockefeller statement just quoted, for example, it is said that certain "non-
material" values are threatened by growth, but these are not
spelled out, nor is their independence of material values
demonstrated.

Despite occasional imprecision, certain major emphases
or areas of value concern do emerge from this literature. Three
distinct sets of values appear to comprehend most of the concerns voiced by these writers. First, there are the values
related to man's physical environment and his setting in nature.
Second, there are the values related to man's social environment: his place within and control over important social
institutions. Finally, there is the value of economic progress
in the sense of growth in real per capita income (or output).
Those who argue that population growth threatens the quality
of life usually have one or more of these values in mind. Let
us look at their claims more closely.

---

[36]Works expressing the quality-of-life view, except
those that do so in economic terms, are listed in Section E of
the bibliography.

a. *Population and the Physical Environment*

        Concern with the impact of population growth on the
world's physical environment is perhaps the most easily understood expression of the quality-of-life view. Because each
individual's share of environmental space is virtually a direct
function of the number of human beings who make a claim to
that space, population growth must necessarily diminish the
amount of room available for each person. At the same time,
increased human density involves greater interference with the
environment and increases the amount of clutter to which open
space is subject. Finally, even where population growth does
not consume all available habitable or recreational space,
it can serve to distance large numbers of men from daily contact with an untrammeled natural environment.

        Some writers concerned with these environmental
effects have argued that excessive crowding and loss of contact
with nature can erode the quality of life by jeopardizing
human physical or emotional health. This view is particularly
popular among biologists, perhaps because of their tendency to
see man in terms of his evolutionary descent from species with
inborn biological mechanisms for controlling spacing and population size.[37] A series of animal studies undertaken in the
early 1960's by John B. Calhoun intended to clarify the effects
of crowding on rats, for example, had the explicit purpose of
uncovering the possible biological effects of crowding on man.
Calhoun's findings proved inconclusive and biologists concerned
with this question appear less sure than ever that population
density has any direct physical or emotional impact on human
beings.[38] Nevertheless, this kind of concern has continued to

---

[37]H. H. Iltis, P. Andrews and O. L. Laucks have supplemented this type of biological concern with crowding by suggesting that man may have a genetically determined need for
contact with a green, natural environment. For a review of
their position, see Paul and Anne Ehrlich, *Population, Resource,
Environment* (San Francisco: W. H. Freeman and Company, 1970),
p. 204.

[38]See Calhoun's article, "Population Density and Social
Pathology," *Scientific American*, CCVI (February 1962), 139-48.
In a later article, "Population," in *Population Control*, ed.

have a prominent place in the quality-of-life literature. In
view of the undisputedly high value men place on health this is
understandable.

Outside the biological literature, the crowding and
reduced contact with nature that population growth can bring
about are viewed less as a direct threat to health than as an
erosion of aesthetic values or experience that contribute to
the quality of life. Those who argue this way place high
value on natural beauty and fear its disappearance under the
clutter of contemporary industrial culture. A series of
remarks by the literary critic F. C. Lucas express this view.
According to Lucas, the population problem is not correctly
understood in terms of food supplies alone. "Even supposing
we could support a vastly increased world population, do we
really want to?" he asks. "Do we want the earth turned into a
human ant-heap . . . with its wild nature disfigured and
defiled . . . ."[39] Lucas' appeal here is presumably to the
concerns and interests of all men. But elsewhere in his
writings he assumes his audience to be narrower. Suggesting
that the loss of natural beauty can lead to a decline in
literary or artistic creativity Lucas appeals to those interested in such values to respond to the population problem.[40]

This latter kind of argument renders acute the
question of whose values and interests are jeopardized by
rapid population growth. Few rational persons would dispute
the importance of physical and emotional health to the quality
of human life. Some, however, might dispute the importance of
access to an uncluttered green environment or the preservation
of broad stretches of wild nature. And many more, presumably,

---

Anthony Allison (Middlesex, England: Penguin Books, 1970),
pp. 110-30, Calhoun reviews some of the further evidence
advanced to dispute the findings of his earlier studies.

[39]*The Greatest Problem of Today and Other Essays* (New
York: The Macmillan Co., 1961), p. 320.

[40]"The Writer in an Overpopulated World," in *The
Population Crisis*, eds. Larry K. Y. Ng and Stuart Mudd
(Bloomington, Indiana: Indiana University Press, 1965),
pp. 267ff.

would not be willing to place great value weight on the
spiritual and aesthetic experiences which, if Lucas is correct,
untrammeled nature can produce. This is not to say that,
other things being equal, many individuals would not like to
see these values preserved. But when speaking of the population problem, other things are not equal. If nothing else,
population limitation means that some individuals must
relinquish a degree of their ability to reproduce. There is,
in other words, the possibility of significant dispute over
which values ought to enter into the quality of life and a
resolution of this dispute might depend on just whose values
are considered to be most important. As we shall see, this
problem is not unique to those who stress aesthetic values;
it is a problem that plagues virtually all expressions of the
quality-of-life view. For the time being, we should note that
those concerned with the integrity of man's physical environment merely express one value preference among others. In
advocating population restraint, they clearly favor those for
whom the natural environment is of great importance.

b. *Population and the Social Environment*

        Besides the physical environment in which human beings
act, there is a social environment shaped by the behavior of
their fellows and by the institutions and practices through
which behavior is ordered. A second major concern within the
quality-of-life literature has to do with the impact of population growth on this human environment. Generally speaking,
those who share this concern believe that population growth
erodes the human environment by diluting or distorting social
and institutional life. But there are at least three different
ways in which this result is believed to come about.
        One line of reasoning holds that population growth
increases subjection to the human environment because the conduct of life under conditions of crowding requires increased
regimentation of human behavior. As densities increase,
activities which were once without social importance become of
concern to society and the sphere of freedom decreases.
Crowding can necessitate the abandonment of formerly casual

patterns of behavior, such as the indiscriminate disposal of
refuse. Or, in a more complex fashion, it can force an
increased degree of coordination and integration of behavior
in order to prevent loss of efficiency in productive enter-
prises.[41]

Some writers note a second major way in which subjection to the human environment can come about. As numbers
increase, the individual's control over the important social
institutions in which he acts or which affect him diminishes.
In politics, for example, his vote becomes less meaningful
when the size of the voting populace increases. The individual
is also distanced from meaningful involvement in the political
process and the political institutions grow more representative
and less direct at every level. Much the same can occur in the
educational, economic, recreational or religious institutions
in which people act.[42]

It is useful to distinguish these two ways in which
population growth can affect the individual's relation to his
social environment. Loss of freedom in the first sense can to
some degree be expressed in economic terms. One can speak of
the "opportunity cost" of population growth; activities foregone as a result of growth have a value expressible in terms
of the amount of income consumers would be prepared to pay
for the right to pursue these activities freely again. The
loss of political power and control over vital institutions,
however, is not so easily converted into an issue of economic
welfare. It seems odd, for example, to think of one's say in
the political or economic process as something traded off for
economic goods, if for no other reason than that these processes play a large part in determining the supply of goods
available and their distribution. This does not mean that a
discussion of these values in economic terms is impossible, but

---

[41]Brown, *The Challenge of Man's Future*, p. 218. Also,
Joseph J. Spengler, "Population Pressure, Housing and Habitat,"
Law and Contemporary Problems, XXXII (Spring, 1967), 202, and
Solly Zuckerman, "Environmental Planning for an Increased
Population," in *Our Crowded Planet*, ed. Fairfield Osborn
(Garden City, N.Y.: Doubleday & Company, 1962), p. 114.

[42]Lucas, *The Greatest Problem*, p. 320.

only that such a discussion seems far more problematical than
in the case of other opportunities foregone as a result of
population growth. When we turn to the economic quality-of-
life view, the matter of political and institutional control
remains an instance where an economic perspective on growth can
be incomplete.

A third and final way in which population growth is
held to erode the quality of the human environment has to do
with the differing fertility rates of various social groups.
Concern with differential fertility as a part of the population
problem can usually be interpreted as concern with the impact
of high fertility on the quality of the human population and
its network of vital institutions.

The most heated argumentation in this area has sometimes revolved around the issue of the direct impact of differential fertility on the biological quality of human populations.
This is the concern that finds expression in the fear that the
high fertility of lower-income groups might inundate the gene
pool and proportionately displace the superior genetic potential of upper income groups. We need not dwell too long on
this kind of concern. Suffice it to say that geneticists
today are extremely reluctant to relate social or economic
performance to genetic inheritance. Those geneticists concerned with the quality of the gene pool are most preoccupied
with the increased incidence of genetic disease as the result
of medical science's ability to enable those with deleterious
genes to reach reproductive age.[43] But this matter has little
direct relationship to differential fertility or population
growth.

Within the traditional argument about the genetic
impact of differential fertility, however, there exists a more
basic concern that still elicits attention in the population
literature. This is the fear that the high fertility of
certain economic, political or racial groups might jeopardize
the ordered institutional life of human communities or might
undermine the conditions of social cooperation on which these

---

[43]For a discussion of this concern on the part of
genetic scientists see Paul Ramsey, *Fabricated Man* (New
Haven: Yale University Press, 1970), pp. 22-32.

communities depend. This concern is possibly implicit in the
arguments of those who used supposed genetic data to express
anxiety over the high growth rates of certain economic or
racial groups. But as a concern in its own right, it predates
genetic science and can be found in the earliest population
literature.[44] As on many other aspects of the population
question, moreover, it is Malthus who provides the classic
expression of this concern.

In Malthus' view, the high fertility of certain
individuals or social groups can constitute a species of
unfairness or injustice to the fellow members of their
society. He illustrates this point with reference to a hypothetical society where goods and property have been equally
distributed at some point in the past. These economic arrangements might remain intact, Malthus argues, so long as population does not grow. But if it does so, future generations are
likely to suffer impoverishment. Or, if it grows differen-
tially, the offspring of the most prolific parents will
experience poverty and distress. Should these offspring demand
a further redistribution of income, they would unfairly
penalize the offspring of those parents who have acted
responsibly, who have reduced their fertility and who have
tried to respect the egalitarian arrangement as well as the
rights of their descendants. Should a redistribution be
prohibited, the egalitarian society would promptly be trans-
muted into a traditional society of rich and poor.[45]

In recent population literature, a similar argument
has been set forth by the biologist Garrett Hardin. Population
growth, Hardin argues, can precipitate "the tragedy of the
commons" whereby resources open to all are overconsumed by
groups or interests which allow their numbers (of humans or

[44]The United Nations study *Determinants and Consequences of Population Trends* (New York: United Nations,
1953), pp. 21-24, has a good discussion of the concern with
differential fertility in pre-Malthusian literature.

[45]*An Essay on the Principle of Population* (1798),
Ch. 10. In *On Population*, ed. Himmelfarb, pp. 64-76.

valued animals) to proliferate.[46] Following Malthus, Hardin
argues that this kind of over-exploitation of resources and
opportunities must lead to the breakdown of fair cooperative
schemes. It can force the replacement of egalitarian distributive arrangements by a system of private property backed by
the threat of coercion. Or it can necessitate employing harsh
restraint directly to prevent overproliferation. In Hardin's
view, groups that allow their numbers to grow unchecked are
guilty of an injustice against their neighbors. They may
therefore be forced to act responsibly. This is especially
true because if such groups are given complete procreative
freedom, their numbers can only grow and further threaten
fellow members of society.[47] Hardin's argument thus naturally
culminates in the suggestion that groups marked by high
fertility today should be compelled to halt their unjust procreative behavior.

It is important to note that in employing this kind
of reasoning to justify coercive population policies, Hardin
also follows in the footsteps of Malthus. Like Malthus, he
moves from a hypothetical argument concerning the possible
implications of high fertility in a justly ordered society to
concrete recommendations for observable social conditions.
Malthus, after all, was not concerned only with the abstract
implications of population growth. He sought primarily to
throw light on the social conditions of England in his day.
He assumed, for example, that the economic distress of the
English working class could be explained in terms of his
population argument. He viewed their poverty as a result of
their own excess proliferation from a basepoint of equal
distribution in the past, and his advocacy of continued class
and property arrangements, as well as his opposition to any
form of economic redistribution, grew out of this view.
Hardin's recommendations for the coercive reduction of population growth today parallel this kind of movement from a

---

[46]"The Tragedy of the Commons," *Science*, CLXII (December 13, 1968), 1243-48. Also, his article, "Multiple Paths to
Population Control," *Family Planning Perspectives*, II (June
1970), 24-26.

[47]"The Tragedy of the Commons," 1245ff.

hypothetical position to concrete policy recommendations.

It should be clear that both Malthus and Hardin err
in interpreting existing social conditions in terms of a
hypothetical possibility. In the absence of evidence that
present fertility rates have followed a period in which all
members of society have been fairly and equally placed, one
cannot legitimately pass moral judgments on the fertility of
existing groups. The employment of coercive measures against
groups marked by high fertility, for example, would have substantially different meaning, even within the terms of Malthus'
or Hardin's analysis, in a case where high fertility is the
result of past inequities and injustices in the distribution
of goods and opportunities. In such a case, coercive policies
might represent yet a further injustice against groups already
unfairly treated by society.

These considerations raise the question of which
individuals or groups form the object of concern of those who
point to the effect of differential fertility on the social
environment. Ostensibly, those who argue as Malthus and Hardin
have done are interested in the welfare of all within an
equitable social order. But when applied to existing social
groups and conditions, their argument can potentially further
disadvantage groups with high fertility and at the lower end
of the income spectrum. Here, the practical effect of this
perspective is similar to that of the crisis view, and it is
not simply an accident that Malthus is the progenitor of each
of these interpretations of the population problem. We have
already noted that Malthus, justifiably or not, was committed
to the interests of the middle and upper classes. His population arguments, by his own admission, therefore aimed at preserving these interests against the attacks of low-income
groups.

This fact points up a serious difficulty in the
position of all those who, following Malthus or Hardin,
identify differential fertility as a problem because of its
tendency to disorder existing social or economic arrangements.
Moral estimates of this differential fertility, and concrete
judgments as to whether it poses a problem or not, cannot be
made apart from a prior estimate of the moral acceptablity of
the social order in which that fertility occurs. In cases

where a society is unjust or discriminatory, high fertility may
not easily be judged a source of concern in its own right, and
the groups marked by high fertility may not simply be labeled
irresponsible. Thus, if it is not to promote injustice, a
view of this sort requires a prior determination of how income
and opportunities are to be justly distributed in a given
society. It requires, in other words, supplementation by a
basic theory of social and economic justice. In the second
part of the thesis, I will turn directly to this issue. But
for the time being it is sufficient to note that this very
basic kind of distributive issue is a problem for all who would
single out differential fertility as a source of concern.
Indeed, as we shall see shortly, the same need for a comprehensive moral theory to determine fair shares in a social
order also makes itself felt in economic discussions of the
population problem. In the case of all these quality-of-life
views, the question of whose values and interests are to be
taken into account must first be settled, and it must usually
be settled in connection with a complete theory of social
rights and responsibilities.

c. *Population and Income*

The view that population growth is a threat to the
quality of life because of its tendency to diminish per
capita income or output is a logical extension of some of the
other perspectives we have examined. Compared with these other
views of the problem, there seem to be several real advantages
in conceptualizing the issue in this way. Indeed, the fact
that the literature dealing with the relationship between
population and income is the most extensive of the population
debate testifies to the importance attached to this way of
understanding the problem.[48]
One advantage of the economic perspective is the
relative ubiquity of the concept "income," that is, the

---

[48]See bibliography, Section F.

interchangeability of this value with most other values.[49]
The various quality-of-life views we have examined up to this
point have all focused on single values believed to be related
to human welfare. Yet, as economists point out, many of these
values can be expressed in economic terms. The value of
uncluttered space and access to nature can be expressed in
terms of the prices consumers of these values would be prepared
to pay for them at different schedules of supply. The loss of
personal freedom associated with crowding or human density
can be expressed as an opportunity cost of growth. It is true,
as I have just suggested, that the value of political power
or institutional control seems hard to express in economic
terms, and some economists seem to be aware of this.[50] This
places some limits on the comprehensiveness of any view which
regards population growth exclusively in terms of its effect
on income. Nevertheless, with this qualification, it appears
true that the economic view is more comprehensive than any
perception of population growth centering on a single value.

A second major advantage of the focus on income is
that this permits a systematic exploration of all the implications of population growth, both positive and negative.
Reducing discussion of the issue to the two variables, population and income, facilitates a balanced assessment of the net

---

[49] In discussing the economic quality-of-life view I
have selected per capita income as the index of welfare rather
than per capita output. It is true that the latter index is
preferable when discussing economic development because
every gain in output need not be reflected in income; output
can be diverted to savings. When discussing the impact of
demographic increase on the quality of life, however, income
would seem a more appropriate measure. I assume that income
comprehends resources devoted to savings. For a discussion
of the relative merits of these indices, see Horace Belshaw,
Population Growth and Levels of Consumption (New York:
Institute of Pacific Relations, 1956), p. xxiv, and Harvey
Leibenstein, *Economic Backwardness and Economic Growth* (New
York: John Wiley & Sons, 1957), p. 10.

[50] See Joseph Spengler, "The Economist and the Population Question," *American Economic Review*, LVI (March 1966),
14, and Paul Demeny, "The Economics of Population Control,"
in *Rapid Population Growth; Consequences and Policy Implications*, Prepared by a Study Committee of the Office of the
Foreign Secretary, National Academy of Sciences (Baltimore:
Johns Hopkins Press, 1971), p. 209.

40

impact of population growth and helps avoid the mistake, common in the non-economic literature, of looking upon growth in population as an unequivocal cause of evils and constant detraction from the quality of life. While it is true that population growth can dilute valued resources and diminish per capita income, it is also true that population growth and differing population sizes can have an independent and some-times positive effect on income. This, indeed, is one key awareness of the theory of an economic optimum of population. Although optimum theory has moved from the center of economic thinking for a variety of reasons, its main assumptions still serve to distinguish the economic approach to the matter of population growth. For this reason, examination of an economic view of the population problem must begin with a brief survey of optimum theory.

Before turning to optimum theory, however, one pre-liminary oddity of economic thinking in the area of population demands attention. This is general use by economists of per capita well-being as the measure of welfare, a measure which, in population questions, tends from the outset to favor the limitation of human numbers. As we might expect, economists have not failed to discuss and justify their selection of income as a measure of the more basic value, human welfare or well-being.[51] But within the economic literature there is no correspondingly systematic discussion or justification of the decision to measure the welfare associated with income at the level of the individual rather than the community as a whole; that is, of the decision to select the average or per capita measure over the aggregate. (It is true, of course, that the per capita measure is also an "aggregate." But I reserve that term for the total sum of a community's welfare.)

This lack of justification is all the more surprising since a minority among economists have not hesitated to

---

[51] See A. C. Pigou, *The Economics of Welfare*, 4th edition (London: Macmillan, 1950), Part I, Ch. . Also Manuel Gottlieb, "The Theory of Optimum Population for a Closed Economy," *Journal of Political Economy*, LIII (December, 1945), 295.

maintain that the aggregate is the appropriate measure. For example, Henry Sidgwick, whose contribution to later welfare economic theory is significant, postulates maximum total as against maximum average satisfaction.[52] More recently, J. E. Meade has argued for the aggregate measure.[53] And even Pigou, one of the major formulators of welfare economic theory, appears to have considered the aggregate measure as one possibly valid measure of welfare.[54]

It is true that there are scattered defenses of the average measure in the economic literature. But on close inspection these defenses are not convincing and serve merely to buttress the impression that economists are uncertain on this issue. A. B. Wolfe, for example, advances a moral argument for this measure. He defends the selection of the average on the grounds that only the individual human being experiences value. Because this is so, he maintains, it is logical to conclude that satisfaction ought properly to be measured as it is experienced by individuals, not communities as a whole.[55] It should be clear, however, that Wolfe's conclusion does not follow from his premise. Even if one believes that only the individual can experience value, there still remains the question of whether a given sum of positive value should be distributed over one or many individuals. Use of the aggregate measure would be appropriate if one believed that value should be distributed and experienced as widely as posible.

A more interesting approach to the issue is taken by Harvey Leibenstein in his *Economic Backwardness and Economic*

---

[52]*The Methods of Ethics*, 7th ed. (New York: Dover Publications, 1907, 1966), p. 415. Also, with somewhat less certainty, in his *The Principles of Political Economy* (London: Macmillan and Co., 1883), p. 522.

[53]See his *Trade and Welfare* (London: Oxford University Press, 1955), Ch. VI. In a more recent article, "Population Explosion, The Standard of Living and Social Conflict," *Economic Journal*, LXXVII (1967), 236, Meade reaffirms his uncertainty over the appropriate measure.

[54]*The Economics of Welfare*, p. 99.

[55]A. B. Wolfe, "On the Criterion of Optimum Population," *American Journal of Sociology,* XXXIX (1934), 585-99.

42

Growth. Leibenstein's topic in this work is the problem of
economic development, which he relates, very generally, to
ethically defined welfare goals.[56] Bearing on development,
however, is the question of which variable should serve as an
appropriate measure of economic advance. Leibenstein chooses
per capita output, but his justification is noteworthy.
Average output, he argues, is more useful in indicating what
is going on in a developing society and economy as a whole
under conditions of population growth than is the total
measure. This is so because population growth can cause the
total to advance at the same time as per capita output
declines or remains stationary. In view of the Malthusian
conditions that prevail in the less-developed economies, however, a rise in per capita output is not likely to be accompanied by a decline in total output. The average measure,
therefore, is a superior "index of observation" because it
comprises the total measure.[57]

Leibenstein's reasoning here seems valid, and has the
advantage of by-passing the moral task of indicating which
measure is preferable on welfare grounds. But that is just
what is so curious about this discussion. Despite the fact
that his labors are devoted to a careful analysis of the conditions of economic growth, Leibenstein nowhere clearly
spells out the value or values growth is intended to promote.
The Malthusian circumstances of the less-developed nations aid
him in circumventing this issue, and his unwillingness, as an
economist, to become involved in a discussion of welfare goals
is understandable. Nevertheless, one is left to speculate
how Leibenstein might measure economic development if the
aggregate and per capita measures moved in opposite
directions.

I have singled out Leibenstein's discussion of this
issue because in some ways it is representative of economic
discussion generally. Although per capita income or output is
almost always selected today as the measure of economic

---

[56]p. 9.

[57]pp. 13f.

advance, this selection is rarely defended even in the limited manner undertaken by Leibenstein. In this sense, one of the root premises of the economic view hangs in a void. To the degree that the economic perspective helps furnish an explanation of why rapid population growth poses a moral problem we may say that this view remains unclear as to who are to be considered recipients of the evils generated by growth. Are they to be actual human beings whose per capita welfare can be diminished by the expansion of human numbers? Or are they to be those individuals in the expanded human community whose very existence may depend upon the larger population sizes permitted by the aggregate measure (since the aggregate measure can justify larger populations at a lesser per capita level of welfare)? Beyond the issue of the per capita or aggregate measures, in other words, lies a question of one's distributive preference for actual or possible human beings. In the Second Part of the thesis I will turn to this issue in greater detail. For the time being, however, it is sufficient to note that the selection of the per capita measure already expresses a distributive preference and one not seriously scrutinized by economists themselves. Moreover, the theory of an economic optimum of population prefigures later discussion of the issue by simply assuming the validity of the per capita measure.

As elaborated in the writings of economists like Mill, Cannan and Wicksell, optimum theory brings together two awarenesses developed in the earlier literature. On the one hand, optimum theorists noted the tendency of demographic increase, in the absence of technological change, or the development of new resources, to reduce average output by diluting capital resources and by precipitating diminishing returns to labor on fixed resources such as land. On the other hand, these thinkers also were aware that larger populations can imply a larger market, increased division of labor, various economies of scale and greater economic efficiency through better inter-industry fit. Demographic increase could thus serve to boost output by permitting increasing returns.

From these awarenesses it was but a short step to the
conclusion that -- given a static technology and constant
level of capital -- a closed economy would have one population size, or one zone of population sizes, which would be
economically optimum in terms of returns per head. This would
correspond to the size at which further growth caused decreas-
ing marginal returns to labor to exceed increasing marginal
returns to scale. According to optimum theory, demographic
increase would be permitted until population reached the
optimal size. Beyond that point, a larger population would
be desirable only if changes in capital or technology rendered
a larger population capable of increasing per capita returns.

The potential importance of changed technology or
capital for the size of an economically optimum population has
been an important reason for the dwindling popularity of
optimum theory among economists. As its critics have noted,
optimum theory tends to be unjustifiably "static" since it
works with a *ceteris paribus* assumption that is neither
realistic nor historically defensible. These critics note
that the experience of technological innovation and capital
growth over the past several hundred years makes this assumption particularly unacceptable.[58] They also note that the
technological change and capital growth which have facilitated
larger optimum population sizes may themselves be the outcome
of population growth. Thus the *ceteris paribus* assumption is
doubly unjustified.[59]

Contemporary defenders of optimum theory have conceded
the truth of these criticisms, but they have insisted that
these considerations do not so much invalidate optimum theory

---

[58]Though they wish to defend optimum theory, Abraham
David and Ching-Ju Huang consider that one of classical
optimum theory's weakest points is its *ceteris paribus* assumption. See their "Population Theory and the Concept of
Optimum Population," *Socio-Economic Planning Science*, III
(1969), 201.

[59]See, for example, the articles by Adolphe Coste,
Maxim Kovalevsky and A. Loria in *Contemporary Sociological
Theories*, ed. Pitirim Sorokin (New York: Harper & Brothers,
1928). Ohlin, in *Population Control and Economic Development*,
p. 57, maintains that population growth rates bear on capital
formation and can alter the optimum population even as population moves toward the optimum.

as complicate it. Manuel Gottlieb, for example, argues that
optimum theory does not logically require the *ceteris paribus*
assumption, although it freely employs it. In defense of the
employment of this assumption, moreover, Gottlieb asks
whether technological or capital change any longer serves to
advance the size of an economically optimum population.[60]

This kind of defense has not apparently been successful in returning contemporary economic thought to a consideration of optimum theory. With few exceptions, economists have
abandoned as too complex and problematical the question of
which size population is optimal; they have turned their
attention instead to the more easily resolved question of how
rapid population growth may impede growth in per capita income
and development from states of economic backwardness. To
understand contemporary economic thinking on the population
problem, therefore, we ought to direct our attention to this
issue. But before doing so, one further difficulty in optimum
theory must be briefly mentioned. It becomes particularly
important to note this difficulty once we recognize that contemporary economic discussion of population is not wholly
sundered from its rootage in optimum theory. Though the
focus on development serves to bypass some of the complex
problems in optimum theory, it does not depart from all the
assumptions or all the difficulties of the earlier position.

This further difficulty in optimum theory involves the
question of the time span over which the optimum is to be
measured. Since society is an ongoing affair, with generation
succeeding generation, it is important to ask which generations
one should consider in measuring the optimum population size.
Clearly the question is important. If one assumes that non-
replaceable resources can be an important factor in production,
it would seem that increments to population can hasten the
exhaustion of these resources and eventually bring about a
decline in average income. Depending upon the time period for
which one projects the optimum, therefore, one's conclusion
about what is an optimum population can vary. In one sense,
this question is related to the difficulty in optimum theory's

---

[60]"The Theory of Optimum Population . . . ," pp. 300f.

46

ceteris paribus assumption; the consideration of population
levels over an extended series of generations further renders
questionable the assumption of fixed capital resources and
unchanged technology. But the time-span difficulty is not
reducible to this difficulty and it cannot be resolved by a
careful consideration of changes in these other variables.
What the time-span issue involves is a prior moral decision as
to the period over which changes in these other variables are
to be considered in the first place.

We may view this problem another way, as a distributive
difficulty. If optimum theory may be thought of as an answer
to the question of why population growth can pose a moral
problem, the matter of the time-span of the optimum raises a
further question of which moral agents are affected by the
evils of growth. Are only a series of immediately proximate
generations important? Or, are distant generations important
as well? Despite the obvious significance of the time-span
of the optimum, however, this issue is virtually neglected
by the theory's defenders. And those few writers alert to
the problem seem incapable of resolving it. Hugh Dalton, for
example, notes that a growth rate that would reduce income in
the near future below what it. would otherwise have been might
raise it in the future above what it would otherwise have
been.[61] But Dalton has no suggestion as to how a choice
between generations is to be made. Gottlieb is no more
specific. "The optimum," he maintains, "should be conceived
of as pertaining to a succession of generations husbanding and
consuming a limited and, in part, an exhaustible resource
supply." In response to the question of just how many generations this succession should include, however, Gottlieb's
reply is an uninformative "as many generations as we are
interested in."[62]

This time-span difficulty may be a factor contributing
to the replacement of optimum theory in contemporary literature
by a concern with the problem of economic growth. It is the

---

[61]"The Theory of Population," *Economica*, VIII (1928), 43.

[62]"The Theory of Optimum Population . . . ," p. 298.

nature of this latter concern that it focuses attention
primarily upon the immediate generations whose economic welfare is imperiled by high fertility. But not even this development focus is free of time considerations. The problem
reappears in the face of short-term inter-generational conflict. Here the debt of contemporary economic thinking to
population optimum theory, and to the inadequacies of that
theory shows through.

If the concentration on problems of development in
recent economic treatments of population stems partly from the
perceived difficulties of optimum theory, contemporary social
and historical conditions have also helped determine the change
in approach. Economists have noted the fact that developed
economies have been able to advance average income despite
sometimes rapidly growing populations, while less developed
economies with rapidly growing populations have been unable
even to begin the process of development. This has led them
to explore the specific relationship between high fertility
and underdevelopment and to shift attention from the theoretical problem of determining an optimum population size to what
Myrdal has called the "practical problem" of achieving improvement in average income in the underdeveloped areas.[63]

This shift in emphasis has led economists to direct
their attention primarily to the negative consequences of
further rapid population growth in the underdeveloped setting.
But a preoccupation with the negative implications of high
fertility has not fully eclipsed optimum theory's earlier
openness to the positive effects of population growth. Contributors to the development literature such as Ester Boserup,
Colin Clark and Albert Hirschman have argued that population
pressure, even in already crowded and underdeveloped regions,
acts more as a stimulus to development than as a depressant.[64]

---

[63]*Asian Drama* (New York: Pantheon Books, 1968), III;
2065.

[64]Ester Boserup, *The Conditions of Agricultural Growth;
The Economics of Agrarian Change Under Population Pressure*
(London: G. Allen & Unwin, 1965), pp. 63-64; Colin Clark, *Population Growth and Land Use* (London: St. Martin's Press, 1967),
pp. 253-78; Albert Hirschman, *The Strategy of Economic Development* (New Haven: Yale University Press), pp. 176-82.

Population growth, according to Clark, can promote development
by facilitating economies of scale, stimulating investment,
accentuating savings (presumably because younger populations
save more than older ones), and by inducing cultural and
technical changes that would not appear without the goad of
necessity.[65] Without fully accepting it, Paul Demeny has
advanced the idea that population growth can render an economy
more flexible in adjusting to structural changes, particularly
changes in demand.[66] Finally, Leibenstein has pointed to a
possible "replacement effect" of growth whereby high fertility
can hasten modernization of the skill composition of a population as older, unskilled workers dwindle in proportion to
skilled newcomers.[67]

If these claims have not been accepted by the
majority of economists, it is not so much because they reject
their theoretical importance as doubt their factual accuracy
or significance. Development-oriented economists have not
abandoned the earlier interest in the income-producing consequences of population growth; but they have minimized the
present value of demographic increase in stimulating underdeveloped economies. The importance of these income-advancing
effects, it is argued, is not as great as their defenders
maintain and not sufficiently great to outweigh the negative
effects of high fertility.[68]

In addition to denying the positive consequences of
high fertility, economists have extensively discussed the
negative implications of population growth in the underdeveloped setting. These consequences may be grouped into those
already dealt with by traditional economic analysis, and other

---

[65]*Population Growth and Land Use*, Ch. VII; also, "The
Economic and Social Implications of Population Control," in
Allison, *Population Control*, pp. 222-37.

[66]Demeny, "The Economics of Population Control,"
p. 204.

[67]Harvey Leibenstein, "The Impact of Population Growth
on Economic Welfare--Nontraditional Elements," in *Rapid Population Growth*, pp. 188ff.

[68]See, for example, Demeny's rejection of these popu-
lation-favoring arguments in "The Economics of Population
Control," p. 204.

non-traditional consequences first suggested in recent discussions. The negative consequences perceived by the traditional economic approach to population have to do with the impact of growth on the assemblage of factors that cooperate with labor in the productive process. These factors, commonly gathered together under the headings "capital" or "resources" include land, non-depletable natural resources of fixed supply, depletable and non-replaceable natural resources, natural resources which are replaceable and whose supply can be augmented, and, finally, equipment in use, including machinery, buildings and the like.[69] The chief effect of population growth is to dilute the quantity of these resources as new members are added to the labor force. Spengler concisely traces the way in which this dilution can lower average productivity:

> If the labor supply continues to grow after the whole of the complex of factors used with labor has been brought into use, average output per unit of labor will fall. The rate of fall will depend upon (a) the *substitutability* of labor for the factors with which it is combined, and the rate of decline in this substitutability and (b) the *convertibility* of labor into the factors with which it is used, and the rate of decline in this convertibility.[70]

In addition to the diluting effects of growth on existing resources, the traditional approach has pointed to the reduction in savings brought about by the dependency burden that accompanies rapid demographic increase. High fertility means that households and governments must devote a portion of income that might have gone to savings or productive consumption (the purchase of better food, for example) to sustaining and educating new members of society. In their now classic study *Population Growth and Economic Development in Low Income Countries*, Ansley Coale and Edgar Hoover seek to bring this dependency effect together with the direct effect of growth on capital per head. By means of a series of

---

[69]Joseph Spengler, "Population and Per Capita Income," *The Annals of the American Academy of Political and Social Science*, CCXXXVII (January 1945), 208.

[70]*Ibid.*, p. 209.

50

hypothetical projections they detail the remarkable advance in
per capita income experienced within decades by a population
whose fertility is halved over a twenty-five year period.[71]

A characteristic feature of this analysis of the
income effects of population growth is that the rate of population growth is seen to affect economic performance but the
reverse relationship between income and population growth is
neglected. However, even within the confines of traditional
theory, this simplified causal relationship has been considered
unjustified and an effort has been made to explore the population effects of income growth. Leibenstein's *Economic Backwardness and Economic Growth* is a principal contribution to
theory at this point. In an effort to provide a theoretical
explanation for the apparently chronic backwardness of the
underdeveloped economies, for their failure to progress despite
the existence of economic forces impelling development,
Leibenstein suggests viewing a backward economy as "an equilibrium system whose state (or states) possesses a degree of
'quasi-stability' with respect to per capita income . . . ."[72]
The cause of this equilibrium is the effect of income on
fertility. As per capita income advances in the underdeveloped
setting, a reduction in mortality comes about which heightens
the rate of population growth and dissolves the income gains.
Thus, average income in this setting is likely to fluctuate
around some low level at the same time as population expands.
Simple increments in income are not enough to help such
economies escape from this kind of demographic trap. What is
needed is an externally induced rise in average income
sufficient to push the economy to that threshold level where
the income-increasing effects of economic growth are sufficient
to outweigh the population-increasing, income-lowering effects.
In Leibenstein's terms a "critical minimum effort" must be made

---

[71]Princeton, N.J.: Princeton University Press, 1958.
See also the article by Coale, "The Economic Effects of
Fertility Control in Underdeveloped Areas," in Roy O. Greep,
ed., *Human Fertility and Population Problems* (Cambridge,
Mass.: Schenkman, 1963) pp. 141-73.

[72]p. 16.

to begin the development process.[73] Once begun, development
can accentuate conditions such as lowered infant mortality,
better education and the institutional and value structure of
a modernized society needed to keep fertility rates low.

Concern with the feed-back effects of income growth
more or less rounds out traditional theory on the negative
implications of population growth. The appellation "traditional"
for this body of awarenesses is particularly appropriate since
many of these effects are suggested, albeit in crude form, in
the work of Malthus. Leibenstein's concern with low-income
equilibrium, for example, represents a sophisticated re-state-
ment of Malthus' claim that population growth can cause income
to remain at or near the subsistence level.

Non-traditional exploration of this issue goes beyond
Malthus and beyond the economists' usual concern with
quantifiable factors. Emphasis here is largely upon the
"micro" or household effects of population growth as these
bear on the performance of the larger economy. The need for
this kind of exploration has been suggested by the work of
Simon Kuznets and others revealing how little traditional
factor inputs such as land, labor and capital appear to have
accounted for the observed growth in output in economies where
substantial economic progress has taken place.[74] This has
turned economists' attention to the role of technological
change and improvements in the labor force in promoting
economic growth, and it has raised the question of how high
fertility might impede the development of key economic and
technological skills. In recent articles, Leibenstein has
addressed himself to this question.[75] He assumes that rapid
population growth implies a greater number of large families
with characteristically higher dependency ratios, larger sib-
numbers and shorter sib-spacing. Together with the increased

---

[73]*Ibid.*, p. 16.

[74]Simon Kuznets, *Modern Economic Growth* (New Haven:
Yale University Press, 1966), pp. 80f.

[75]"The Impact of Population Growth . . ."; also "The
Consequences of Population Growth--The Impact of Non-Traditional Inputs," unpublished MS in this writer's possession.

52

chance of poor nutrition and the higher maternal morbidity
that exist in large families, these factors can adversely
affect speech or personality formation, I. Q. and other
qualities instrumental to economic growth. The household
effects of high fertility, therefore, can bear upon the
economy as a whole. Leibenstein concedes that the data to
support these claims are elusive and, at best, suggestive.
But he maintains that the new evidence underscoring the
importance of labor-force quality in economic development
ought, nevertheless, to encourage economists to give greater
attention to the impact of fertility on the factor of "human
capital."[76]

This departure from traditional theory has the curious
effect of approximating contemporary economic discussion of
the population problem to the series of concerns usually a
part of the family-planning view. In each case, it is the
household consequences of population growth that are at the
center of attention. Of course, the ultimate object of the
economist's concern (as economist) remains quite different
from that of family-planning spokesmen. While the latter
places family welfare at the top of his priorities, the
economist is presumably concerned about the wider matter of
economic performance. If he advocates fertility reduction,
it is because he believes smaller families are conducive to
the development of skills upon which income growth, and
increased social welfare, depend. Even in its recent focus
on the family, therefore, economic discussion stays within
the general framework of the quality-of-life perspective,
with its attention to values beyond the family that are
believed jeopardized by population growth.

Discussion of the family in this economic context,
however, raises a difficulty already touched upon in our
earlier examination of quality-of-life views. In the name of
social welfare, economists are prepared to advocate a reduction
in the sizes of families. This policy recommendation is based
on the assumption that children do not figure importantly in
one's calculation of social welfare. But is this assumption

---

[76]"The Impact of Population Growth . . .", p. 194.

justified? Can one assume that whatever income gain is
effected by reduced fertility necessarily compensates parents
for the loss of their opportunity to have and enjoy children?
And, if so, why should people have children at all? If
children do not enter into social welfare, why should any
resources be spent on their production and maintenance?

We should note that economists are not unaware of this
difficulty, even though they have not really resolved it.
In a treatment of the relationship between income and population growth, for example, T. Paul Schultz observes that
children "yield intangible and important rewards to parents
that elude national income accounts." And he adds, "one
simply cannot consider per capita income as an adequate indica-
tor of personal welfare for evaluating the effects of demographic trends."[77] Similarly, Leibenstein notes that efforts
to calculate the economic value to society of a prevented
birth cannot be fully evaluated until there exists a more
complete understanding of the place of children in a social
welfare function.[78] These remarks point up the fact that it
is essentially arbitrary to select a value like income as
determinative of social welfare on the issue of population
growth. If the economic perspective is to have any relation
to the genuine moral question of social welfare, the value of
children cannot simply be neglected. We can put this another
way by saying that the economic view, as presently expressed,
favors those who value income over offspring. But if economic
discussions of population growth are not to disregard those
with a differing set of preferences, and if these discussions
are not to become the rationale for public policy that unfairly
favors one group of interests over the other, this subordina-
tion of the value of offspring must either be justified or
qualified.

The problem of how the value of offspring is to fit
into a social welfare function is common to all the quality-

---

[77]"An Economic Perspective on Population Growth," in
Rapid Population Growth, p. 166.

[78]"Pitfalls in Benefit-Cost Analysis of Birth Prevention," *Population Studies*, XXIII (July 1969), p. 164.

of-life views, as I have said, and it is a problem that points up the fact that any estimate of the population problem involves a prior determination of how goods and evils are to be distributed in a social order. Here this problem partly takes the form of a conflict between those who value offspring and those for whom additional children, because of their effects on income, are an evil. To settle this conflict, some general way of ranking and ordering these different preferences is required. But, in addition to this, the problem of placing children in a social welfare function also raises some fundamental questions about the very general distribution of income and opportunities in society. For children not only have emotional value to parents, but concrete economic value as well. And this value is closely enough correlated with parents' economic status in many societies so that programs of population limitation, whether voluntary or coerced, can have a marked effect on the social distribution of income. But if this is so, no moral assessment of population growth or population limitation can proceed without some prior understanding of the way in which income and opportunities are to be justly distributed in a community. Here, a problem we discussed in connection with the claim that population growth threatens social and political institutions, makes its appearance in the economic context.

We can perhaps understand this problem better by looking more closely at the value of children as this has been discussed in the economic literature. In an effort to relate reproductive behavior to economic analysis, a number of economists have sought to elaborate a theory of fertility according to which a couple's decision to have or not have an additional child is likened to a consumer decision in which the benefits and costs of securing an item are weighed against one another.[79] Those who have worked out this theory

---

[79]See Leibenstein, *Economic Backwardness*, pp. 159-70; Gary Becker, "An Economic Analysis of Fertility," in *Demographic and Economic Change in Developed Countries,* A Conference of the Universities-National Bureau Committee for Economic Research (Princeton, N.J.: Princeton University Press, 1960), pp. 209-31; Richard Easterlin, "Toward a Socio-Economic Theory of Fertility: A Survey of Recent Research on

do not wish to affirm that all children are the result of
rational calculation of this sort, although they believe a
substantial number of reproductive decisions can be understood
in this way.[80] Nor do they affirm that all the benefits or
costs of children are really expressible in economic terms.
They concede that such benefits as the joy taken in children,
or the religious value of surviving offspring, escape strict
economic analysis. And the same is true of costs involved in
childrearing such as parental anxieties or loss of time that
does not directly impede economic activity. Nevertheless,
these theorists wish to maintain that a substantial number of
the advantages and disadvantages of children can be expressed
in economic terms.[81]

The economic costs of having an additional child
according to this position include direct costs involved in
the bearing and rearing process, such as costs of prenatal
care, delivery, food, clothing, shelter, and medical and educational expenses. Opportunity costs in the form of the wife's
income foregone or the cost of extra-parental child care also
enter here. Economic benefits include the contributions of
children to the family's income, directly through their aid
in production and, in the future, as a form of retirement
annuity which parents can "purchase" in their youth to draw
upon when their own ability to work is diminished by old age
or ill health. Economists who have reflected on these costs
and benefits seem agreed that the benefits of additional
children most clearly outweigh costs when levels of average
income are low. As income rises, this relation is reversed,
except perhaps at the very highest levels of income.[82]

Economic Factors," in *Fertility and Family Planning: A World
View,* eds. S. J. Behrman, L. Corsa and R. Freedman (Ann Arbor:
University of Michigan Press, 1969), pp. 127-56.

[80]Leibenstein, *Economic Backwardness,* p. 160.

[81]For a synthetic treatment of all these costs and
benefits see Warren C. Robinson, "Population Growth and
Economic Welfare," *Reports on Population/Family Planning,*
No. 6 (February 1971), pp. 22-27.

[82]Leibenstein, *Economic Backwardness,* pp. 161ff.

56

The fact that the economic benefits of having children
may be greater at the lowest income levels poses the very basic
distributive problem I have spoken of. It may be true, as
economists have observed, that fertility reduction is needed
to begin the development process and to facilitate growth in
per capita income. But whose income, really, is advanced by
such lowered fertility? When an economy is organized so that
the lowest income classes possess no economic security for old
age or sickness, or when these classes earn their livelihood
by the application of sheer labor to resources owned by others,
it may not be in their advantage to lower their fertility.
They may well worsen their economic position by reducing their
numbers. In addition, if there exists any kind of government
transfer program by which families receive income or benefits
on a per capita basis, it may be sharply to their disadvantage
to lower fertility. One can imagine, for example, that in a
given society the expense of educating children is underwritten
by the government, which draws revenues for this purpose from
progressive taxes on the income of families. Under such a
system, additional offspring might greatly advantage low income
families. The costs of these children would be low, their
education would be free, and their prospects of economic improvement greatly enhanced. Thus, low-income individuals may
have no reason to reduce fertility under these or similar
conditions and they may have every reason to expand the size
of their families.

It may still be true, of course, that high fertility
has a deleterious effect on average income in this setting.
Swelling numbers of lower class individuals may overwhelm a
society's ability to equip present generations with the capital
and skills needed for development, and, where transfer
arrangements exist, high fertility may even drain income from
those higher-income, low-fertility groups at the forefront of
the modernization process. In the name of "social welfare,"
therefore, it is natural to demand fertility restraint and
when voluntary programs prove ineffective, as they well might,
it would be natural to seek to effect this restraint by one
or another coercive policy. But do such policies really promote social welfare? In view of the substantial number of
low-income families disadvantaged by reduced fertility, this

is not at all clear. As with many proposed social policies
population reduction has distributive implications that render
its welfare consequences uncertain. How does one balance the
gains to those individuals and groups that profit by higher per
capita income against the immediate losses experienced by those
individuals and groups forced to restrain their numbers?

Generally speaking, when faced with this kind of distributive problem, welfare economists have sought to circum-
vent it by means of a compensation principle. They have
argued that if a particular redistribution has the effect of
increasing income overall, but works to the detriment of some
representative group, then this difficulty can be overcome by
transferring some of the increased income back to the losers
in the distribution. Such compensation can render everybody
at least as well-off as they were before the redistribution and
render some individuals better off. For this reason, they
argue, income-maximizing decisions can always be seen to
maximize welfare, irrespective of their distributive
implications.[83]

Recently, some economists have tried to apply this
reasoning to the population problem of the developing regions
and, particularly, to the distributive difficulty a decision
to maximize average income by reducing fertility can involve.
Warren Robinson, for example, has suggested that the bonus
or incentive schemes proposed by Stephen Enke and Paul Demeny
may be thought of as transfer or compensation mechanisms of
the sort indicated by the welfare economists. By means of such
bonus schemes, high-income, low-fertility groups in a society,
who might be the principal beneficiaries of a lower rate of
population growth in the society as a whole, would be able to
transfer back to the low-income, high-fertility groups some of
the income these groups might lose if fertility is lowered.
According to Robinson, so long as the tax burden imposed by

---

[83]For discussions of this "compensation" principle see
Nicholas Kaldor, "Welfare Propositions and Interpersonal Com-
parisons of Utility," *Economic Journal*, XLIX (1939), 549-52;
John R. Hicks, "The Foundations of Welfare Economics,"
Economic Journal, XLIX (1939), 696-712; and Melvin Reder,
Studies in the Theory of Welfare Economics (New York: Columbia
University Press, 1947), Ch. VIII.

58

these incentive schemes did not outweigh the higher income
groups' gains from lowered fertility, it would be rational
for these groups to support these schemes. And, so long as
the incentive payments received by the low-income groups
equaled or outweighed their benefits from children, these
groups, too, would find it rational to cooperate with these
schemes.[84]

Robinson himself notes a difficulty in this reasoning,
however. It may be the case, he says, that the losses in such
schemes offset the gains, that is, "that the subsidy and bonus
required to effect the desired reduction in fertility may be
too great in the judgment of the gainers to permit them to
pay for it out of their gain and leave anything left over."[85]

In this case a program of fertility reduction cannot
bring about a certain increase in social welfare, and, in such
cases, population would continue to grow. Nevertheless, what
is welfare maximizing for one generation may not be so for
future generations. There are costs of high fertility that
can be external to entire generations, such as the exhaustion
of once readily available but non-replaceable natural resources.
Where this is true, a future generation would gain from
fertility reduction in an earlier generation, and might even
be prepared to transfer back some of its gains to its predecessors. But how can such compensation be effected? It should
be clear that the whole idea of compensation, real or hypothetical, breaks down when one views demographic increase as
a source of concern to several or more generations.

Population growth thus forces a series of distributive
decisions that cannot be by-passed by means of a compensation
device. The first of these decisions presents itself at the
generational level, and involves choosing between the groups
that are affected in different ways by high fertility. In view
of the fact that low income groups seem immediately to benefit
most by unrestrained population growth this kind of decision
has unavoidable welfare implications. For any policy that

---

[84]"Population Growth and Economic Welfare," p. 31.

[85]*Ibid.*, p. 32.

seriously disadvantages those closest to a subsistence level
of income must have grave effects on social welfare as a whole.
It would thus seem impossible to estimate the effect of population restraint without some comprehensive prior estimate of how
the social product ought to be distributed in a given society.
Only with such an estimate in hand could one then proceed to
alter existing distributive arrangements in the confidence
that welfare would not be reduced.

It is possible, of course, to try to by-pass this
difficulty by means of a compensation device. But this poses
numerous difficulties in itself. Without a prior estimate of
just distributive shares, for example, compensation may only
serve to perpetuate arrangements detrimental to welfare.
Thus, groups wrongly drawing a share of income by high fertility
might have that share sustained when compensation is paid.
More serious than this, however, is what compensation payments
might mean for the welfare of future generations. On the one
hand, if reduced fertility is needed to promote growth in
income, and if the gains are great enough over the course of
one generation, compensation is feasible. But the very payment
of compensation to high fertility groups can have the effect
of siphoning off much of the income gain in their direction,
and future generations may be disadvantaged. On the other
hand, the gains to one generation may not be sufficient to
permit compensation, and fertility could then proceed unaltered.
In this case, members of future generations might be disadvantaged by larger population sizes. Either way, in other
words, it is the future that is penalized by high fertility.
While use of a compensation device might help by-pass
distributive decisions between groups in the present, it cannot do so across generations. At some point, the question
must be answered of which generations are to count in estimating the welfare implications of fertility. Which generations
are to make the sacrifices involved in any decision in this
area? And once this question is answered, the benefits or
losses produced by lowered fertility must be distributed within
generations in a morally acceptable way without the aid of a
compensation device.

The difficulty pointed up by the impossibility of
compensation across generations brings to mind the older

optimum theory's uncertainty over the time-span that is to
enter into population decisions. The insistence that population size or rates of growth be maintained at an income-
maximizing level may have some meaning when applied over the
very short run, say, over the space of a single generation.
But once it is recognized that demographic problems necessarily
involve more than one generation, a prior determination must
be made concerning the generations whose income is to be
maximized. We can see now that despite the focus on the much
narrower issue of population growth in the underdeveloped
setting, economic thinking on population has not fully
escaped this earlier problem. Even over the space of several
generations conflict is possible and requires adjudication.
Should population be reduced in order to promote development
from backwardness? If so, how much? And how much should be
demanded from the various income groups in any one generation
that participate in this task?

Interestingly, once the possible conflict between
generations is recognized on this issue, it is not clear any
longer that the economic literature's virtual preoccupation
with the fertility problems of the underdeveloped nations is
justified. Earlier, I noted that one reason for the movement
away from the question of optimum population for a developed
economy was the relative immunity of those economies to per-
turbations caused by population growth. The experience of the
developed nations has been one of constant growth in income
regardless of demographic conditions. This had encouraged
the belief that once development had begun, matters of population could largely be left disregarded. But the recent
decline in environmental quality in many of the industrialized
nations has challenged this earlier confidence. Ecologists
and conservationists have occasionally engaged in bitter
criticism of the economists' attention to the relation between
population and income and their inattention to the effect of
population on values not entered into national income accounts,
such as the quality of the physical environment.[86] And some

---

[86]See, for example, Paul and Anne Ehrlich, *Population,
Resources, Environment,* p. 279.

economists have responded sympathetically to this criticism.
Spengler, for example, notes that the concept "income" has been
too narrowly construed by many economists. Properly understood, he argues, this concept should include values jeopardized by demographic pressure even in a developed setting,
values such as non-agricultural recreational land, or "parameters of space" such as atmosphere, topography, and climate
on which human and other species depend.[87]

A similar point has been made recently by Demeny. He
observes that the high levels of income and advanced techno-
logies of developed economies create unprecedented demands on
the physical environment. At the same time the elasticity of
demand for environmentally-related values such as recreational
space is likely to be very high in economies of this sort.[88]
These considerations lead Demeny to conclude that continued
population growth in a developed economy can jeopardize the
advancing living standard of present and future generations.
And he even argues that population size, not simply growth,
must be considered in relation to these economies. Since
higher income can increase both the value of the environment
and the pressure upon it, growth in income may reduce the
population size that is optimal at higher income levels.[89]
Should population grow at this stage, therefore, or should
large populations be handed on to the future, welfare in its
fullest sense may be lowered.

Attention to these environmental issues has tended to
point up the fact that inter-generational conflict as a
result of demographic pressure can occur at any stage of the
developmental process. At every stage, population growth or
larger population sizes can cut into the income of future
generations or, in some cases, of existing groups in present
generations who are disadvantaged by high fertility. It is

---

[87]"The Economist and the Population Question," *American
Economic Review*, LVI (March 1966), 10. Also see his "The
Aesthetics of Population," *Population Bulletin*, XIII (1957),
61-75.

[88]"The Economics of Population Control," pp. 207ff.

[89]*Ibid.*, p. 208.

not enough in these cases to recommend, as economists have
been accustomed to do, that income be maximized. For once it
is clear that not everybody's welfare increases as a result of
fertility restraint, indeed, that not everybody's income does
so, the real question becomes whose income or whose welfare
should be given priority. Unless this question is answered,
a recommendation that income be maximized by fertility reduction works out to be a distributive preference for those who
cherish income and who belong either to future generations or
to low fertility groups in the present.

I should add that some economists are not unaware of
these basic distributive issues. I have already indicated
Schultz's and Leibenstein's recognition that children deserve
a place in a social welfare function. I have also noted the
unsuecessful efforts to employ the idea of compensation to by-
pass recognized distributive difficulties within a generation
that can be occasioned by population limitation. Finally, I
might point to Leibenstein's effort to resolve several of these
difficulties by means of a concept of "long run" welfare
criteria.[90] In Leibenstein's view, policy decisions that
affect a series of individuals and generations should not be
made with a focus on the effect of specific redistributions.
Rather, attention should be given to the choice of economic
"games" or larger and enduring patterns of economic activity.
By their nature such choices are long run; practices and
institutions extend for generations into the future. Now, if
the matter of regulating reproductive behavior were included
among the choice of "games" regulated by this welfare procedure,
then the procedure might possibly correct the lack of long run
distributive consideration that presently characterizes
economic discussions of population growth. Such a procedure
might also help arrange some of the unavoidable distributive
conflicts within generations raised by high fertility or
fertility reduction. But Leibenstein has not worked out his
view that far. Nor is it to be expected that he should. The
kind of viewpoint he suggests moves beyond many of the

---

[90]"Long-run Welfare Criteria," in *The Public Economy
of Urban Communities,* ed. Julius Margolis (Washington, D.C.:
Resources for the Future, Inc., 1965), pp. 39-51.

traditional areas of concern to economists and raises basic
questions of moral and political philosophy. In the second
part of the thesis I shall seek to approach some of these
issues directly with a moral theory not dissimilar to the viewpoint or procedure suggested by Leibenstein.[91] Whichever view
is selected, it is clear that the need for such an approach
arises from difficulties involved in any claim that population
growth poses a problem because of its threat to income or
other values believed central to the "quality of life." No
claim of this sort can, in its own right, be taken as an
adequate assessment of the moral issues raised by high
fertility.

B. *Views Denying that Population Poses a Moral Problem*

I want to turn now briefly to several perspectives
whose common feature is a denial that population growth poses
a moral problem. These positions result from one or several
separate claims: that population growth is not a cause of
evils for moral agents (or that it is more properly thought of
as a cause of goods); that it is a cause of evils but is not
subject to control; or that it is a cause of evils but ought
not to be subject to moral control. Each of the views we
shall examine characteristically contains statements of this
sort, although the reasons for these statements can differ.

1. *Catholic Views*

In speaking of a Catholic viewpoint on population
growth, or a Catholic denial of the population problem, one
encounters the immediate difficulty of speaking of a unified
Catholic view of any moral problem today. It is commonly recognized that the Church of the post-Vatican II era no longer
speaks with a single voice on moral or doctrinal matters. Any
treatment of Catholic moral teaching today, therefore, must

[91]For a comparison of Leibenstein's position with the
contract theory of justice, see below p. 102, f.n. 6.

proceed on the assumption that there is not only the authoritative position of Popes, Councils and recognized moralists--the Magisterium in the usual sense--but also the views of dissenting moralists and laymen that must be taken into account. The Catholic viewpoint we shall be examining largely coincides with the position of the Magisterium, but it includes, as well, a good deal of conservative interpretation of that teaching. I give less attention to the views of those progressive moralists and laymen according to whose interpretation the Magisterium does not deny the existence of a population problem. My approach to Catholic teaching is, therefore, selective. I want to accentuate the conservative interpretation in order to bring out what has been unique in Catholic thinking in this area.[92]

A second difficulty in approaching Catholic thinking on this issue derives from the temptation to make the view of population merely an appendage of the Church's teaching on contraception. Since contraception plays a part in any program of population limitation, it is natural to suppose that only a question of legitimate method separates Catholics from non-Catholics on the population issue. Certainly, there are many inside and outside the Catholic Church who have viewed the issue in this way.[93] Nevertheless, as important as the matter of birth control might be in shaping Roman Catholic thinking on the population problem, it is mistaken to believe that Catholic opposition to programs of fertility control and to other demographic efforts to remove social evils is based exclusively on the objection to birth control. There does

---

[92]For references to the variety of Catholic views of the population problem, see bibliography, Section G.

[93]Non-Catholic writers who have reduced Catholic population theory to a matter of birth control include Alvah Sulloway, *Birth Control and Catholic Doctrine* (Boston: Beacon Press, 1959), p. xix and William Vogt, *People! Challenge to Survival* (New York: William Sloane Associates, 1960), pp. 211ff. Catholic thinkers who take this position include John Kane in "A Sociological View," in *What Modern Catholics Think About Birth Control*, ed. William Birmingham (New York: The New American Library, 1964), pp. 151-63, and John Rock, *The Time Has Come* (New York: Alfred A. Knopf, 1963), Chs. 1-3.

exist a distinct and authoritative Catholic viewpoint on overpopulation amounting to an assessment of the goods and evils
associated with demographic increase and a series of recommendations concerning a morally permissible response to these evils.
These recommendations do not include fertility reduction but
for reasons having as much to do with the assessment of the
problem as with the ban on birth control. Applied to overpopulation in national communities, this viewpoint predates
the Second World War.[94] Since the war, with little alteration
in its major contentions, this viewpoint has been applied to
the global population situation. It has found consistent
expression in the encyclical literature of this period and has
been articulated in additional papal statements.[95] It appears,
as well, to have received support in the Pastoral Constitution
on the Church in the Modern World, *"Gaudium et Spes,"* issued by
the Second Vatican Council.[96] Finally, this view has been
amplified in a body of non-authoritative literature written by
Catholic moralists specifically concerned with population
growth.[97]

I may briefly summarize this position by stating that
it amounts to a refusal to permit manipulation of the

---

[94]See, for example, John A. Ryan, "Population," *The
Catholic Encyclopedia* (New York: The Encyclopedia Press, 1907-
1912), XII, 276-78.

[95]See, for example, Pius XII, "Christmas Message of
1952," in *Major Addresses of Pius XII*, ed. V. A. Yzermans (St.
Paul, Minnesota: N. Central Publishing Co., 1961), II, 159-
83. Also, John XXIII, Encyclical Letter *Mater et Magistra*
(Providence: Providence Visitors Society, 1961). Also Paul
VI, Encyclical Letter *Populorum Progressio* (New York: Paulist
Press, 1967); Encyclical Letter *Humanae Vitae* in *The Catholic
Case for Contraception*, ed. Daniel Callahan (London: Mac-
millan Co., 1969), pp. 212-38; "Address to the General
Assembly of the United Nations, 1965," in *The Fourth Session;
The Debates and Decrees of Vatican Council II, September 14
to December 8, 1965*, ed. Xavier Rynne (New York: Farrar,
Straus & Giroux, 1966), pp. 285-91; and his "Statement on
Population," *New York Times*, November 18, 1970.

[96]In Walter Abbott, ed., *The Documents of Vatican II*
(New York: Guild Press, 1966), pp. 301ff.

[97]See bibliography, Section G, especially the writings
of Rupert Ederer, George Kelly, Stanislas de Lestapis, Arthur
McCormack and Anthony Zimmerman.

population variable. Whether or not high fertility is esteemed
as one of the causes of social evils, fertility itself is not
considered subject to control for the purpose of eliminating
those evils. Attention is instead focused on other contributory
causes, such as low levels of productivity, or inadequate
distribution of goods. Manipulation of these variables to
alleviate shortages and situations of "overpopulation" is the
recommended course.

At the heart of this Catholic viewpoint stands the
extremely high value placed upon family life and upon the
importance of the family as a procreative unit. The integrity
and health of the family forms, for Catholic thinking, a major
object of social and personal concern. And the family on
which Catholic thought focuses is not simply an association
oriented to the satisfaction of its members, but a social
group whose highest responsibility is the procreation and
nurture of offspring. For Catholic teaching, procreation is
not just a right of families but a duty. In replacing themselves and augmenting the numbers of mankind, the couple is
viewed as selflessly and generously cooperating in the
creative activity of God.[98]

This valuation of the family as a procreative unit
certainly plays a part in shaping Catholic thinking on birth
control. But in a sense, this valuation precedes the birth
control ban and serves as its basis. As a result, the value
placed upon the family as a procreative unit has significance
beyond the realm of sexual morality and enters into Catholic
social and political thought as well. The Catholic position
on population derives from this more fundamental valuation
and belongs really to Catholic social theory. Evidence for
this, in part, is the fact that some Catholic writers who
accept the technical legitimacy of birth regulation by means
of the rhythm method still resist suggestions that this means

---

[98]For a full account of the historical development of
this stress on familial procreative responsibility, see John
T. Noonan, *Contraception; A History of Its Treatment by the
Catholic Theologians and Canonists* (Cambridge, Mass.:
Harvard University Press, 1965) and Derrick Sherwin Bailey,
The Man-Woman Relation in Christian Thought (London: Long-
mans, 1959).

be used for population limitation. Their valuation of the
family in its procreative capacity leads them to resist efforts
to limit the family's exercise of its procreative responsibility.[99]

Catholic valuation of the family as procreative unit
is not confined to the past. Recent authoritative statements
on the family have consistently reaffirmed the obligation of
married couples to bear the largest number of children that
their circumstances allow.[100] It is true that this responsibility is not unqualified. Catholic moral teaching has always
maintained that the duty to procreate also includes an obligation properly to rear and educate one's children.[101] Thus,
conditions within the family circle which can hinder the
proper education of children are among the reasons which can
excuse a couple from fulfilling their procreative duty. But
it is not equally clear that conditions in the surrounding
society which do not directly affect the individual family's
ability to rear its young also constitute an excuse from this
obligation. Moralists have argued on both sides of this
question.[102] Nor have recent Papal utterances clarified the

---

[99]Stanislas de Lestapis, for example, admits the
general permissibility of birth limitation by the rhythm
method, but he does not advocate the use of rhythm for population control and calls, instead, for steps to facilitate
a growing population. See his *Family Planning and Modern
Problems* (New York: Herder and Herder, 1961), p. 282. See
also George Kelly, *Overpopulation: A Catholic View* (Glen
Rock, N.J.: Paulist Press, 1960), p. 72.

[100]See, for example, *Gaudium et Spes* in Abbot, ed.,
pp. 251ff.

[101]In his treatments of human sexuality, Thomas Aquinas
provides the foundation for what has been consistent Catholic
teaching in this area. See his *Summa Theologica* Ia-IIae,
Quest. 94, Art. 2; IIa-IIae, Quest. 154, Art. 2; and Supplement,
Quest. 41, Art. 1.

[102]Zimmerman argues in his *Overpopulation: A Study of
Papal Teachings on the Population Problem with Special
Reference to Japan* (Catholic University of America Press,
1957), pp. 89ff., that demographic reasons are not among the
indications which legitimate use of the rhythm method.
Louis Janssens, "Catholics and Non-Catholics: Their Collaboration in Family Planning," *World Justice*, V (1963-64),
34, and Paul Anciaux, "Ethical Aspects of Demographic Policy,"
World Justice, V (1963-64), 291, take an opposite view.

issue. In his encyclical *Humanae Vitae*, for example, Paul VI
specifies that the couple's procreative responsibility extends
to God, themselves, their family and society in a "correct
hierarchy of values."[103] But the Pope nowhere indicates what
that correct hierarchy is.

Within the framework of Catholic thinking, therefore,
we can continue to speak of a very weighty *prima facie*
obligation to procreate incumbent upon every family. The
seriousness with which this obligation is understood is further
evidenced by the rights which correspond to it. Catholic
teaching has consistently maintained that the couple's right
to procreate and the right to determine the size of their own
family are both absolute and may not be infringed by government.
The Second Vatican Council, for example, speaks of an "inalien-
able right to marry and beget children," and adds that "the
question of how many children should be born belongs to the
honest judgment of the parents. The question can in no way
be committed to the decisions of government."[104]

This insistence on an absolute right to procreate and
to determine the size of one's family is not without its
difficulties. It appears, for example, to undercut the traditional Catholic moral awareness that the common good of the
community takes precedence over individual or private goods.[105]
But some Catholic writers deny that there is any contradiction
here, and their remarks serve to illuminate the logic which
has supported Catholic thinking on the priority of the family

---

For a general discussion of the place of demographic considera-
tions in use of the rhythm method, see Gerald Kelly and John C.
Ford, "Periodic Continence," *Theological Studies*, XXIII
(December 1962), 590-624.

[103]In Callahan, ed., p. 219.

[104]Abbot, ed., p. 302.

[105]Joseph Fuchs, *Natural Law; A Theological Investigation*
(New York: Sheed and Ward, 1965), p. 131; also Gerald Kelly,
"The Common Good and the Socio-Economic Order," *Proceedings
of the Catholic Theological Society of America*, VII (1952),
91. Recently, some Catholic writers have argued that this
priority can justify state intervention in familial reproductive decisions. See, for example, Daniel Callahan, *Ethics and
Population Limitation* (New York: Population Council, 1971),
pp. 16-18. But this remains a minority viewpoint.

as a procreative unit. These writers contend that there is a
proper ranking of ends served by a just social order. Society
aims to serve the individual and the family; individuals and
families do not exist for society. Thus, they conclude, the
rights of families are not to be manipulated for broad social
or economic purposes. State intervention must be confined to
the sort which directly enables the family to achieve its
proper end, as when the state prohibits individuals from marry-
ing at an age when they are too young to responsibly raise
offspring.[106]

Yet another writer has argued that this priority of
family over community is drawn from the basic priority in
Catholic thought of the sexual and procreative aspects of
human existence over the social aspects. This priority, for
example, is reflected in the Catholic ranking of sexual sins,
where masturbation is judged to be a graver violation of the
natural moral law than rape. While the latter represents a
disruption of the rational communal life, which man is called
to shape, the former constitutes a direct violation of the
basic pattern of desires implanted directly in man by his
Creator. It is therefore considered a more serious violation
of God's moral will.[107] Whether or not these considerations
enter directly into Papal thinking on family and society today
is open to question. But it should be kept in mind that when
Paul VI asks couples to order their responsibilities to family,
community and God within a "correct hierarchy of values," he
utilizes terminology with a history that tends to underscore
the essential priority of family interests to those of society.

This heavy stress on the family's right and duty to
procreate serves as a fixed reference point for Catholic
thinking about population growth. For many Catholic writers,
the effect of this stress is to thrust the burden of proof upon
all those who would urge married couples to limit their number

---

[106]See Heinrich Rommen, *The Natural Law* (St. Louis:
Herder Book Co., 1947), p. 238, and Jacques Maritain, *The
Rights of Man and Natural Law* (New York: Charles Scribner's
Sons, 1943), pp. 78ff.

[107]Louis Janssens, *Mariage et Fécondité* (Gembloux:
Editions J. Duculot, 1967), pp. 46ff.

of offspring for demographic or economic reasons. Proponents
of birth limitation--by whatever means--are called upon to
show the clear necessity for that recourse. If many Catholic
writers have refused to concede that population control is
justified, it is because they perceive alternate ways of
handling pressing social evils, ways that do not require interference with familial reproductive liberty.

The principal alternative emphasized by these thinkers
is the increased production and wider distribution of goods.
Catholic spokesmen frequently note that the "population problem" is not a global or national one. Despite the existence
of areas or regions where there are too many people for
available resources, there also exist areas, nations or entire
regions where productivity is high and material goods are
plentiful.[108] Thus, they argue, it would be possible to
alleviate the suffering and distress of areas experiencing
demographic pressure if their more prosperous neighbors would
share their goods, their know-how and even their territory with
the less advantaged. In recommending this course, Catholic
thinkers do not appeal to the charity of the more advantaged.
Rather, they maintain that such sharing of material resources
and skills is a demand of justice. They appeal to a firm
tenet of Catholic moral theory, one that has been expanded
into a substantial body of social teaching, that the goods of
the earth exist for the common use of men. The validity of
private property is not denied, but it is insisted that
property must, in justice, be shared.[109]

Applied to the matter of population this position leads
to the demand that "population problems" be solved not by
birth restraint but by greater sharing of goods and technology.

---

[108]John XXIII, *Mater et Magistra*, p. 39.

[109]This teaching can be traced to Thomas Aquinas, *Summa
Theologica* IIa-IIae, Quest. 61; Arts. 1, 2, 3. For an account
of Catholic teaching on national and international justice see
Jean-Yves Calvez and Jacques Perrin, *The Church and Social
Justice* (Chicago: Henry Regnery Co., 1961) and Richard Camp,
The Papal Ideology of Social Reform (Leiden: E. J. Brill,
1969). Also, Arthur McCormack, *World Poverty and the Christian*
(New York: Hawthorne Books, 1963).

John XXIII, for example, maintains that the "true solution" to the difficulties associated with population is "cooperation on a world scale that permits an ordered and fruitful interchange of useful knowledge, of capital and manpower."[110] And Paul VI, while still Vatican Pro-Secretary of State, maintained that the "industrious solidarity of all peoples" is the remedy for overpopulation.[111]

In this emphasis on the sharing of goods to ease localized situations of population density, Catholic teaching supports the principle that nations or regions are not responsible for limiting their population in order to meet their indigenous economic capability. This, of course, follows from the very heavy stress in Catholic thought on the right and duty to procreate and from the relative priority given the family over the community. Pius XII expresses this principle and its rationale concisely when he maintains that to suggest that the number of inhabitants of a given region be regulated according to the public economy is "equivalently to subvert the order of nature."[112] Here Catholic thinking is poles apart from that of Malthus and some of his intellectual descendants. Justice in this area is not taken to mean that families should restrain their reproductive activity for the sake of community welfare, as was true for Malthus, but that social resources should be employed for the aid of the family as a procreative unit.

This series of concerns and priorities commonly leads Catholic thinkers to deny that one can speak of "overpopulation" in any meaningful sense. The evils usually attributed to demographic pressure, in their view, are a result, not of population, but of the lack of solidarity between men and nations. What is called the "population problem" is really a problem of human injustice and greed. Furthermore, when this perception of the issue is joined with the traditional Catholic objection to methods of artificial birth control, it leads to

---

[110]*Mater et Magistra*, p. 39.

[111]Quoted in Zimmerman, *Overpopulation*, p. 305.

[112]"Christmas Message of 1952," in Yzermans, ed., p. 167.

a vigorous condemnation of programs of contraceptive aid.
These programs, whether on the national or international level,
are viewed as doubly immoral. Not only do they violate the
sexual moral order dictated by the natural law, but they violate the natural law order of justice as well. Pius XII
expresses this view when he terms birth control programs
"simply a pretext used by those who justify avarice and
selfishness." Such programs, he adds, are the work of those
groups and nations "who fear that the expansion of others will
pose a danger to their own political position and cause
general lowering of the standard of living."[113] One moralist
has argued that birth control programs reflect the uneasy
conscience of the well-to-do nations. These nations, he says,
are fearful of the burgeoning, clamoring populations of the
less developed world, but, at the same time, they refuse to
take generous steps to remedy poverty. They soothe their
consciences and serve their interests by disseminating contraceptive devices instead. The ostensible generosity of these
programs, therefore, conceals a strong measure of egoism and
selfishness.[114]

Because they see these programs as violating the dictates of sexual and social morality, moreover, some Catholic
writers predict that they cannot be successful in eliciting
mass support in the underdeveloped world. George Kelly, for
example, argues that the instincts of normal people everywhere
aim at parenthood and family life so that the residents of
poorer nations can be expected to resist contraceptive aid
programs, just as they have resisted using the ancient means
of birth control known to all cultures.[115] Other writers argue
that the basic selfishness implicit in contraceptive aid programs will lead to their failure. "People in the developing
countries," says Anthony Zimmerman, "are not so naive as to

---

[113]"Address to Large Families of Rome and Italy, 1958,"
quoted in Zimmerman, *Overpopulation*, p. 116.

[114]de Lestapis, *Family Planning and Modern Problems*, p. 9.

[115]Kelly, *Overpopulation*, pp. 64ff.

confuse real aid from advanced nations with aid in birth prevention."[116] Presumably, they can be expected to resist accomodation to these programs. Arthur McCormack adds that not only the economic but in many cases the racial overtones of these programs can render them unsuccessful. When residents of poor ex-colonial nations receive contraception instead of economic aid, he argues, they are likely to see this aid as a form of racial or national genocide, and seek to resist its incursions.[117]

The Catholic viewpoint on overpopulation is thus a unified and inclusive perspective. It involves not only a diagnosis and solution for the evils associated with population growth, but it generates a rationale which condemns other solutions to failure. The consistency and forcefulness of this view probably results from the way in which it draws together some of the more important insistences of contemporary Catholic moral teaching: the objection to methods of artificial birth control, the more basic valuation of the family and of its reproductive function, and the strong encouragement to a just distribution of the goods of the earth.

At the core of this Catholic viewpoint is the assumption that fertility ought not to be subject to moral control. It is true that even some of the more extreme Catholic spokesmen like Zimmerman would allow population control in the hypothetical state of "absolute overpopulation," where no more resources existed on a global scale to sustain human life. Other thinkers, perhaps the Popes themselves, would urge population limitation somewhere before this point in order to maintain an adequate level of material existence. But all these thinkers seem agreed that the reproductive responsibility of the family, the obligation to co-create with God in populating the earth and to display generosity to new life is so weighty as to take priority over strictly material values. And all are agreed that this is a demand of the natural moral law known to all men.

---

[116]*Catholic Viewpoint on Overpopulation* (Garden City, New York: Hanover House, 1961), p. 188.

[117]*World Poverty and the Christian,* p. 50.

The sharing and just distribution of goods, itself demanded by
the natural law, also extends to sharing in order to sustain
families, groups or nations in their reproductive function.
The Catholic denial of a "population problem," therefore,
fundamentally expresses a concern with the family and with the
future offspring that the family produces in the exercise of
its natural function. And it is a concern that extends not
only to the well-to-do but to the least privileged members of
society. In view of this series of distributive preferences,
it is not surprising that Catholic population thinking should
be so opposed to the Malthusian tradition.

2. *Marxist Views*

Next to Roman Catholicism, Marxism represents the one
major school of thought which has sought actively to deny the
existence of a "population problem." In the case of Catholicism, we have seen, this denial proceeds from the assumption
that the demographic variable ought not to be manipulated
because the safeguarding of the family in the exercise of its
procreative responsibility takes high moral priority. The
Marxist position, however, has a different point of departure.
In terms of our paradigm of what it means to say that something poses or does not pose a moral problem, Marxists have
generally based their denial of a population problem on the
claim that population growth is not causally related to the
social evils with which it is associated. They have insisted
that poverty, illiteracy and other evils have a social or
economic, not demographic explanation. And in defense of this
claim, they have advanced elaborate social and economic analyses of the conditions that create the appearance of overpopulation. We shall look at these shortly. But it is useful to
note at the outset that the air of scientific precision which
surrounds Marxist discussions of population growth can be
misleading. As on many issues, Marxist analysis serves to
express and give substance to a series of moral concerns that
are more than scientific. In this case, this concern is
directed toward the working class whose welfare is believed

jeopardized by proposals for population restraint. To understand this better, however, it is useful to look briefly at
the foundation of Marxist thinking in this area, Marx and
Engels' discussions of population.

Marxist population theory actually stands in a continuing tradition of opposition by radical social theorists to
Malthusian population doctrine.[118] To radical thinkers,
Malthus' *Essay on the Principle of Population* was more of a
political challenge than a scientific treatise. As the full
title of the first edition of the *Essay* indicates, Malthus had
sought to employ the "principle of population" to demonstrate
the foolishness of the proposals for social change advocated
by Condorcet, Godwin and other defenders of the French Revolution.[119] If population advances always to the limits of subsistence, Malthus argued, any attempt at the redistribution of
social wealth would end in failure since redistributed wealth
would only serve to aid the proliferation of new, hungry
mouths.[120] Against the mere speculation of the rationalists
and social utopians, Malthus held up the hard facts of
"science" in the form of the differential progressions or
"ratios" of population and nourishment. According to these,
population growth must always outstrip food supplies.

Malthus had handed all those who would "improve"
society by social reorganization the task of demonstrating the
falsity of the principle of population. This demonstration
might involve showing that one or another of Malthus' ratios
was erroneous. Or it might involve the demonstration that
Malthus' attention to population had no scientific basis, that
the observable social evils which Malthus attributed to overpopulation have another explanation entirely. The former

---

[118]For a listing of Marxist and radical treatments of
population, see the bibliography, Section H.

[119]*An Essay on the Principle of Population, as It
Affects the Future Improvement of Society, With Remarks on the
Speculations of Mr. Godwin, M. Condorcet, and Other Writers*
(1798), in *On Population*, ed. Gertrude Himmelfarb.

[120]*Ibid.*, Ch. 5.

approach was tried by earlier radical thinkers and receives
some attention from Engels.[121] The latter approach is unique
to Marx.

In rejecting the Malthusian account of poverty and other
social evils Marx did not deny the gross fact of overpopulation,
that there were too many people for the existing stock of goods
and other factors of production. What he disputed was Malthus'
contention that this excess population resulted from the operation of permanent laws of nature requiring population always
to outstrip resources. Against Malthus, Marx insisted on the
historically conditioned nature of human population dynamics.
Just as every stage of human economic development has its own
pattern of political, familial and cultural relations, so does
every stage have its own law of population. "It is only for
plants and animals that there is a law of population in the
abstract," Marx declares.[122] Overpopulation, in his view,
forms a part of the law of population for capitalist society.
It is no more permanent than the other evils generated by the
capitalist system.

Tracing the exact relationship between capitalist production and overpopulation occupies Marx's attention in the
course of his treatment of the process of capitalist accumulation.[123] The creation of a constantly growing population of
redundant laborers, a population too large with respect to the
means of employment is, according to Marx, a necessary consequence of the growth of private capital. Wealth produced
by labor is progressively siphoned off in the course of production by the owners of the means of production. Capital is
thus in constant expansion. But, as accumulation proceeds,

---

[121]For an account of the approach taken by some utopian
socialists see Alfred Sauvy, "Marx et les problemes contem-
porains de la population," *Informations sur les Sciences
Sociales,* VII (August 1968), 28ff. Also, his article, "Les
marxistes et le malthusianisme," *Cahiers Internationaux de
Sociologie,* XLI (1966), 2ff.

[122]*Capital* (London: Allen & Unwin, 928), Vol. I, p. 698.

[123]*Ibid.,* Ch. 23.

the composition of capital undergoes change. Progressively
less capital is employed in the payment of wages to labor
(variable capital) and more is employed as means of production
(constant capital). This change in the composition of capital
is ineluctable because it is forced on the capitalist class
by the advance of technology and by the conditions of competition. The consequences of this change in the composition of
capital is a progressive fall in demand for labor, since this
demand arises from the relatively declining variable component
of capital. Growth of capital thus produces an "apparent"
increase in the laboring population, an increase, as Marx says,
"always moving more rapidly than that of the variable capital
or the means of employment." Marx points up the irony of this
process:

> The law in accordance with which a continually
> increasing quantity of the means of production
> can, thanks to the advance in the productivity
> of social labour, be set in motion by a pro-
> gressively diminishing expenditure of human
> energy--this law, in a capitalist society
> (where the worker does not make use of the
> means of production, but where the means of
> production make use of the worker) undergoes
> a complete inversion and is expressed as
> follows: the higher the productivity of labour,
> the greater is the pressure of the workers on
> the means of employment; and the more pre-
> carious, therefore, becomes their condition of
> existence, namely, the sale of their own labour-
> power for the increasing of another's wealth, or
> to promote self-expansion of capital. Under
> capitalism, likewise, the fact that the means
> of production and the productivity of labour
> grow more rapidly than does the productive
> population secures expression in an inverse way,
> namely that the working population always grows
> more quickly than capital needs for self-
> expansion.[124]

Overpopulation is thus an unavoidable consequence of
capitalist production. But it is more than that. It serves
as well as the "lever" of capitalist accumulation.[125] The
surplus population formed by this system, according to Marx,

---

[124]*Ibid.*, p. 713.

[125]*Ibid.*, pp. 698-700.

78

forms a "disposable reserve army" by means of which exploitation and accumulation are accelerated. Swelled by technological unemployment--and by the increasing movement of women and
children into the factory labor market--this reserve army perpetuates its condition. Because of the intense competition for
few job openings, wages are bid down and the working day
lengthened. The rate of exploitation--the ratio between paid
and unpaid labor--increases, capital expands rapidly and unem-
ployment extends ever more widely. The impoverished, unemployed
and continually growing proletariat is thus the product of
economic mechanisms and not the result of demographic factors
as is wrongly implied by the name "proletarian."[126]

Within the framework of this analysis, Malthus'
perspective is made to appear foolish and perverse. Population
does not exert pressure on the means of subsistence, says Marx.
Rather, the means of employment exert pressure on population.
Equally perverse, in Marx's view, is the suggestion tentatively
advanced by Malthus in the first edition of the *Essay* and
elaborated in later editions that the working class might
ameliorate the effects of the principle of population by
practicing "moral restraint," i.e. abstention from early
marriage. According to the classical tradition, which Malthus
represents at this point, the simple laws of supply and demand
regulate the wages of labor. Should the supply of labor
decline relative to the available capital, wages will rise and
the welfare of individual workers increase. In Marx's view,
however, this account ignores the dynamics of capitalist
accumulation and the power wielded by the capitalist class.
It ignores the fact that the owners of the means of production
cannot tolerate diminution in the rate of exploitation of
labor and must take steps to see that such diminution does not
occur. According to Marx, ". . . such a keeping down of the
labouring population, diminishing the supply of labour, and,

---

[126]Herman Daly states that Marx's use of the term
"proletarian" for the class created by the operation of the
capitalist economic system represents a deliberate effort to
undercut the demographic account of poverty. See his article,
"A Marxian-Malthusian View of Poverty and Development,"
Population Studies, XXV (March 1971), 25-37.

consequently, raising its price, would only *accelerate* the application of machinery, the conversion of circulating into fixed capital, and, hence, make the population artificially 'redundant' . . . ."[127]

Marx's opposition to birth limitation is thus based upon an assessment of its implications within the capitalist system and not, as in the case of Catholic thought, on a positive favorance of procreation. The method of birth limitation itself does not appear to have played a significant part in his thinking. To Marx, Malthus' proposal for voluntary restraint from marriage presumably is in no way better than contraceptive methods of birth limitation. Any means of fertility control renders the proletariat superfluous with respect to the means of production. We can distinguish Catholic and Marxist thinking on this issue by stating that for Marx fertility restraint is inadmissible primarily because it *cannot* eliminate observed social evils, whereas for Catholic thinkers it is inadmissible because fertility *ought not* to be subject to manipulation. The difference is important because it has had the effect of freeing Marxists from restraints on the use of birth control, so long as this could be justified on other than economic grounds. Thus societies such as the Soviet Union and China have displayed the curious pattern of liberal contraceptive and abortion programs, usually justified in the name of maternal welfare, side by side with often vociferous condemnations of birth control as an instrument of economic policy.[128]

---

[127]*Theorien über den Mehrwert, Werke* (Berlin: Dietz Verlag, 1967), Band 26, Zweiter Teil, s. 581. The English in this quotation is Marx's own.

[128]Lenin's remarks in his 1913 article, "The Working Class and Neomalthusianism" are typical: "We are unconditionally the enemies of neomalthusianism, suited only to unfeeling and egoistic petty-bourgeois couples who whisper in scared voices, 'God grant we manage somehow by ourselves. So much the better we have no children.'

"It goes without saying that this does not by any means prevent us from demanding the unconditional annulment of all laws against abortion or against the distribution of medical literature or contraceptive measures, etc. Freedom for medical propaganda and the protection of the elementary democratic

If Marx's method aimed at revealing the ironies (or "contradictions") within the capitalist system, his critique of Malthus and the principle of population represents a singular example of that method. Marx and Malthus' confrontation on the matter of overpopulation in fact typifies the confrontation between Marxian and classical economics. It is therefore a further irony that the analyses and projections of both men on the matter of population have not fully withstood the test of historical experience. As William Petersen has noted, Malthus (or at least the Malthus of the first edition of the *Essay*) did not accurately predict the rise of the working class standard of living concomitant with an unprecedented increase in population, nor did he foresee the decline in fertility among the lower classes in the West. Marx, on the other hand, was unable to predict the improved condition of the working class within the Western nations. Where Malthus neglected the future importance of growth in productivity and the use of artificial contraception, Marx underestimated the developing significance of the trade unions and the political power of labor.[129]

But I am not concerned here with the accuracy of Marx's analysis so much as with its moral implications. In this respect, I should note that Marx's critique, whatever its scientific value, expresses a strong moral position. Malthus' principle of population was offensive to Marx because it proferred a false account of the evils associated with population growth in order to preserve and defend existing social injustices. Marx was above all resentful of the general ideological role of Malthus' thinking in defending the capitalist mode of production and deflecting the barbs of its critics. Malthus' attribution of existing social problems to the prolificness and irresponsibility of the working class was

---

rights of citizens, men and women, are one thing. The social theory of neomalthusianism is quite another."--V. I. Lenin, *Collected Works* (Moscow: Foreign Languages Publishing House, 1963), Vol. XIX, p. 237.

[129]Petersen, *The Politics of Population* (Garden City, N.Y.: Doubleday & Company, 1964), p. 88.

an audacious slander in his view. The poor were being held
responsible for circumstances foisted upon them by the rich
and by an unjust social system. The dire conditions which
should have alerted the working class to their exploitation
were being used by Malthus to further the subjection and
oppression of that class.

The injustice implicit in Malthus' assessment of the
problem was compounded, in Marx's view, by his solution.
Malthus, in keeping with his insistence upon individual
responsibility, had recommended that members of the working
class better their condition by frugality, diligence and
"moral restraint" from early marriage. By working hard and
preventing themselves from being overburdened with excessive
children early in life, the workers could not only profit
most from their own wages, but they might also help drive up
the rate of wages generally. We have seen, however, that Marx
denied this claim. However much the isolated worker could
advantage himself in the short run by diligence and abstention,
so long as the means of production remained in the hands of
an alien and exploitative class the net result of individual
restraint would be to depress the wages of all workers. A
parallel illustration of Marx's view here may be found in
his estimate of piece work. Wherever this system of remunera-
tion was introduced, Marx noted, its initial effect was to
increase the pay of the hardest workers. In the long run,
however, the piece-work system drives down wages generally,
intensifies labor and lengthens the working day. Seeking to
extricate themselves from the condition of their class,
individual workers actually worsen their condition.[130] In the
last analysis, according to Marx, the only hope for workers
lies in strengthening their class consciousness and undertaking
joint action against the capitalist system. Because Malthus'
"moral restraint" serves to undercut the formation of this
common purpose, it further perpetuates the misery of the
proletariat.

It is not clear whether Marx also objected to Malthus'
solution because of its direct effect on the numbers of the

[130]*Capital*, Vol. I, p. 606.

proletariat. Certainly he believed that the swelling number
of poor provided one of the conditions for the eventual over-
throw of the capitalist system. But Marx was aware that the
formation of a powerful revolutionary class depended upon many
more factors than increase in numbers by birth. Whatever the
case, it is true that later followers of Marx--Lenin among
them--interpreted his objection to Malthus' "moral restraint"
to include the effects of birth limitation upon the numerical
strength of the proletariat.[131] Outside the Marxist camp this
theme has recently been picked up by spokesmen for the American
black minority and by some leaders of "Third World" nations.[132]

By diverting the workers from the true source of their
misery and by holding out a false solution to their problem,
Malthus' position, in Marx's eyes, thus perpetuated the workers'
suffering. But in two other respects, Marx appeared convinced
that Malthus' viewpoint actually worsened the condition of the
proletariat. It did so, first, by promoting abandonment of
the older English poor law, the so-called Speenhamland System
which, on a parish basis, provided modest sums to maintain
the indigent in their own homes. As we have noted, one of the
direct aims of the first edition of Malthus' *Essay* was to
demonstrate the folly of this system. The passage of a new
poor law in 1834 terminating in-home assistance and requiring
all who would receive aid to enter a workhouse thus represented
a victory for Malthus' ideas. The principle of population
proved an effective instrument for eliminating what had become
a costly drain on the revenues of the propertied classes, a
fact of which Marx was fully aware.

---

[131]Lenin, "The Working Class and Neomalthusianism,"
p. 236. Also, the remarks by Rosa Luxembourg in opposition
to socialist proposals for birth limitation, quoted in Sauvy,
"Les marxistes et le malthusianisme," p. 7.

[132]See, for example, Robert F. Murray, Jr., "The
Ethical and Moral Values of Black Americans and Population
Policy," Documentary Study prepared for the Commission on
Population Growth and the American Future (Hastings-on-Hudson,
N.Y.: Institute of Society, Ethics and the Life Sciences,
1971). See, also, the articles by Stycos listed in the
bibliography, Section H, for a treatment of the views of
minority group spokesmen.

Finally, Marx resented the corrosive effect of Malthus' thinking on the family life of the workers. Having sought to deprive the worker of even a subsistence dole, Malthus would also deny them a normal sex and family life. "Parson Malthus," said Marx, "reduces the workers to beasts of burden for the sake of production, and even condemns them to die of hunger and to celibacy."[133] Marx saw Malthus' view as accentuating the inroads made by capitalism on the family life of the working class. In its quest for cheap labor, capitalism had already forced the employment of the worker's wife and children. Malthus would not just disrupt the home but deprive the worker of even the simple pleasures of bed and hearth. In stressing this point Marx most closely approximates the central moral concern of Catholic population thinking, although this issue remains a subordinate one in his considerations.

It is well known that Marx deliberately eschewed the role of moralist or social reformer. He condemned all appeal to morality as unscientific sentimentality. Nevertheless, students of his thought have noted that his attack on morality is more properly understood as an attack on moralism, and they have pointed out that Marx's entire position has a profound moral basis with a large measure of borrowing from the thought of Kant and Hegel.[134] Certainly, Marx's treatment of Malthus displays a sharply critical moral content, which must partly account for its lasting popularity among radical social theorists. In this respect, we can interpret Marx's position as raising some of the pointed distributive questions neglected by Malthus and other advocates of birth limitation. Malthus, like many thinkers after him, believed population growth to be adverse to social welfare. He believed birth restraint beneficial to all those who practice it and to society as well. But Marx, as champion of the working class,

---

[133]*Theorien über den Mehrwert, Werke,* Band 26, Zweiter Teil, s. 112.

[134]See, for example, Eugene Kamenka, *Marxism and Ethics* (London: Macmillan Co., 1969), pp. 9ff., and Herbert Marcuse, "Ethical Tenets," in *Soviet Marxism,* Vintage edition (New York: Random House, 1961), pp. 184ff.

84

disputes these contentions. Within the circumstances of
unjust capitalist society, he seems to say, population
restraint disadvantages the lower-income groups and enhances
the wealth and power of those at the top of the social order.
His denial that there is any such thing as a population problem can partly be interpreted, therefore, as the claim that
population growth need not diminish the welfare of those
groups entitled to our moral concern. The more complex
assertion that population growth does not cause existing
social evils also stems from and draws upon Marx's primary
concern with the welfare of the working class and its disadvantageous circumstances in capitalist society.

Whether or not Marx is correct in his various judgments
on population is not easily settled. Resolution of the issue
requires a comprehensive estimate of just distributive shares
and some understanding of the relationship between population
growth and the welfare of representative social groups. But
Marx's sharply critical perspective still has the virtue of
pointing up basic distributive issues ignored by Malthusian
theory and all those viewpoints which draw upon it.

Some writers have argued that this critical content
exhausts Marx's perspective.[135] To an extent this is true.
Marx was certainly more concerned with exposing the flaws in
Malthus' reasoning--especially as these flaws revealed
defects in the capitalist system--than he was in formulating
a positive response of his own to the phenomenon of population
growth. Thus while Marx was reasonably clear in his statement
of the "population law" of capitalist society, he was markedly
less informative when it came to stating the laws of population
for any other stage of economic development. He does not discuss the "laws of population" for primitive or feudal society,
for example.[136] More important, nowhere in his writings do we

---

[135]See Alfred Sauvy, *General Theory of Population* (New
York: Basic Books, 1969), p. 524.

[136]For one effort to fill in these gaps in Marxist
theory, see J. Fréville, *L'Epouvantail malthusien* (Paris:
Editions Sociales, 1956).

find an explicit statement of the population law of communism, or classless society, a law which one would think to be of primary value in demonstrating the falsity of Malthus' eternal laws of population. The absence of such a statement is troubling because it deprives us of an authoritative Marxian perspective on the moral problems posed by population growth in a society which is considered to be fully just.

Nevertheless, as Marx's defenders have noted, criticism is not without its positive implications. In Marx's criticism of capitalist "overpopulation" there are indications of what he believed to be the population dynamics of communist society and the significance of population growth in such a society. Moreover, these indications are made a good deal more explicit by Engels. It is Engels, in fact, who assumes most of the responsibility for articulating a communist law of population.

As we might expect, Engels' discussions of population follow the course set down by pre-Marxian socialist literature. The core of his viewpoint is an attack on Malthus' famous "ratios." In a variety of statements Engels claims that the productivity of communist society is capable of outpacing population growth indefinitely, or alternately (and perhaps jointly), that population under communism will grow at a diminished rate, if at all. Actually, two separate lines of argument are involved here since each of Malthus' ratios is brought under criticism. Each line of argument correspondingly deserves separate attention.

We have already examined Marx's ironical reduction of the dynamics of population in a capitalist society. Implicit within this critique is a view of the state of the worker within communist society. Under communism, where the full value of each worker's labor will accrue to him without being drained away by a property-owning class, the worker will experience a state of increasing well-being. Expansion of technology and the growth of the means of production will facilitate a constant increase in material productivity and a reduction in the amount of labor expended. Whether it will also make possible growth in population, or whether it should make possible such growth, is not clear. Marx is silent on this matter.

Engels is less reticent. He insists that growth in technology, combined with a radical reorganization of society, will enable men to cope with a constantly growing population. This view is repeatedly set forth by Engels, but his remarks in a letter to Lange of 1865 are representative:

> You ask yourself how increase of population and increase in the means of subsistence are to be brought into harmony . . . . We begin with the assumption that the same forces which have created modern bourgeois society--the steam-engine, modern machinery, mass colonization, railways, steamships, world trade--and which are now already, through permanent trade crises, working toward its ruin and final destruction--these same means of production and exchange will suffice to reverse the relation in a short time, and to so increase the productive power of each individual that he can produce enough for the consumption of 2, 3, 4, 5, 6 individuals . . .

> Too little is produced, that is the whole trouble. But *why* is too little produced? Not because the limits of production--even today and with present-day means--are exhausted. No, but because the limits of production are determined not by the number of hungry bellies but by the number of *purses* able to buy and to pay. Bourgeois society does not and cannot wish to produce more.[137]

If increasing productivity is to be the remedy for future population pressure, of course, it must be assumed that productivity can grow at least proportionately to population. This means that any fears about diminishing marginal returns to labor must be dispelled. It is evidence of how much reliance Engels places on this response to the problems associated with population growth that he goes out of his way to deny the possibility of diminishing returns. In his *Outlines of a Critique of Political Economy*, for example, Engels directly challenges Malthus' "arithmetical" progression as well as the assumption on which it is finally based; what Malthus and his sympathizers overlook, says Engels, is the crucial factor of science:

> The extension of land is limited--certainly.
> But the labor power to be employed on this area

---

[137]Karl Marx and Friedrich Engels, *Werke*, Band 31 (Berlin: Dietz Verlag, 1965), s. 467.

increases with the population; and even if we
accept the fact that the increase of output
achieved by increase of labor is not always
proportionate to the latter, there still remains a third element--which is certainly never
worth anything to the economists--namely
science, the progress of which is just as
limitless and at least just as quick as that
of population.[138]

Elsewhere in the same work, Engels underscores the point:
"The productive capacity of the land can be increased ad
infinitum by the application of capital, labor and science."[139]

Engels' optimism is not explicitly supported by Marx
and it remains unclear whether Marx himself would have advocated this response to population growth. Nevertheless, it
is Engels' view that has been carried over into the thought
of both men's followers. Indeed, it might be said that
Engels' "productivity" solution to the evils associated with
rapid population growth--the belief that a reorganized society
can and should produce more than a growing population demands--
has largely dominated later Marxist thinking on the matter of
population. Soviet statements on population, for example,
have consistently celebrated the productive power of the
socialist state. Unlike capitalism, Russian thinkers have
argued, communism is able to absorb a constantly expanding size
of population.[140] And Chinese leaders have frequently held
up their large and growing population as a unique sign of
socialist strength.[141] It is true, as observers of the Soviet

---

[138]Karl Marx and Friedrich Engels, *Werke*, Band 1 (1970),
s. 521.

[139]*Ibid.*, s. 517.

[140]For one account of traditional Soviet population
theory see W. Parker Mauldin, "Fertility Control in Communist
Countries: Policy and Practice," *Population Trends in Eastern
Europe, the USSR and Mainland China* (New York: Milbank Memorial
Fund, 1960), pp. 179-223. Also David Heer, "Abortion, Contra-
ception, and Population Policy in the Soviet Union," *Soviet
Studies*, XVII (July 1965), 76-83. For a treatment of recent
shifts in Soviet population theory away from this stress on
production see Robert C. Cook, "Soviet Population Theory from
Marx to Kosygin: A Demographic Turning Point?" *Population
Bulletin* (October 1967), 85-115.

[141]For accounts of early Chinese Communist attitudes

population situation have noted, that the official optimism
concerning the nation's ability to outproduce population is
based upon realities not fully consonant with Marxian theory.
These include drastic losses of population because of two
world wars and repeated bouts of political repression, as well
as the existence of an implicit population policy in the form
of very permissive abortion laws. [142] Nevertheless, the fact
that the Chinese, who have faced genuine problems associated
with population, have sometimes insisted on "outproducing"
demographic increase reveals this response to be a genuine
motif in Marxist thinking.

The importance which this approach to population growth
assumes in later Marxist theory stands in strange contrast to
the lack of even a basic moral justification for its adoption.
We have already noted some of the efforts made by Engels to
defend the factual assumptions on which this approach rests,
particularly the effort to uphold science's ability to maintain
constant or increasing marginal returns to labor. This assumption makes it possible to believe that population growth will
not substantially hinder the development process or inflict
the evil of negative income growth rates on a population. But
even if this factual assumption is accepted a further moral
assumption is implicit in Engels' response: that a share of
the resources of a growing economy should be applied to

---

toward population see Robert C. North, "Communist China and the
Population Problem," in Stuart Mudd, ed., *The Population
Crisis and the Use of World Resources* (The Hague: Dr. W. Junk,
1964), Vol. II, pp. 176-87. Also, Dorothy Nortman, "Population
Policies in Developing Countries and Related International
Attitudes," in Charles B. Nam, ed., *Population and Society*
(Boston: Houghton Mifflin, 1968), pp. 659f. There are a
number of good treatments of the ups and downs of Chinese popu-
lation theory since 1953. See, for example, John S. Aird,
"Population Policy in Mainland China," *Population Studies*,
XVI (July 1962), 38-57. And W. F. Wertheim, "Recent Trends in
China's Population Policy," *Science and Society*, XXX (Spring
1966), 129-35.

[142]See, for example, Clement Mertens', "Le Marxisme et
les problèmes de population," *Vie Economique et Sociale*, XXXIII
(May 1962), 211. Also, William Petersen, "The Evolution of
Soviet Family Policy," in *The Politics of Population*, pp. 103-
24. H. Kent Geiger's *The Family in Soviet Russia* (Cambridge,
Mass:: Harvard University Press, 1968) remains the best

equipping an increasing population with capital. The future classless society which Engels sketches, and which many later Marxists have sought to bring into being, is one which has made the moral decision to devote a share of its savings, its accumulated capital, to demographic investment, and, as a consequence, it has chosen to reduce the highest rate at which growth in income per capita can advance. Important distributive decisions, in other words, underlie a commitment not to manipulate the population variable, yet neither Engels nor his followers appear to explain why these decisions have been made.

We can, of course, speculate on some of the reasons why Engels' thinking might have been led in this direction. There is, for example, the fact that Malthus had already established the terms of the debate. Initially, Malthus had employed the principle of population to argue against attempts to "improve" or reorganize society, but as his argument developed it changed: improvement was possible so long as birth limitation (through delayed marriage) was practiced. Now it is conceivable that in rejecting Malthus' offensive ideological position, Engels might have been led to reject the prospect of birth limitation as well. It was natural for him to affirm not only that society could be improved, but that it could be so without the need to limit births at all.

Another reason why Engels may have been led to favor outproducing population growth has to do with the offensive connotations attached to economically motivated birth limitation as a result of Malthus' work. According to Marxian analysis, not only was birth limitation of this sort unnecessary but, when practiced by the individual worker, it represented a selfish and counter-productive effort to extricate oneself from the plight of one's class. Within the orbit of Marxist thought, therefore, birth limitation practiced for economic reasons comes to be associated, rightly or wrongly, with the egoism of bourgeois society. Interestingly, Marxists and Catholics here share a common resentment at the selfishness they believe to be associated with a "contraceptive mentality."

---

introduction to the theory and practice of family life in the Soviet Union.

It is true that Marxists place particular emphasis on class solidarity, as Catholics do not, but both viewpoints share a common opposition to the prudential and individualistic orientation of bourgeois culture which Malthus represented.

Either of these explanations, if correct, tends to reduce the specific moral content of Engels' position. Rather than being based upon a well thought out moral rationale or consideration of the proper response to population in a just society, Engels' view would be merely an expression of resentment at Malthusian theory. A third possible explanation of his view, therefore, carries greater moral significance. It may be that Engels' consideration of the issue is shaped by the currents of utilitarian moral theory prevalent in nineteenth century England. In general, neither Marx nor Engels were sympathetic to utilitarianism. They were alert to the way utilitarianism's encouragement to maximize the sum total of well-being neglected distributive considerations and could lead to great economic inequalities. Both men had enough rootage in Kantian and Hegelian moral theory to bristle at suggestions that persons be ignored, abused or exploited for the sake of "national" wealth.[143]

But while Marx and Engels strongly condemned the economic inequalities possibly sanctioned by utilitarianism, it is not clear that either thinker rejected one distributive pattern also justified by classical utilitarian moral theory: the pattern whereby a fixed (or growing) sum of value is distributed among a growing number of human beings. So long as per capita utility does not fall so fast as to reduce the sum total of welfare, this kind of distribution can admirably fit the utilitarian requirement that welfare be maximized.[144] Such a distribution can, of course, cause a slower rate of

---

[143]See, for example, Marx's criticism of the bourgeois stress on aggregate accumulation and production in *Capital*, Vol. I, pp. 654, 697.

[144]The clearest expression of the classical utilitarian position may be found in Henry Sidgwick's *The Methods of Ethics*, 7th ed. (New York: Dover Publications, 1966), p. 415.

growth of per capita welfare, and can even allow per capita
welfare to decline. But if we recall Engels' belief in constant or increasing marginal returns, then the latter is not
likely to come about. Thus, the most offensive moral prospect
associated with this kind of classical utilitarian position
(the prospect of declining individual welfare) is eliminated.
In view of this, it may well be that Engels assumed a
utilitarian norm to be appropriate in this area. If this is
so, his productivity response has genuine moral foundation and
reflects a preference for distributing income over an expanding
number of human beings. It represents one distributive preference among those we have looked at, and like the others
requires further moral justification. But Engels himself does
not furnish this justification.

To this point I have tried to show that Engels'
thinking on population eventuates in a pro-natalist policy,
or at least one favoring demographic investment. But I must
now point out that this is not the only response to population
growth in Engels' thought. Side by side with the view I have
been discussing, Engels expresses a quite different attitude
toward population, and he does so in at least two statements.
The first of these is contained in his remarks in the *Outlines of a Critique of Political Economy* of 1844. Engels
begins by emphasizing his productivity response, but he shifts
his argument in mid-course:

> The Malthusian theory, however, has been an
> absolutely necessary transitional stage, which has
> taken us infinitely further forward. Because of
> it, as because of economics generally, we have
> become aware of the productive power of the soil
> and of humanity, and after conquering this
> economic despair, we are forever secure from the
> fear of overpopulation. From this theory we
> derive the most powerful economic argument for
> a reorganization of society; for even if Malthus
> were altogether right, it would still be neces-
> sary to carry out this reorganization on the spot,
> since only this reorganization, only the enlighten-
> ment of the masses which it can bring with it,
> can make possible that moral restraint on the
> reproductive drive which Malthus himself sets
> forth as the most effective and easiest counter-

measure to overpopulation.[145]

Having bowed momentarily to Malthus, Engels then proceeds in
the passages that follow to demonstrate the falsity of the
Malthusian productivity progression.

The second statement of this view is found in Engels'
letter to Kautsky of 1881. Here, Engels concedes the "abstract
possibility that the number of people will become so great that
limits will have to be set to their increase." But he
immediately adds:

> . . . if at some time it should appear necessary to
> communist society to regulate the production of
> human beings, just as it has already come to regu-
> late the production of things, it will be precisely
> this society, and this society alone, which can
> carry out this without difficulty. It does
> not seem to me that it would be too difficult in
> such a society to achieve by planning a result which
> has already been produced spontaneously, without
> planning, in France and Lower Austria. In any case,
> it is for the people in the communist society them-
> selves to decide whether, when, and how this is to
> be done, and what means they wish to employ for
> this purpose . . . .[146]

Clearly, Engels' viewpoint in both of these statements
is quite distinct from the one we have just examined. Having
been told that communist society can and should handle population growth by outproducing it, we are now told that population will not grow substantially in such a society. An attack
on the Malthusian food progression has been replaced by an
attack on the population progression. Whether Engels openly
contradicts himself here, or whether this new point is meant
to supplement the latter is not clear. Some later Marxist
writers have maintained that both arguments are closely
related, with Engels envisioning communist society as undergoing a period of population growth, met by rising production,
followed by a period of enduring population stabilization.[147]

---

[145]*Werke*, Band 1, s. 520.

[146]*Werke*, Band 35 (1967), s. 151.

[147]Two of the most important expressions of this interpretation are those by Tchang Pei-Gang, et al., "La Loi de
population en régime socialiste et le problème de la population

93

If this is a valid interpretation, my earlier remarks deserve qualification. Instead of reflecting a permanent distributive preference on Engels' part, the decision to outproduce rising population may simply be based on the belief that this is an expeditious and morally acceptable way of responding to growth in the interim before a stationary population is reached. Even here, of course, certain distributive preferences are operative. Engels would, in this case, be prepared to accept a slowed rate of growth in income per capita rather than interfere with the liberty of those individuals or groups marked by high fertility during the interim period. Indeed, some later Marxist population writers have argued that this concern for the liberty of high-fertility groups or individuals is demanded by Marxist theory.[148]

More important than this for our purposes, however, is the fact that Engels' argument in these two texts represents, to some degree, a repudiation of the claim that population growth poses no problem for a fully just society. By indicating the desirability of a stationary population as the long term prospect for a just society, Engels implicitly concedes that population growth can sometimes inflict evils on moral agents. Indeed, his remarks may be taken to mean that, in view of these evils, a just society may be required actively to regulate the reproductive behavior of its members.

In an effort to preserve the claim that overpopulation need never trouble a just society, some later Marxist and radical thinkers have insisted upon the primarily spontaneous and unregulated nature of fertility reduction in such a society. They have argued that the liberated status of women in this society, the extension of educational opportunity, and the vastly enhanced economic opportunity and security will naturally remove many of the traditional causes of high

en Chine," *Etudes Economiques: Cahiers Mensuels d'Economie Socialiste*, No. 114-115 (1959); and P. Podyashchikh, "Impact of Demographic Policy on the Growth of Population," in *World Views of Population Problems*, ed. Egon Szabady (Budapest: Akadémiai Kiadó, 1968), pp. 231-51.

[148]Podyashchikh, *Ibid.*, pp. 239, 243.

94

fertility and will keep growth rates low.[149] And they have
maintained that this is the meaning of Engels' claim that only
a reorganized society can facilitate the enlightenment of the
masses that is needed to make birth restraint possible.

These claims have considerable importance. They
suggest a link between concrete institutional expressions of
social justice and lowered fertility. If correct, they may
support the Marxist objection to fertility reduction in an
unjust society, and they certainly point up and express the
Marxist stress on the relationship between population growth
and the larger issue of just distributive shares. But for the
time being, it is important to note that there is a strain
in Engels' thinking which concedes that population can pose
a problem in a just society. Whether that problem is self-
eliminating, as those who point to the direct population-
effects of social reform believe, or whether it remains a
problem with which the just society would actively have to
wrestle remains unclear. But low fertility is nevertheless
seen by this line of thought as possibly good, and high
fertility is at least sometimes viewed as an evil.

This brief review of Marxist thinking on the matter of
population growth reveals that we cannot speak of a single
Marxist perspective on this issue, nor even of a clear-cut
denial that population can pose a moral problem. Nevertheless,
despite the genuine unclarity of Marxism on the full moral
status of population growth, there is a unity to the Marxist
position. Arching over the several different views of growth
is sharp moral criticism of the injustice of Malthusian population theory. In the circumstances of bourgeois society,

---

[149]For an extended discussion of the economics of fertility from a Marxian perspective, including the suggestion that
high fertility results largely from social injustice, see Sidney
Coontz, *Population Theories and Economic Interpretation*
(London: Routledge & Kegan Paul, 1957), especially pp. 110ff.
Podyashchikh, "The Impact of Demographic Policy," pp. 250ff.
sums up the Marxist view of the relationship between economic
and social reform and lowered fertility. August Bebel's *Die
Frau und der Sozialismus* (Stuttgart: J. H. Dietz Nachfolger,
1904) is one classic treatment of the relationship between
social reform, women's liberation and lowered fertility.

unjust society, Marx and Engels believed that Malthus'
teaching only inflicted further injustice on what for them was
the most important social group, the working class. An
estimate of the Marxist criticism of Malthusian theory, therefore, requires some general conception of the just distribution
of values in a social order and the relationship between this
conception and population growth.

Part II

A Deductive Moral Approach to the Population Problem

A. *The Need for a Theory of Justice*

      To this point I have been engaged in a survey of differ-
ent assessments of the moral problem posed by rapid population
growth. If that survey has revealed anything, it is that there
is wide disagreement concerning the moral significance of this
problem. Not only are there different views about which values
are threatened by high fertility, but there are at least two
schools of thought, the Marxist and Roman Catholic, which tend
vehemently to deny that population growth really ever threatens
values of concern to moral agents. The term "population
problem" is itself at dispute in this controversy.

      As sharp as some of this conflict appears to be, I have
tried to suggest in the course of examining these views that
there exists a common ground of contention. The various
parties to the population debate may be thought of as divided
most fundamentally on the question of who it is that suffers
and ought to suffer the evils caused by high fertility. It is
true that in some respects, Catholic and Marxist thinkers deny
that population growth is a significant cause of evils. But
I have tried to indicate that these claims can usually be
understood as a denial that growth inflicts evils on groups
for whom they are concerned. In some cases, these claims
involve the further belief that population growth is a source
of goods, either for oppressed economic groups, individual
families or possible members of future expanded generations.

      Those who affirm the existence of a population problem
generally are agreed that high fertility is primarily a source
of evils, but they differ in turn on just who it is that most
suffers the various evils associated with growth; more importantly, they differ on who ought or ought not to do so. The
family planning perspective looks first of all to the welfare
of individual families. Those concerned with the impact of
growth on the quality of life favor the welfare of larger
social groups. In some cases, however, this larger society
proves more exclusive than it first appears since it does not
include those who highly value children, and very frequently,
it does not fully include those income groups or classes that
have least to benefit by population restraint. The indecision

of the economic perspective concerning just whose welfare it
is that is advanced by the growth in per capita income effected
by population restraint points up and reflects all these conflicts over distributive preference.

Seen in this way the population debate is a dispute of
justice. Characteristically, disputes of justice have the
following features: several parties co-exist in a common
territory where their behavior comes into conflict; natural
and other resources are not so abundant that each party can
avail himself of them without encountering competing claims to
the same resources; and the parties themselves are similar
enough in physical and mental powers so that enduring domina-
tion by any one of them is impossible.[1] In such circumstances,
strident verbal controversy over how resources and liberties
are to be distributed is natural.

In terms of its most general characteristics, we can
see that the dispute over the moral implications of rapid
population growth is a dispute of justice. The territory in
which the dispute takes place may be the earth itself, but
has more commonly been the various national communities in
which men are gathered. The contested scarce resources are
those which virtually all men desire: land, water, accumulated property and the like. Without a scarcity of these
goods it is hardly likely that men would be interested in the
fact of population growth at all. Finally, the parties to
the dispute are spokesmen for various ideological positions
who claim to represent the interests of concrete human beings.

At stake in the dispute itself is the question of how
these resources shall be distributed among those who lay
claim to them. This involves the question of the extent to
which resources should be used to facilitate growth in population and the extent to which the liberty to reproduce may be
exercised in a world of scarce material goods. It also
involves the question of the relation between the principles

---

[1]This characterization of a dispute of justice draws
loosely on Hume's description of the conditions that make
principles of justice necessary. See his *A Treatise of Human
Nature*, bk. III, pt. II, sec. ii.

of justice in this area and the principles that otherwise
govern the distribution of scarce goods among individuals in
various social positions.

When the various interpretations of rapid population
growth which we have examined are looked upon as contending
positions in a dispute of justice, the need for an adjudicatory
perspective or "high order" theory of justice becomes evident.
Such a perspective must have several features. First, it
would have to be based on widely held, commonly accepted
premises in order to elicit assent from all parties to the
dispute.[2] Second, it would have to be capable of effectively
ordering and ranking the various claims advanced by parties to
the dispute. This means that it would have to be able to
dictate when the demographic variable might be considered an
unacceptable source of evils, for which agents and under what
circumstances. Finally, its ordering of claims would have to
be complete so as to preclude further dispute. We may think
of this adjudicatory perspective or higher order theory of
justice as furnishing a deductive approach to the matter of
rapid population growth. Up to now, I have been concerned with
surveying and gathering different opinions on the nature of
the population problem. In the face of extensive disagreement,
however, we require a viewpoint which, by working only from
reasonably evident premises and assumptions, is capable of
generating a comprehensive understanding of the issue.

B. *The Contract View*

1. *Basic Structure of the View and the Original Position*

The aim of the following section is to present such a
higher order perspective and explore its implications for the
population issue. The specific view I have in mind is John
Rawls's contract theory of justice. This position has been
elaborated by Rawls in a series of articles since 1958, in

---

[2]This requirement for any kind of adjudicatory procedure
is stated by Ch. Perelman in *Justice* (New York: Random House,
1967), p. 74.

several unpublished manuscripts, and, most recently, in his
work, *A Theory of Justice*.[3] I select the contract view
because I believe that it is one view capable of meeting the
requirements of a higher order theory in a dispute of the sort
represented by the population debate. Obviously, the claim
that this is an acceptable higher order view requires justification. But I shall have to postpone the task of justification
for the time being. A defense of the claim that the contract
view serves as an acceptable higher order theory in disputes
of justice must await some explanation of the contract view
itself.

The aim of Rawls's theory is to present a conception
of justice which restates in a general form and renders more
acceptable the traditional theory of the social contract, as
found in the work of Locke, Rousseau and Kant (*Theory*, p. 11).[4]
The intuitive idea of the theory is to think of the first
principles of justice as derived from an original agreement
made by contending parties in a suitably defined, but hypothetical, initial situation (*Theory*, p. 118).[5] The need for

---

[3]Cambridge, Mass.: The Belknap Press of Harvard University Press, 1971. Earlier unpublished manuscript versions
of the theory are *Chapters on Justice* (1964-65) and *Justice
as Fairness* (two editions, 1967 and 1969). All further
references to these three works will be made in the body
of the text. For other articles by Rawls, see bibliography,
Section I. The most important critical treatments of Rawls's
position include those by R. P. Wolff, Ch. Perelman,
Brian Barry, Norman Care, Dorothy Emmett, Charles Frankel,
Michael Lessnof, R. L. Cunningham, and Dan W. Brock.

[4]The leading works of the contract tradition on which
Rawls draws include John Locke's *Second Treatise of Govern-
ment*; Immanuel Kant's *Foundations of the Metaphysics of Morals,
Critique of Practical Reason, Metaphysical Elements of Justice*
and *Religion within the Limits of Reason Alone*; and Jean
Jacques Rousseau's *The Social Contract*.

[5]It is the emphasis upon this initial situation and
its definition which places Rawls's theory within the contract tradition and which distinguishes it from a rationa-
list universalizationist theory of the sort proposed by
R. M. Hare in his *The Language of Morals* (New York: Oxford
University Press, 1964) and his *Freedom and Reason* (New
York: Oxford University Press, 1965).

such an agreement and the specification of its conditions derive from certain assumptions about human society and the kinds of circumstances in which disputes of justice arise. Generally speaking, these are the circumstances I have already suggested in connection with the population dispute. Rawls assumes, for example, that human society is a cooperative venture for mutual advantage, but one marked by conflict as well as identity of interests. The identity of interests stems from the fact that cooperation and free collaboration make possible a better life for all. But there is conflict, as well, because members of society "are not indifferent as to how the greater benefits produced by their collaboration are distributed"; each prefers a larger to a lesser share of scarce social goods (*Theory*, p. 4). This conflict, finally, is enduring. Since human beings are roughly similar in physical and mental powers, and since they are vulnerable to attack, all may have their plans blocked by the force of others. Nor can any one individual securely dominate the rest (*Theory*, pp. 126f.). Because of this conflict, a society requires a set of principles to aid in determining the proper division of advantages. These principles, as Rawls says, are the principles of social justice: "they provide a way of assigning rights and duties in the basic institutions of society and they define the appropriate distribution of the benefits and burdens of social cooperation" (*Theory*, p. 4).

Assuming these circumstances of justice obtain, the contract view seeks to provide a common vantage point from which the differing claims may be adjudicated and principles selected. Rawls terms this vantage point the "original position" (*Theory*, p. 17). It is, in fact, a hypothetical and fictional device designed to express the conditions under which acceptable principles of justice might be formulated.[6] The

---

[6]Outside the contract tradition, a similar device for economic theory has been suggested by J. C. Harsanyi. See his article, "Cardinal Utility in Welfare Economics and in the Theory of Risk Taking," *Journal of Political Economy*, LXI (1953), 434-35. The best approximation of the device of the original position, as well as contract theory as a whole, however, is to be found in the article by Harvey Leibenstein, "Long-run Welfare Criteria," in *The Public Economy of Urban*

hypothetical character of the original position must be
stressed. Rawls differs sharply from some classical advocates
of the contract view in refusing to understand the original
position as an historical occurrence.[7] His claim is not that
the principles of justice *have been* agreed upon in some
original position, but rather that these principles must be of
the sort that could be agreed upon in such a position (*Theory*,
p. 12).

The operation of the original position within the contract theory may be thought of in the following way. Assume
that a society is characterized by the kind of conflict over
the distribution of rights and goods that I have just sketched
out. In the face of this conflict, members of the society
would be asked to imagine themselves within the original position of equality. (In his early writings, Rawls suggests
viewing the original position as a kind of imaginary conference

---

Communities, ed. Julius Margolis (Washington, D.C.: Resources
for the Future, Inc., 1965), pp. 39-51.
    Leibenstein's position approximates that of the con-
tract view in several ways. First, he suggests that welfare
economics concern itself not with specific economic redistributions, but with the choice of economic "games," pp. 40f. This
corresponds to Rawls's stress on concern with the basic
structure rather than specific allocations (*Theory*, p. 88).
Second, he stresses the importance of evaluating institutions
from a pre-game rather than mid-game situation and illustrates
the choice of institutions as a choice made on behalf of
shipwrecked children, about whose specific tastes and nature
we know nothing (p. 43). This parallels the veil of ignorance.
Third, he links the stress on pre-game judgments to inter-
generational concerns, noting that welfare decisions in which
the fate of future generations is involved very largely are
of a pre-game nature (p. 49). Finally, on the basis of
criterion of "fairness" he suggests that players in economic
games be given "as equal a start as possible" (p. 50). Unlike
Rawls, Leibenstein believes that pre-game preferences of
rational men can be researched and determined empirically,
avoiding the need to determine consent rules on an a priori
basis (p. 51). But with the exception of this insistence, his
program for welfare decisions is remarkably similar to that
of the contract view.

[7]Of the classical advocates of contract theory, Kant
alone seems to have stressed the hypothetical and normative
function of the "original contract." See his *The Metaphysical
Elements of Justice*, Library of Liberal Arts Edition (Indianapolis: Bobbs-Merrill, 1965), p. xxx.

hall to which members of society might retreat to arbitrate
their disputes.[8]) Once in the original position, the parties
pass behind a "veil of ignorance." This, too, is a hypothetical and fictional device. It functions to deprive each
party of the knowledge of those facts which are particular
to him or to his social group. Rawls's own remarks serve best
to delineate the effects of the veil of ignorance:

> First of all, no one knows his place in society,
> his class position or social status; nor does he know
> his fortune in the distribution of natural assets
> and abilities, his intelligence, strength and the
> like. Nor, again, does anyone know his conception
> of the good, the particulars of his rational plan
> of life, or even the special features of his
> psychology such as his aversion to risk or liability
> to optimism or pessimism. More than this, I assume
> that the parties do not know the particular circum-
> stances of their own society. That is, they do not
> know its economic or political situation, or the
> level of culture it has been able to achieve. The
> persons in the original position have no information
> as to which generation they belong. (*Theory*, p. 137)

It is important to note that these effects of the veil
of ignorance are not arbitrarily chosen. They are needed,
according to Rawls, precisely to secure principles of general
value in adjudicating social disputes. Two ideas, really,
are involved here. First, these restrictions are needed to
facilitate the formulation of principles of general usefulness
in resolving social conflicts. Thus, unless the parties'
knowledge as to their generation were restricted, the original
position would be of no value in settling possible disputes
between generations (for example, an appropriate rate of
capital savings). Second, these restrictions are needed if
any kind of enduring agreement on principles is to be secured.
Were members of the original position to possess knowledge of
their particular strengths and weaknesses, they might be
reluctant to favor any principles which did not benefit them
directly. Thus, no agreement could be secured. Alternatively,

---

[8]In the *Chapters on Justice* (1964-65), p. 64, Rawls
elaborates a "fantasy" in which the original position is
described as a building to which the disputing parties might
retreat.

it might be possible for those with particular advantages
(physical strength, wealth or intelligence) to impose principles
on the less advantaged individuals. But since principles
secured this way reflect only a particular and possibly
temporary distribution of advantages, they are likely to be
repudiated when the distribution of advantages is altered. The
veil of ignorance, therefore, is designed to facilitate an
enduring and stable conception of justice. It does so by
insuring that no one is advantaged or disadvantaged in the
choice of principles. In Rawls's terms, the original position
is "fair between individuals as moral persons" (*Theory*, p. 12).
Indeed, Rawls himself offers the phrase "justice as fairness"
as an alternate name for his entire theory (*Theory*, p. 12). I
shall return to the function of the veil of ignorance when I
discuss its justification in greater detail. But for the
moment, I might observe that each effect of the veil of
ignorance has a justification derived from the function of the
original position as a whole.

It is important to observe that the veil of ignorance
does not deprive contract parties of all their knowledge.
They know "whatever general facts affect the choice of
principles of justice" (*Theory*, p. 13). They understand
political affairs and economic theory. And they retain knowledge about the general features of human psychology and the
facts of human social organization. This includes, among
other things, the knowledge that every society is characterized
by various "representative" positions, defined in terms of
social status and expectations (*Theory*, p. 64). As we shall
see, this knowledge is important because it enables members of
the original position, though deprived of the knowledge of just
who they are, to consider their possible welfare as particular
representative individuals in different social orders. They
continue to be deprived of the knowledge of which representative person they are or which representative positions their
society contains, of course. But the only knowledge which they
can clearly be said to be without is particular knowledge about
themselves or the social groups to which they belong.

Behind the veil of ignorance, and within the original
position, the contract parties also share several general

106

characteristics. All are assumed to be rational. Rawls's
concept of rationality is "the standard one familiar in social
theory" (*Theory*, p. 143). According to this concept, a
rational person is thought of as having a "coherent set of
preferences between the options open to him" and he is capable
of ranking these options "according to how well they further
his purposes" (*Theory*, p. 143). He is able to choose effective
means to advancing his end. He is able to select that plan
which satisfies more of his preferences rather than less
(the more "inclusive" plan). And he is able to select the plan
which displays a higher probability of being successfully
executed. The concept of rationality for Rawls, then, is a
formal one involving only general principles of choice, and it
relies minimally on appeals to self-evidence. Nor does it
appear to involve a specification of the ends or purposes which
the rational agent pursues. In fact, this is not quite true.
As we shall see, Rawls's own description of the original
position seems based upon the assumption that there are
certain concrete desires which all rational persons possess,
such as the desire to live, to avoid physical suffering and
the like. But to insist on the presence of these desires in
Rawls's use of the term "rationality" does not seriously
compromise the minimal reliance on self-evidence at this point. [9]

---

[9]Bernard Gert, in his *The Moral Rules* (New York:
Harper and Row, 1970), Ch. 2, advances a substantive concept
of rationality making explicit some of the ends or desires
assumed, but not discussed by Rawls. In Gert's view, a
desire or belief is rational if it is not "prohibited by
reason," that is, if it is not one which all persons of
ordinary intelligence would deem it irrational to act upon
or possess. "Irrationality" for Gert is thus a metaphor for
the unanimous negative judgment of all persons of ordinary
intelligence. But certainly the desires or beliefs which
members of the original position would condemn in the process
of making moral rules are of this sort; that is, they are
desires or beliefs which no rational person of at least ordinary
intelligence would risk holding when choosing under conditions
of uncertainty. Thus the substantive irrational desires
listed by Gert (such as the desire to suffer pain for no
reason) are to be presumed as desires not shared by members of
the original position. Gert's minimal substantive account of
reason and irreason, therefore, accords with the contract view
and fills out Rawls's purely formal account.

In addition to being rational, each party in the original position possesses a "sense of justice" and knows that every other member of the original position does so as well. This does not mean that each party holds some particular conception of justice, for it is to choose a conception of justice that they gather in the original position. Rather, it means that "once principles are acknowledged, the parties can depend on one another to conform to them" (*Theory*, p. 145). The reason for this assumption is obvious. If members of the original position could not count on one another to obey the principles to which they agree, then the whole enterprise of the original position would be pointless. All must assume, therfore, that the principles agreed to will be acted upon and respected. We should note, however, that while it is required that each member of the original position possess a sense of justice, it is not necessary at every stage of their reasoning for them to assume that these principles will be strictly obeyed. The device of the original position can be used, once ideal principles for situations of "strict compliance" have been secured, to generate principles for "partial compliance" situations where it is supposed that some members of real society might not obey the ideal principles. We shall have occasion to examine the process of partial compliance reasoning in a short while. But I should note that the possibility of assuming partial compliance at some later stage in the reasoning process does not alter the assumption of a sense of justice. Whether securing principles for a fully compliant society or for a partially compliant one, members of the original position are themselves assumed to be prepared to act strictly upon whatever principles are selected.

Finally, members of the original position are assumed to be "mutually disinterested." Each is eager to advance his own plan of the good but has no interest in the good of other members of the original position. The provision for mutual disinterestedness should not be understood to mean that contract parties are necessarily selfish in real life. Their real plan of the good may contain substantial provision for the welfare of other persons, and may even be consummately altruistic.

The assumption of mutual disinterestedness, as Rawls states, is partly made "to insure that the principles of justice do not depend on strong assumptions" (*Theory*, p. 129). It is also made to avoid the conceptual difficulties involved in generating principles of justice for a society of purely benevolent persons (*Theory*, p. 148). When they are restored to real society, members of the original position may use the rights and goods secured for them by the principles of justice in whatever manner they please.

Once behind the veil of ignorance, and possessed of these qualities, the contract parties are permitted to propose and select principles of justice. The process proceeds in the following way. Each party is permitted to propose principles which he thinks might be to his advantage. Only those principles which elicit consent from all other members of the original position are selected. Actually, the requirement of unanimity is redundant. One effect of the veil of ignorance is to render the parties so similar that whatever principles are selected by one party will necessarily be accepted by all.

It may be objected here that the constraints of the veil of ignorance render a choice of principles impossible. How can any party select principles which advance his good if he is unaware of what his plan of the good might be? Rawls responds to this difficulty with the concept of primary goods. These are the values which every rational man, regardless of his particular plan of the good, can be expected to want. They are, in a sense, instrumental values, since with more of them, individuals can be assured of carrying out their plans and securing their ends, whatever these may be (*Theory*, p. 62, 92). Among the primary goods are those at the disposition of society, such as rights and liberties, powers and opportunities, income and wealth. Rawls terms these the "social primary goods" (*Theory*, p. 62). One further social primary good of great importance is self-respect, which Rawls defines as the secure conviction that one's plan of life is both worth carrying out and capable of being fulfilled (*Theory*, p. 440). In addition to these social goods there are "natural primary goods" such as health, vigor, intelligence and imagination. Although the possession of these goods is influenced by the

basic structure of society, they are not directly under
society's control (*Theory*, p. 62). Since a conception of
justice seeks to furnish principles for the basic structure
of society, it directly concerns itself only with the distribution of the social primary goods.

The concept of primary goods functions to provide
contract parties with sufficient information for them to know
how best to secure their interests in the original position.
Without this concept, no principles could be agreed upon.
With a more complex conception, agreement would be similarly
impossible. The problem of qualitative interpersonal comparisons (of utility or satisfaction) is raised in this connection.
Rawls does not believe that it is impossible to make such
comparisons, nor does he believe that the reliance on interpersonal comparisons necessarily invalidates an alternate
conception of justice like utilitarianism (*Theory*, p. 91).
But he does believe that the prospect of unanimity among
contract parties would be severely impeded by making such
comparisons the basis of distribution, since there would
probably be disagreement on how to estimate satisfactions in
the first place. The concept of primary goods thus operates
as a necessary simplifying and enabling assumption for the
contract view.

It is interesting to note here that Rawls's concept of
primary goods functions much like the "index of welfare" concept in economic theory.[10] In neither case is it asserted
that the good or goods involved are intrinsically valued by
all men. Rawls assumes that most rational men would desire
more rather than less of these goods in order to advance other
ends. The welfare economist assumes that an increase or
advance in the index he selects (usually "income") is
accompanied by advance in the indices of many widely cherished
values. There are obvious differences in the use of these
concepts, of course. The economist needs only an empirical
verification of the adequacy of his index, while Rawls must

---

[10]See Harvey Leibenstein, *Economic Backwardness and
Economic Growth* (New York: John Wiley & Sons, 1957), pp. 9ff.

110

assume that most rational men would in fact desire the primary goods. But this difference aside, it remains true that for both the contract view and welfare economics, the impact of social institutions and policies on the good of income is of great concern. This suggests that much economic discussion of the income effects of rapid population growth is relevant to the contract view. It also suggests, as we shall see, that the concept of primary goods may be as inadequate as the income index in fully comprehending all the issues raised by high fertility.

2. *The Principles of Justice*

If the description of the original position and the choice procedure it establishes constitutes the first part of the contract theory of justice, a description of the actual choices made by contract parties forms the second part. The contract view aims not only at providing a method by which principles of justice are produced, but seeks to identify the principles themselves. This is done by asking which principles members of the original position would agree upon to determine and regulate the basic structure of their society. The concern with principles for the basic structure of a society is, by the way, a major aspect of the contract view. Rawls carefully differentiates his understanding of the purpose of a theory of justice from those views which concern themselves with providing principles for selecting among possible bundles of goods.[11] This latter kind of theory has natural appeal, but in Rawls's view it wrongly abstracts from the real circumstances of social justice where goods are not merely allocated but are produced by their recipients within existing cooperative relations (*Theory*, p. 88). More important than the question of how any particular batch of goods may be distributed, therefore, is the question of how social relations and the major social institutions that govern political and economic life

---

[11]For one such view see Nicholas Rescher, *Distributive Justice* (Indianapolis: Bobbs-Merrill, 1966), pp. 18-22.

are to be regulated.

Applying the device of the original position to the problem of basic social structure, Rawls derives two fundamental principles of justice and some priority rules. The first principle of justice applies to the basic political and social liberties which are the concern of the political institutions of a society. This principle states that in a society "each person is to have an equal right to the most extensive total system of equal basic liberties compatible with a similar system of liberties for all" (*Theory*, p. 302). The second principle of justice Rawls terms the "difference principle." It applies to the economic and social institutions of society and regulates the distribution of goods and authority within those institutions. According to this principle, "social and economic inequalities are to be arranged so that they are both: (a) to the greatest benefit of the least advantaged, and (b) attached to offices and positions open to all under conditions of fair equality of opportunity" (*Theory*, p. 83).

Among the priority rules relating these principles is a rule rendering the second principle of justice subordinate to the first. The principles of justice, as Rawls says, are to be ranked in "lexical order" such that equal liberty takes priority. Thus, it is not generally permissible, according to the contract view, for basic political and social liberties to be sacrificed for the sake of economic advantage. Basic political and social liberty may be sacrificed only under two conditions: (a) "a less extensive liberty must strengthen the total system of liberty shared by all" and (b) "a less than equal liberty must be acceptable to those with the lesser liberty" (*Theory*, p. 302). A similar priority rule obtains *within* the difference principle, rendering its first part subordinate to its second. This means that the requirement of fair opportunity must be satisfied before the difference principle is put into effect: representative positions within the economic and social institutions must always be open on a basis fair to all.

3. *Explanation of the Principles*

The entire second part of *A Theory of Justice* is devoted
to the derivation of these two principles and their priority
rules. It is impossible to detail all the arguments and
assumptions that undergird the selection of these principles.
But it is important to point to the main modes of reasoning
employed in their defense. In general, each of the two
principles can be thought of as a maximin solution to the problem of choice under uncertainty.[12] Placed within the confines
of the original position, contract parties seek to rank
alternatives by the worst possible outcomes, as though each
party were to end up in the least-off representative position
determined by the principles they select (*Theory*, pp. 152f.).
This is not to say that members of the original position are
required to believe this. If the outcome of their reasoning
process is a maximin solution, this is because the nature of
the situation which the original position represents tends to
generate a conservative attitude to choice (*Theory*, p. 152).
Explaining the two principles of justice, therefore, involves
showing why this conservative attitude is rational within the
original position and why this attitude leads to each of these
two principles.[13]

According to Rawls, there are three chief features of
situations which render a maximin rule of choice plausible.
First, there must be some reason for discounting estimates of
probabilities. Under ordinary circumstances the natural procedure for choice between different patterns of distribution

---

[12]A good discussion of the maximin rule may be found
in W. J. Baumol, *Economic Theory and Operations Analysis*,
2nd ed. (Englewood Cliffs, N. J.: Prentice-Hall, 1965),
Ch. 24. Within moral philosophy a maximin rule is also
advocated by Marcus G. Singer in his *Generalization in Ethics*
(New York: Alfred A. Knopf, 1961), pp. 202-03.

[13]Resher, *Distributive Justice*, p. 38, rejects the
maximin rule on the basis of its allocative implications.
While Rawls does not ignore these difficulties, he believes
the total choice situation of the original position favors a
maximin solution (*Theory*, pp. 157f.).

would involve computing the likelihood of gain for each
distributive pattern and selecting the best one. Estimating
which pattern is best would, in turn, depend upon an estimate
of the gain accruing to each specific representative position
within that distribution and an estimate of the probability
of realizing that specific position within the distribution.
If the maximin rule is selected by members of an original position it must partly be because they are not capable of estimating likelihoods in this fashion.

Rawls notes that this is the case. The veil of
ignorance, as he says, "excludes all but the vaguest knowledge
of likelihoods" (*Theory*, p. 155). While this is true, the
important question is why the original position should be
defined so as to exclude a knowledge of the likelihood of
belonging to representative positions in real society. An
answer may be found in the contract view's focus on the basic
structure of society. As we have noted, Rawls believes a
theory of justice must eschew discussing principles for particular allocations. When the concern is with generating
principles to regulate the basic structure of society, its
enduring social institutions, a clear determination of the proportion of representative positions is out of the question.
As a society develops over time the configuration of social
positions is subject to extensive change and much of this
change is conditioned by the prior choice of a basic structure.
Thus, we see that while the focus on basic social institutions
derives from a particular conception of the aim of a theory of
justice, it also conditions the choice of principles within
that theory.

The second and third features of a choice situation
prompting a maximin solution have to do with the meaning of
gain and loss in a particular situation. In a situation of
choice under uncertainty, an individual may seek to maximize
the least-off representative position if "he cares very
little, if anything, for what he might gain above the minimum
stipend that he can, in fact, be sure of by following the
maximin rule" (*Theory*, p. 154). The second feature of a
maximin situation, in other words, is that additional gain
is neither essential nor sufficiently enticing from the

individual's point of view. The third and final feature
prompting a maximin solution prevails when it is not worth-
while for the individual to take a chance for the sake of
further gain, because in so doing he stands to lose a great
deal of importance to him. Here the risk of his choice is
all important.

When all three features work together in significant
degree, a maximin solution is the likely outcome of a situation of rational choice. Of course, it may be that there are
variations in the degree to which these features are operative.
In that case, the maximin rule may be qualified. In fact,
this seems to be the case with respect to the two principles
of justice. Their differing subject matter renders the
maximin rule slightly less rational in the case of economic
institutions and this accounts for the special features of the
difference principle as well as the priority of the principle
of equal liberty. Let us look at this more closely.

It is Rawls's view that the question of choosing
principles for the regulation of basic social and political
institutions fully displays the features of a situation that
elicits the maximin rule. The implication of such a rule in
this case is a principle of strict equal liberty. It is
Rawls's claim that in their efforts to minimize possible
losses, members of the original position would resist any kind
of utilitarian rule for the distribution of basic liberties
(*Theory*, pp. 175-83). They would not, for example, accept a
distribution in which the aggregate sum of these liberties
was considered important apart from their possession by each
representative individual. Nor would they tolerate a pattern
of distribution in which a lesser share of these basic liberties for some members of society was held to be justified by
a greater share for others. Each individual would demand the
largest share of these liberties that he could command in
any possible representative position. By its nature, this
share would have to be an equal one.

In addition to indicating the contract parties' absence
of knowledge of likelihoods, Rawls advances a number of arguments to demonstrate that rational persons in the original
position would adopt this kind of maximin solution. These

arguments turn, essentially, on the claim that contract parties have few reasons to wish to augment these liberties and the most pressing reasons to fear their loss. The nature of the basic political and social liberties conditions this claim. These liberties include freedom of conscience and thought, liberty of person, equal political liberty (including freedom of speech, freedom of assembly, and the right to vote or to be eligible for public office), freedom to hold personal property and freedom from arbitrary arrest and seizure (*Theory*, p. 61). Most of these liberties are of the sort that gain little by being distributed unequally. With the possible exception of the strict political liberties, it is not clear how a degree of these freedoms greater than that possessed by other persons could materially advantage the individual. Once an equal satisfactory minimum of any of these liberties is secured, the individual does not have reason to be seriously enticed by the prospect of further gain (*Theory*, pp. 156, 542).

Quite the opposite is true with respect to the possible loss of any of these liberties. Rawls discusses a variety of reasons why contract parties would be most reluctant to accept a less than equal share of any of these basic liberties. The political liberties and freedom of person, for example, are so instrumental to one's pursuit of the good that any loss of them would be intolerable. Moreover, since members of the original position are assumed by Rawls to represent not only themselves, but family lines extending into the future, the case against the loss of these liberties is strengthened (*Theory*, p. 169). However willing a single individual may think himself to be to sacrifice these basic liberties, he must be prepared to defend their possible loss to children who are affected by his acts. The extended implications of a loss of basic liberties, in other words, decreases the rational person's willingness to gamble with them. A similar, but somewhat different line of reasoning applies to liberty of conscience. Here the rational individual must be thought of as possibly possessing a deep obligation to worship and serve his God. Faced with this obligation, Rawls argues, the rational member of the original position would be unwilling to

risk the loss of his ability to fulfill it. Whatever
advantage may be attached to a greater share of these liberties
is far outweighed by any possibility of loss.

A final major consideration inducing reluctance to
gamble with these liberties, according to Rawls, is their
close relationship to the primary social good of self-respect.
By participating as an equal in political life and by exercising his equal sovereignty in society, the individual affirms
his own worth (*Theory*, pp. 178, 536). By relinquishing any of
these fundamental rights, however, the individual opens himself
up to the contempt of others and to self-contempt (*Theory*, pp.
179, 500). Furthermore, if, as Rawls maintains, rational
agents in the original position would adopt the difference
principle, permitting some degree of unequal distribution of
income, the case for insisting upon equal basic liberties is
strengthened. Because unequal income shares are roughly
correlated with nature's own unequal distribution of skills
and talents, it is especially important that other aspects of
the basic structure do not erode an individual's self-respect.
By agreeing to a strict equal division of the basic social
rights and liberties, the individual preserves one of the most
important expressions of his equal worth.

Acceptance of the first principle of justice serves as
a precondition for the second principle. Rawls believes that
when their basic equal liberties are preserved, members of the
original position might be willing to depart from a strictly
equal division of income and authority within the economic
and social institutions of society. This departure from
equality is expressed by the difference principle. It permits
inequalities in the distribution of economic goods and
authority within the economic and social institutions so long
as these inequalities work out to the long term advantage of
the least-off members of society and are attached to offices
open on a basis fair to all. The difference principle represents, on the one hand, a continuation of the conservative
kind of reasoning which supports the principle of basic equal
liberties. Since they are deprived of the knowledge of their
likelihood of being in any representative position, and since
they are intensely desirous of advancing their ends without

jeopardy, members of the original position are inclined to agree upon an equal distribution of income. On the other hand, the difference principle represents a slight departure from this cautious attitude. Being familiar with the general circumstances of human life, contract parties have some reason to qualify a strict principle of equality. The parties know, for example, that some men have received talents and capacities in the "natural lottery" of birth which enable them to make special contributions to the social and economic life of a community. They know, also, that these capacities may not be exercised or developed if these individuals are deprived of the additional resources they need to secure education or training, or if they are not stimulated to employ these capacities by incentive payments. In view of these facts, members of the original position are prepared to depart from a strictly equal distribution in order to evoke the exercise of those capacities which might benefit, over time, all members of society, and particularly the least-off representative persons. Considering themselves to be in this least-off position, contract parties know that they are immediately disadvantaged by inequality. But they are prepared to put up with this in order to improve their long-term prospects.

It should be noted that in some respects, the difference principle represents a slight relaxation of the maximin criterion as a principle of choice. This can be seen when the difference principle is compared with the first principle. It is true that Rawls believes contract parties would permit a less extensive basic equal liberty when this is needed to strengthen the total system of liberty shared by all (*Theory*, p. 302). This forms one of the priority rules of the contract view and functions, in many ways, as a difference principle for the basic equal liberties (*Theory*, p. 83). But this priority rule is not exactly like the economic difference principle. It does not, for example, permit marginal increments in the basic equal liberties of some representative persons in order to increase the long-term advantage of the least-off. Or, at least it does not do so in ordinary circumstances. The question, then, is why the difference principle is applied so willingly by contract parties to social and

118

economic inequalities, but not to the basic equal liberties.
Why is there a greater willingness to permit inequality in the
case of income and authority?

The answer to these questions seems to be that the
distributions of basic political and social liberties and the
distribution of income or authority are not entirely identical
problems. On reflection, we can detect an assymetry between
the political liberties and a good like income. For one thing,
it seems rational for contract parties to exert themselves to
attain an additional share of income. Below the stage of
abundance or material comfort, they have good reason to believe
they will be advantaged by each increment in this primary good.
But the same is not true, as I have said, of the basic social
and political liberties. For another thing, contract parties
may have less reason to fear a marginal loss of income than
a loss of political rights. Above some minimal level a loss
of income may not be fatal to the pursuit of one's interests,
while a loss of basic social and political liberties can well
be. What all this suggests is that the question of distributing a good like income involves somewhat less urgency concerning the second and third features which prompt individuals
to adopt a maximin solution. And this relaxation leads contract parties to agree to possible short-run losses of income
(or authority) in order to enhance their long-run prospects;
to agree, in other words, to the difference principle.

When the reasoning behind the difference principle is
viewed this way, however, a further question arises. Since
the possible losses involved in distributing income are less
important, and the possible gains more important than in the
case of political liberties, why must contract parties adopt
a maximin solution in this area at all?[14] Why should they be
as intensely concerned about their prospects in the least-off
position as Rawls contends they are? And why might they not

[14]The view that the original position, as a situation of
choice under uncertainty, should produce a utilitarian maximization principle, at least for economic distribution (if not
for basic liberties), is perhaps the most common criticism of
Rawls's earlier published statements of his theory. See the
articles by Barry, Brock, Cunningham and Emmett in the
bibliography, Section I.

display a greater willingness to gamble with their prospects
by selecting a utilitarian maximization principle? Concretely,
this might amount to accepting a system of "natural liberty"
whereby economic distribution is taken care of by the efficient
operation of the market on the basis of those natural and
social assets or failings received by each individual in the
lottery of birth (*Theory*, p. 72). Or, it might amount to
accepting a system of "liberal equality" where efficiency is
still the primary aim, but in which some effort is made to
insure equal prospects for those with similar abilities and
talents (*Theory*, p. 73). Or, finally, if either of these
systems seem too extreme, it might amount to structuring the
basic institutions according to some mixed conception of
justice whereby the principle of efficiency is operative but
is constrained by the establishment of a social minimum for
the least advantaged (*Theory*, p. 316).[15]

Rawls suggests several reasons why contract parties
would not be led to gamble with their prospects in any of these
ways. For one thing, contract parties have some reason to
believe that gambling may not be necessary to achieve an
efficient economy. By permitting incentive payments to stimulate economic activity, the difference principle is compatible
with efficiency. So long as the circumstances of the least-
off can be improved by differential payments, these payments
are allowed. And when the difference principle is fully
satisfied, a situation that is at least Pareto-optimal is
obtained: "it is impossible to make any one representative
man better off without making another worse off, namely the
least-advantaged representative man . . . " (*Theory*, p. 79).
This compatibility with efficiency, of course, should not be
taken to mean that a fully just society is the only efficient
one, or that it is even the most efficient (in the sense of
having the highest average level of expectations). The

---

[15]William Frankena presents a mixed view of this sort in
his *Ethics* (Englewood Cliffs, N.J.: Prentice-Hall, 1963), pp.
35-42. See also Rescher, *Distributive Justice*, pp. 35-38, for
the use of a standard deviation measure, instead of a minimum,
to forestall or minimize inequities arising from a utilitarian
position.

difference principle is only compatible with efficiency with
respect to the position of the least-off representative person.
It is always his position that is to be improved, and it is
from his position that resulting distributions (or structures)
are judged. Strictly speaking, the difference principle omits
from consideration the circumstances of the better-off
representative men.[16] Evaluation of the basic structure is not
affected by the way that structure contributes to the prospects
of the better-off, even if these prospects are so great as to
increase the mathematical average of expectations. In this
sense, the difference principle may still prohibit distributions
on which rational members of the original position might be
willing to gamble.

A further reason why Rawls believes that contract
parties might not contemplate gambling has to do with the
assumption that inequalities in expectations may be "chain
connected" and expectations themselves "close knit." Chain
connectedness means that "if an advantage has the effect of

---

[16]This statement deserves qualification. Rawls does
advance a form of the difference principle which he calls the
"lexical difference principle" (*Theory*, p. 82f.). This
principle is stated by Amartya K. Sen in his *Collective
Choice and Social Welfare* (San Francisco: Holden-Day, 1970),
p. 138, and is designed to handle some of the most difficult
cases presented by the maximin criterion, those in which the
expectations of the least-off do not vary from distribution to
distribution, but those of the better-off do. The maximin
criterion renders these distributions equivalent, which seems
unacceptable. The lexical difference principle seeks to
correct for this unacceptable conclusion. As stated by Rawls,
in a basic structure with n relevant representatives, it
enjoins: "first maximize the welfare of the worst-off representative man; second, for equal welfare of the worst-off
representative, maximize the welfare of the second worst-off
representative man, and so on until the last case which is, for
equal welfare of all the preceding n-1 representatives, maximize
the welfare of the best-off representative man" (*Theory*, p.
83). Though this lexical principle represents a slight
departure from the contract theory's concern with the least-
off, that concern is preserved both by the lexical nature of
this principle and by the fact that it is presumably not to
replace the difference principle in working out principles for
institutions. Rawls discusses the regular difference principle in all concrete instances, which perhaps reflects his
belief that the lexical principle is not likely to have much
relevance to real social circumstances.

raising the expectations of the lowest position, it raises the
expectations of all positions in between" and close knitness
implies that "it is impossible to raise or lower the expectations of any representative man without raising or lowering the
expectations of every other representative man, especially that
of the least advantaged" (*Theory*, p. 80). Taken together,
these assumptions lead to the result that the difference
principle has "the same practical consequences as the principles
of average utility and efficiency" (*Theory*, p. 82). By increasing the expectations of the least-off, one increases those of
the better-off, and vice versa. When chain connectedness and
close knitness apply, therefore, contract parties might not
feel impelled to gamble upon a utilitarian principle since they
can achieve its benefits by the difference principle and protect their interests as the least-off men at the same time.

It is important to note that Rawls does not really
base the difference principle upon the truth of these assumptions. It is not contingent, he maintains, on the relations
of chain connectedness or close knitness being satisfied
(*Theory*, p. 82). At best these provide further support for
the difference principle, but the fact that contract parties
would select this principle must rest on other grounds.

We are thus returned to Rawls's essential contention
that the difference principle represents a rational choice
for members of the original position. In part, he believes
this to be so because of the inherent importance of income and
the unwillingness of contract parties to gamble on its loss.
But there is a further reason for this unwillingness that is
not flatly stated by Rawls but which might be reconstructed
out of several of his most important awarenesses.

It is useful to observe that the application of
utilitarian reasoning to real social systems involves the
utilization of the natural fact that human beings possess
different talents and failings and are recipients of different
shares in the lottery of birth. In one way or another,
utilitarian systems tend to distribute income disproportionately to those who have already won in the natural lottery.
What this means, however, is that a utilitarian social system
has the effect of doubly rewarding those who have won in the

natural lottery. To their natural advantages, it adds the advantages of authority and greater income. On the other hand, those who have lost in the natural lottery are doubly disadvantaged. Not only do they lack a share of desired personal goods (intelligence, vigor and the like), or socially esteemed personal qualities, but they are denied the additional social goods of higher income or authority.

Contract parties may thus be thought of as being involved in an interconnected double lottery, or two-fold risk situation.[17] On the one hand, before they know their natural talents or failings they are, in a sense, participants in the natural lottery of birth and are in a position of keenly awaiting its outcome. On the other hand, in considering the distribution of income and authority, they are involved in gambling with their prospects as recipients of certain social and natural assets or failings. Taken together, these two related risk situations induce a special note of caution. Should they prove to be losers in the natural lottery, contract parties have good reason not to wish to accentuate their losings. In particular, incentive payments keyed to natural capacities represent a threat. If a contract party is among the least-off, such payments can markedly undercut his self-respect once he returns to real society. This does not mean that the contract parties envy those who are better-off and base their dislike of incentive payments on this propensity. Rawls defines envy as "the propensity to view with hostility the greater good of others even though their being more fortunate than we are does not detract from our advantage" (*Theory*, p. 532). Contract parties must not be considered to be envious, first, because to do so would be to import a special psychological assumption into their description and, second, because

---

[17]The idea of a double lottery presented here is suggested by Brock in his article, "Contractualism, Utilitarianism and Social Inequalities," *Social Theory and Practice*, I (1970), pp. 40f. He states that contract parties might themselves be thought to distribute natural assets in lottery fashion. Certainly Rawls believes that contract parties participate in the natural lottery of birth. But he does not explicitly discuss this double risk situation as a reason for contract parties' caution in the area of economic distribution.

envy is a collectively disadvantageous and irrational propensity. Those who envy are prepared to injure others even at
their own expense.

But if contract parties have reason to fear incentive
payments for winners in the natural lottery, it is not necessarily because they envy these persons. Rather, it is to their
own circumstances that they look. As possible losers in the
lottery of birth, contract parties know that they already
stand perilously near the prospect of self-contempt. Any
patterns of social reward or esteem which enhance this prospect,
therefore, are proper objects of concern.

In view of these considerations, contract parties have
good reason to accept a principle of redress. Such a principle
would distribute primary goods so as to compensate those who
have lost in the natural lottery. Rawls recognizes the appeal
of this principle (*Theory*, pp. 100f.), and the fact that he
does so reveals how much the problem of the natural lottery
concerns him. But he rejects redress as a comprehensive
principle of justice. The reason for this seems to be that
redress can be irrational. By agreeing to reward those who
are are least advantaged by nature, contract parties help to
perpetuate backward economic circumstances over time and
further disadvantage themselves, even as losers in the natural
lottery. Furthermore, contract parties need not accept the
principle of redress since they can adopt the difference
principle. By means of the difference principle, they protect
themselves as possible losers in the natural lottery but
insure the long-run improvement of their economic circumstances, as well.

It is true that the difference principle exposes contract parties to the peril of self-contempt. Like any
principle employing incentives, it favors those who have won
in the natural lottery. But taken together, the constraints
of the difference principle minimize the psychologically
unacceptable aspects of incentive payments. The difference
principle operates to make the greater winnings of some
persons in the natural lottery a public asset for the losers
in that lottery. "In justice as fairness," says Rawls, "men
agree to share one another's fate" (*Theory*, p. 102). The

very arbitrariness of the natural lottery is employed to the reciprocal benefit of all members of society, and where this is known, the psychological tendency to mistrust incentives is mitigated. It is for this reason that Rawls maintains that the difference principle corresponds to the traditional moral concept of fraternity. When it is accepted, all members of society agree not to have greater advantages, either of a natural or social nature, unless those advantages are to the benefit of others who are less well off (*Theory*, p. 105).

Viewed in terms of this double risk situation, therefore, the difference principle seems a rational choice for members of the original position. Utilitarian distributions or principles are a logical abstract form of solution to the problem of choice under uncertainty. But the maximin solution of the difference principle is even more rational when the psychological and social stakes associated with the distribution of income are fully appreciated.

It is important at this point to stress the hypothetical nature of the difference principle. Inequalities of income or authority are permitted *only if* they work out to the advantage of the least-off representative individuals. Rawls does not consider it his task to prove that such inequalities are ever necessary (*Theory*, p. 78). He does, however, suggest certain social circumstances, such as an undeveloped peasant economy, where inequalities are hard to justify. Such economies are not really schemes for mutual benefit. Distribution and redistribution of wealth is like a zero-sum gain where one individual's gain is another individual's loss (*Theory*, p. 539). In this kind of economy, therefore, extensive social inequality might be unjustifiable. Furthermore, this might remain true during a transition stage when economic conditions have changed but attitudes and orientations from an earlier period continue to linger.

Application of the difference principle also implies an existing social and political structure regulated by the first principle of justice. The importance and priority of this first principle has already been suggested. When we understand that the difference principle represents a departure from a strict maximin solution to the problem of economic distribution, the priority of the first principle, as well as the second part of the difference principle, become especially clear. Contract parties may be prepared to accentuate their economic disadvantage for a short period of time in order to increase their long run economic gain. But they would probably be most reluctant to worsen their condition by relinquishing their basic political and social liberties. Nor would they willingly trade off these liberties for economic gain, except perhaps at the very lowest levels of economic development (*Theory*, p. 152). Finally, they would insist that different offices and positions within the society and economy be open not only in a formal sense, but on a basis fair to all. "Fair equality of opportunity" as demanded by the second part of the second principle means that those with similar abilities and skills should have the same life chances, irrespective of the income class or social group into which they are born (*Theory*, p. 73). Rawls points out that the economic purposes of the difference principle can be fulfilled without insisting on fair equality of opportunity (*Theory*, p. 84). But economic gain is not paramount for members of the original position. Their self-respect and ability to pursue a desired plan of life is of greater importance. By preserving fair equality of opportunity, members of the original position protect this self-respect as well as the possibility of realizing themselves through "the skillful and devoted exercise of social duties" (*Theory*, p. 84). Here again caution characterizes the reasoning of members of the original position. The loss of basic equal liberties is not something which contract parties would wish to risk.

This survey of the two principles and of some of the reasoning which underlies them is by no means complete. We shall have occasion to look at these principles again when we apply the contract theory to the matter of rapid population growth. What is important is that the major components of the contract theory, both in terms of the description of the original position and of the principles it is believed to generate, be reasonably clear. The device of the original position and the two principles of justice form the basis of my own approach to the population issue.

Since this is so, one further aspect of the contract theory must be mentioned. This is the absence of a clear principle governing population growth within a society. In his extended discussions of the basic social liberties, for example, Rawls nowhere discusses the particular liberty of procreation. Nor, in elaborating the difference principle, does he explore the implications of population growth for economic distribution. Clearly, this issue comes within the scope of the contract view. Rawls does not fail to formulate related economic principles, such as the just savings principle which regulates distribution of the benefits of economic cooperation between generations. And in an earlier statement of the contract view, he suggests that institutional principles affecting the size of families and rates of population growth may be part of a theory of justice (*Justice as Fairness*, 1967, p. 68). But Rawls has not himself advanced or discussed such principles.[18]

This does not mean that he entirely ignores the matter of population growth. His extended argument against the classical principle of utility, for example, rests upon a rejection of the idea of an indefinitely expanding population which prevents growth in per capita income or allows a per capita decline (*Theory*, pp. 161-66). I shall look at Rawls's dismissal of the classical principle when I discuss the per capita income measure. But it is important to note that Rawls's treatment of population in connection with classical utilitarianism does not really represent a population principle for the contract view. All that Rawls manages to do is reject one extreme population principle. He nowhere advances a comprehensive assessment of the moral implications of population growth in its place. He does not, for example, indicate precisely what rates of population growth members of the original

---

[18]In his book, *A Theory of Reasons for Action* (Oxford: Clarendon Press, 1971), David Richards, a former student of Rawls, suggests some principles governing population growth and population policy (pp. 132ff.). His discussion, however, follows the main lines of Rawls's limited treatments of different, population-related issues throughout *A Theory of Justice*.

position would be prepared to see prevail in their society. Indeed, in his one other mention of population growth, in the course of a discussion of capital savings, Rawls is entirely non-committal on this subject (*Theory*, p. 298). Nor does he indicate the kind of institutional principles contract parties would agree upon to regulate or restrain rates of growth. Thus, apart from the rejection of the classical principle, a rejection motivated less by a concern with population growth than by the desire to dismiss classical utilitarianism, Rawls does not indicate whether, why or how members of the original position would face the matter of high fertility. My task in the sections that follow is to fill in this neglected portion of the contract theory of justice. I hope to utilize the device of the original position to produce contract principles regulating growth between and within generations and, if that proves possible, I hope to suggest a contract population policy as well.

C. *The Contract View and Natural Law: The Problem of Justification*

1. *The Importance of Natural Law*

Use of the contract theory to assess population growth proceeds from the assumption that it is a valid conception of justice and one capable of adjudicating widely divergent viewpoints. This impels us to a discussion of the justification of the contract theory. Rather than proceeding directly to this matter, however, I want first to raise a more general question: in what sense is the contract theory a "natural law" view of ethics? This question has direct bearing on the task of justifying a conception of justice. It is the claim of traditional natural law theory that there exists a single moral code or moral method known to all men. This code or method is assumed to have final authority in settling disputes between all rational moral agents.[19] Clearly, if such a code or

---

[19]For a good statement of the claims of natural law moral theories see James Luther Adams, "The Law of Nature:

method exists, it would have great value in arbitrating disagreement on the population question and in providing a
foundation for universally acceptable policy in this area.
Moreover, if the contract view could be shown to be a natural
law view, the justification of its use for population purposes
would be virtually complete.

There is a further reason for asking whether the contract theory may be thought of as a natural law position. In
examining various views of the population problem, we have
looked at the Roman Catholic perspective and the wide-spread
repudiation of the existence of a population problem that one
finds in that religious tradition. I noted that many Catholic
thinkers trace this repudiation to emphases within a theory of
natural law. By measuring the contract view against the traditional Catholic understanding of natural law, therefore, we
can gain some immediate insight into the correspondence
between the Catholic view of this issue and that likely to be
generated by contract theory.

2. *Catholic Natural Law Theory*

The classic Roman Catholic discussion of the natural
law is found in that part of the *Summa Theologica* of Thomas
Aquinas known as the "Treatise on Law" (Ia-IIae, Quests.
90-97).[20] Aquinas here offers two related but distinct
definitions of the natural law. The first definition is
derived from his general theory of law. According to Aquinas,
there are four generic subtypes of normative prescription
which properly bear the name "law." These include the
"eternal law," that set of prescriptions by which God governs
all creation; the "natural law," the law for the community of
rational human beings; "divine law," the revealed legislation

---

Some General Considerations," *Journal of Religion*, XXV (1945),
88-96.

[20]All quotations are from the edition translated by
the Fathers of the English Dominican Province (London: Burns
Oates & Washbourne, 1912-1925).

of the Church; and "human law," the specific legislation pertaining to each human political community. What distinguishes
each of these sub-types is the nature of the community at
which they aim. Thus, eternal law serves the entire created
universe, while natural law serves only the community of
rational human beings. But the four types of law nevertheless
share a common basic definition. All law, in Aquinas' view is
"an ordinance of reason, for the common good, made by him who
has care of the community, and promulgated" (Quest. 90, Art.
4). Combining this general description of law with the
special aim of natural law, we obtain the first definition of
natural law: it is that rational ordinance (or series of
ordinances) made by God at creation and promulgated for the
common good of the community of rational human beings.

The second definition of natural law is directly
advanced by Aquinas. Natural law, he says, may be understood
as the "participation" of the eternal law in the rational
human being (Quest. 91, Art. 2). According to Aquinas, the
eternal law, or God's rational plan of the universe, governs
the behavior of all created entities. But not all these
entities respond to the dictates of the eternal law in the
same way. When inanimate objects or when animals obey the
eternal law, they do so moved by external forces or inner
drives. But men, in Aquinas' view, are free, rational beings.
When they act, they are not driven to their end but rather
seek what they believe to be good for them. If beings of this
sort are to obey the eternal law, therefore, they must do so
in a special way: by following the dictates of their reason.
This means that their reason must somehow lead men to accord
their behavior with God's plan for the universe; reason must
somehow conform to the eternal law. Aquinas believes this to
be so. The eternal law, he argues, is "imprinted on men's
reason" and "participates" in the rational faculty. By looking
to their reason, men can discern the natural law.

As we can see, these two definitions of the natural
law are somewhat distinct. On the one hand, the natural law
is understood as what is conducive to the good of all rational
human beings. This suggests that the natural law may be known
empirically by observing what is desired by all such beings or

what satisfies their desires. On the other hand, the natural
law seems contained within reason itself, as an *a priori*
principle or set of principles stamped on men's minds. In
fact, Thomas believes that each of these awarenesses is correct. At least the first precept of the natural law, he
maintains, is known *a priori*. A scrutiny of our reason as it
applies to the choice of ends and actions, that is, our
"practical reason," reveals one precept inherently bound up
with our choice procedure. This is the precept that "good is
to be done and ensued, and evil is to be avoided" (Quest. 94,
Art. 2).

But if the first precept of the natural law is known
a priori, all the other precepts are known inductively by
applying this first precept to the conditions of human life.
Since the natural law is what is good for the whole community
of rational men, Aquinas reasons, the precepts of this law
must be derived from a knowledge of those habitual desires or
as Aquinas calls them, "inclinations," which all men commonly
possess and seek to satisfy. Aquinas believes that such
desires exist, and he proceeds to list them. First, there is
that desire which men share with all inanimate or animate
objects: the desire to preserve their own being and stay
intact. In men, this desire expresses itself as the wish to
stay alive and, presumably, to avoid injury or pain. Second,
there are those desires which men share with other animals:
the desires to reproduce and rear their offspring. Finally,
there are those desires unique to men as rational and social
beings: these include the desire to live in society and to
"know the truth about God" (Quest. 94, Art. 2).

It is useful at this point to note an important simi-
larity between Aquinas' view of natural law and Rawls's contract theory of justice. It will be recalled that the purpose
of the veil of ignorance within the contract view is to deprive
the contract parties of the knowledge of all but their common
human nature. I have noted that Rawls does not specify the
desires or ends attached to this nature, preferring to rely
upon a purely formal account of contract parties' deliberative
process. But the assumption that contract parties know they
are human beings necessitates a knowledge of common desires or

ends. Once behind the veil of ignorance, therefore, members
of the original position must know that they are mortal and
sentient beings who are rational, who must live in society and
who possess some plan of the good, although they know nothing
more. Now these qualities known about themselves by contract
parties are very similar to the basic set of desires which
Aquinas attributes to all rational men. It is true that
Aquinas specifically lists men's sexual desires while Rawls
nowhere does so explicitly. But certainly Rawls must include
sexuality in that knowledge of the basic conditions of human
existence which contract parties possess. By clearly specifying the common sexual capacities of men, Aquinas does not
differ from Rawls, and he perhaps even illuminates a fact which
the contract view, in its present form, somewhat neglects:
the fact that much social conflict revolves around problems
created by man's sexual nature. A moral perspective which
neglects this nature may be unsuited to adjudicate conflicts
of this sort. For this reason, when discussing a contract
principle of population I shall greatly have to elaborate
Rawls's implicit acceptance of the sexual nature of man. But
I mention this here only to underscore the validity of
Aquinas' stress on sexuality in listing the basic desires
possessed by men.

A somewhat sharper problem is presented by Aquinas'
inclusion among these basic desires of the desire to know the
truth about God. Rawls nowhere speaks of such a desire and
with good reason, for there are many human beings whose plan
of life is thoroughly non-religious or non-theistic, such that
a religious end of this sort is not a common aspect of the
human condition. Furthermore, inclusion of this desire could
have the effect of skewing the principles of a moral system
in a markedly theological direction, converting it into a
special religious ethic. Both these difficulties in understanding Catholic natural law theory can be avoided, however,
if we simply note that Aquinas here reflects his Aristotelian
heritage. In Aristotle's view, man seeks not only the good
but the highest good of which he is capable.[21] Aristotle

---

[21]*Nicomachean Ethics*, Book VI, Ch. 12; VII, Ch. 7.

believed that human activities find their culmination in
philosophic contemplation, but Aquinas, true to his Christian
background, transmutes Aristotle's highest good into the
knowledge and vision of God (*Summa Theologica*, Ia-IIae, Quest.
3, Art. 8). It is true, therefore, that man's final end for
Aquinas is religious. But this should not obscure the fact
that in terms of the tradition he has inherited, Aquinas is
fundamentally saying that man is a purposive and goal oriented
being who seeks to advance his most satisfying plan of life.
Furthermore, since the natural law is understood by Aquinas to
be the law for all rational men, he is never led to assume
that this purposive capacity always leads all men to a
religious vision. Within the context of his discussion of
natural law, therefore, Aquinas' stress on man's religious end
amounts to little more than the claim that, in addition to
being rational, men possess a plan of the good which informs
all their actions. Certainly, this is a claim with which
Rawls agrees and which the contract view assumes.[22]

Properly understood, therefore, Aquinas' list of basic
human desires does not substantially differ from the knowledge
which members of the original position may possess about themselves. This suggests that the natural law of which Aquinas
speaks may not be very distinct from the kind of moral position
represented by the contract view. But before one can say with
any confidence that these two views are similar, there are
certain questions that must be answered, the most important of
which concerns Aquinas' understanding of reason and the way it
generates principles of morality (the "precepts" of the
natural law). Within the contract view, as we have seen,
reason is understood in the sense standard in economic theory.
The rational individual is one who is able to rank the
various choices open to him according to how well they further

---

[22]It should be noted that Rawls does not accept the
kind of "dominant end" or single end view of happiness apparently shared by Aristotle and Aquinas. Following W. F. R.
Hardie, "The Final Good in Aristotle's Ethics," *Philosophy*,
XL (1965), 277-95, Rawls considers a life organized around
a single dominant end as somehow inhuman or fanatic (*Theory*,
p. 553).

his purposes. He prefers a more inclusive to a less inclusive plan, and a plan more probable of fulfillment to one less probable. He is able to select effective means to his end (*Theory*, p. 143). The principles of justice themselves (as well as principles of right more generally) are produced when a rational individual confined behind the veil of ignorance selects principles to advance his possible conception of the good. Now, is it fair to say that Aquinas' account of reason and of the choice procedure by which the rules of natural law are selected approximates this contract view understanding?

These are difficult questions to answer, because Aquinas himself is never clear on the way in which he moves from a delineation of the common human desires to the concrete precepts of natural law. At best, there are suggestions of how precepts are generated, but some of these suggestions clearly do not accord with the methodology of the contract view. This is particularly true with respect to the sexual precepts of the natural law. Aquinas insists that a variety of sexual acts, including homosexual behavior, masturbation and non-procreative heterosexual intercourse are prohibited by the natural law (IIa-IIae, Quest. 154, Arts. 11, 12). How does he arrive at these prohibitions? On the basis of his view that all men share with animals the desire to reproduce and rear their offspring, I can suggest an answer to this question. It is worth recalling here Aquinas' belief that the natural law represents the rational human being's "participation" in the eternal law. This means that human beings are called upon rationally to conform their behavior to an order which animals obey instinctively. Now, as far as sexuality is concerned, it appears that Aquinas understands this literally. In the animal kingdom, where most higher creatures operate on the estrus cycle, sexual intercourse is always procreative, and if men are to use their reason to discern and follow this pattern, they too would forbid non-procreative forms of sexuality. It thus seems to be Aquinas' view that human reason, when arriving at principles of the natural law operates largely to identify, confirm and mandate modes of

134

behavior observable in the natural order.[23]

Clearly, this understanding of reason and its operation
in the process of moral choice bears no relation to the understanding of the contract view. It is not evident, for example,
that rational members of the original position would find it
to their advantage to restrict the exercise of sexuality to
its procreative function alone. Nor does it seem consistent
with the whole reasoning process of the contract parties for
them to insist upon conforming to a pattern of behavior dis-
cerned in nature. Indeed, we might say that without a knowledge
of their own plan of the good, it would probably be irrational
for contract parties to agree to make nature in this sense the
norm of their action.

Seeking to defend these precepts of the natural law,
some Catholic thinkers have maintained that Aquinas employs a
special understanding of reason. According to Jacques Maritain,
for example, all the precepts of the natural law are known by
a "co-natural insight" or immediate rational intuition of what
is right to do.[24] In Maritain's view there is a rational link
between man's sexual nature, the "natural" pattern of procreative sexuality, and morally right behavior. This rational
link is only intuitively evident and defies further rational
explanation. Maritain's interpretation of reason and the
natural law has the advantage of overcoming most common-sense
objections to the rationality of these sexual precepts. But
it has the disadvantage of doing so in a manner that simply
eliminates further rational defense of the principles themselves.

It may be that Maritain's understanding of law, reason
and the natural law is a correct interpretation of Aquinas'
position. If so, the Catholic theory of natural law bears no
relationship to the contract view. It amounts to an intuitionist

[23]Janssens, *Mariage et Fécondité* (Gembloux: Editions
J. Duculot, 1967), p. 46, insists on the "confirmatory" role
of reason for Aquinas at this point.

[24]*Man and the State* (Chicago: University of Chicago
Press, 1951), pp. 91f.

ethical theory.[25] Before accepting this conclusion, however,
it is useful to look a bit more closely at some other precepts
of the natural law suggested by Aquinas. Both in the
"Treatise on Law" and elsewhere in the *Summa*, Aquinas advances
a number of non-sexual precepts. Many of thse are ideal
precepts, in that they are believed to have obtained in Paradise, before man's fall. They are, therefore, what Rawls would
call "strict compliance" rules since they are not predicated
upon an assumed possibility of wrong-doing or non-compliance.
Among these ideal precepts are some that pertain to individual
moral behavior. These include a prohibition against killing
or injuring one's fellow human beings (IIa-IIae, Quest. 64,
Art. 6); the insistence that promises be kept and other
responsibilities voluntarily assumed be respected (IIa-IIae,
Quest. 88, Art. 3); and the prohibition against lying or
deception (IIa-IIae, Quests. 109, Art. 1; 110, Art. 3; 111,
Art. 1). Other ideal precepts are of a social and political
nature since they govern the practices of human society as a
whole before the Fall. These include a prohibition on the
use of coercion in social affairs, the equal liberty of each
human being within society, and the common sharing of the
goods of the earth (Ia-IIae, Quest. 94, Art. 5).

These ideal precepts are remarkably similar to the
personal and institutional principles generated by the contract
view.[26] The prohibition against killing and injury, for
example, is equivalent to what Rawls terms the "natural duty"
of non-injury and the insistence on keeping promises and truth-
telling conforms to the "obligation" of fidelity (*Theory*, pp.
342-50). The stress on equal liberty in paradise and on the
common sharing of the goods of the earth also closely

---

[25]This seems to be the view of Kai Nielsen in his
assessment of Aquinas' theory. See Nielsen's "An Examination
of the Thomistic Theory of Natural Moral Law," *Natural Law
Forum*, V (1960), 112-19.

[26]Rawls does not seek to elaborate an entire contract
theory of right in *A Theory of Justice*, although he suggests
in sections 18-19 and 51-53 the derivation of some of the
natural duties and obligations that belong to such a theory.

approximates the two principles of justice. It is true that,
unlike Rawls, Aquinas does not believe these ideal precepts
have significant bearing on the way ordinary men must live
their lives. But that is because, like many other Christian
thinkers, Aquinas believes that since the Fall, men cannot
respect these ideal modes of behavior and therefore require
harsh restraint in all their actions.[27] Thus, he argues,
hierarchical political authority and institutions of property
have had to replace the primitive equality of Eden. But
Aquinas' preoccupation with problems of partial compliance
(or non-compliance) should not distract our attention from the
content of the ideal norms themselves. Furthermore, it is
important to note that many of the non-compliance or partial-
compliance norms suggested by Aquinas are similar to those
produced by the contract view.[28] Thus Aquinas' theory of just
war, as well as his view of the permissibility of resistance
to unjust authority (*Summa Theologica*, IIa-IIae, Quest. 40)
conform to contract view non-compliance norms (*Theory*, pp.
371-91).

There seems, therefore, to be a substantial correspondence between most of the non-sexual precepts of the Catholic
theory of natural law and the principles generated by the
contract view. This propels us back to the suspicion that
these positions may share a common methodology. Indeed, on
reflection there is reason to believe this is the case, since
one of the definitions of natural law offered by Aquinas
suggests a procedure for deriving moral principles almost

---

[27]For an excellent account of the history of Christian
thinking on this less-than-ideal, "secondary" or "relative"
natural law, see Ernst Troeltsch, *The Social Teachings of the
Christian Churches*, 2 vols., Torchbook edition (New York:
Harper & Brothers, 1960).

[28]For a good account of scholastic thinking on the issue
of war, see A. Vanderpol, *La Doctrine scholastique du droit
de guerre* (Paris: A. Pedone, 1919). A clear line of con-
tinuity can be traced on this issue from Aquinas through
the neo-scholastics Victoria (*On the Laws of War*) and Suarez
(*Disputation XIII: On Charity*), through secular natural
law thinkers like Grotius (*On the Laws of War and Peace*)
and Kant (*Perpetual Peace*), and finally to Rawls.

identical to the contract view. This is the definition that
the natural law constitutes that set of rational ordinances
which are to the "common good" of all rational human beings.
On the face of it, this definition is odd, for it is by no
means clear that all rational human beings have a "common
good," in the sense of a shared series of ends at which they
all aim. Rational persons, after all, possess many quite
divergent goals or desires. It is true that if we assume a
highly intuitive understanding of this common good or insist,
as some Catholic thinkers have, that there is one "common
good" despite men's apparently different ends, the claim that
there is a common good can make sense. But we need not deny
common sense and empirical observation in this way. Rather we
can take Aquinas' definition in a very literal and strict
sense as meaning that the natural law is for the common good
of all rational human beings insofar as they are *nothing more*
than rational human beings; that is, insofar as they are beings
who know nothing more about themselves than that they are
rational, sentient, social, sexual beings with a plan of the
good.

There is considerable justification for interpreting
Aquinas in this way. He believes, for example, that the human
nature which forms the basis of the natural law is an
"essential" nature, a nature given to all men by God at
creation. But an essence, for Aquinas, is always that set of
ordered properties of an entity that is codified in its definition.[29] In the case of a human being, the essential nature
would presumably include the properties of rationality,
sentience, sociality and the like. Thus, from the relationship between man's essential nature and the natural law, we
can support the suggestion that the "rational human beings"
of the natural law are nothing more than rational human beings.
Moreover, since this is so, the suspicion of a methodological
correspondence between contract theory and Catholic natural law
is borne out.

---

[29]See D. J. O'Connor, *Aquinas and Natural Law* (New
York: St. Martin's Press, 1968), p. 15.

Contract theory, as we have seen, proceeds by having members of the original position select principles which are to their individual advantage. That one set of principles can be selected is a result of the restraint of the veil of ignorance which effectively reduces all members of the original position to a common and symmetrical vantage point. But what are contract parties if not Aquinas' "essential" men seeking their individual good? And are not the principles they agree upon to their "common good" since all possess an identical, if general, set of ends? A moment ago I noted that it is odd to assume that rational persons have any one "common good." But when we specify that rational persons are to be considered as *nothing more* than rational persons, a common good does emerge, in the form of principles protective of basic interests and useful for promoting ends, whatever they may be. The correspondence between the non-sexual precepts of the natural law and the principles of the contract view, therefore, is not merely fortuitous. It reflects the fact that the underlying methodology of these perspectives, especially the conceptions of reason and the moral restraints under which it operates, may be identical.

If this is so, we are nevertheless still left with the problem of Aquinas' sexual precepts and all the particular prescriptions in the area of sexuality to which these precepts give rise in later Catholic moral theory. The presence of these precepts, as we have seen, has led some Catholic defenders of natural law to advance intuitionist interpretations of the entire theory and of the operation of reason within it. And it has led many non-Catholics to reject natural law theory outright.[30] A brief review of the historical background of these sexual precepts, however, may enable us to avoid both these extremes. I might simply observe here that

---

[30]Reinhold Niebuhr in *The Nature and Destiny of Man*, I (New York: Charles Scribner's Sons, 1941), p. 281, singles out the sexual implications of Catholic natural law theory as a principal reason for the unacceptability of this doctrine. His thinking here is generally representative of Protestant criticism of natural law theory.

in his treatment of the natural law, Aquinas seems to be
trying to hold together and express two equally ancient, but
fundamentally different conceptions of the natural law. Both
conceptions have their roots in the Stoic doctrine of natural
law.[31] On the one hand, many of the Stoics viewed the natural
law as a law of reason, a law known only by rational human
beings and containing precepts unique to man. On the other
hand, some Stoic sages viewed the natural law as a human
replication of what transpires unreflectively in the animal
kingdom. According to a formula expressed by the jurist
Ulpian, and later handed down as part of Roman Law, the natural
law is "that which nature has taught all animals" (*Quod natura
omnia animalia docuit*).[32]

These two interpretations of the natural law were
picked up at an early date by the Fathers of the Christian
Church. The idea of the natural law as a law of reason and
unique to men served to buttress the Christian view of the
essential equality and dignity of men. The idea of natural
law as reflecting behavior found among animals buttressed the
Church Fathers' dislike of all non-procreative expressions of
sexuality. In treatments of the natural law prior to Aquinas,
these two views are usually differentiated and selected between

---

[31]Treatment of the development of natural law thinking
from antiquity to Aquinas may be found in A. P. d'Entreves,
Natural Law, Torchbook edition (New York: Harper & Row,
1965), pp. 17-47; R. W. and A J. Carlyle, *A History of
Medieval Political Theory*, II (Edinburgh: Blackwood and
Sons, 1909); Walter Farrel, "Sources of St. Thomas' Concept
of Natural Law," *The Thomist*, XX (1957), 237-94; Felix
Flückiger, *Geschichte des Naturrechts* (Zolliken-Zürich:
Evangelischer Verlag, 1954); O. Lottin, *Le droit naturel
chez Saint Thomas et ses prédécesseurs*; *Ephemerides Theo-
logicae Lovanienses*, vols. 1-3, 1925-26; and Heinrich
Rommen, *Natural Law* (St. Louis, Mo.: Herder, 1947), pp. 3-69.

[32]*Institutes of Gaius and Rules of Ulpian* (Edinburgh:
T. & T. Clark, 1904), II, i. Later Roman Law distinguishes
between a *ius naturale* containing precepts common to men and
all animals and a *ius gentium* containing precepts specific
to rational men. Aquinas, however, does not fully accept
this distinction but prefers to consider *ius gentium* a part
of positive human law (Ia-IIae, Quest. 95, Art. 4).

by individual thinkers.[33] Aquinas is unique in trying
systematically to bring both views together. He does so by
considering the natural law primarily as a law of reason but,
when discussing the sexual precepts, by accepting the view
that man's sexual life must follow the pattern found among
animals. Indeed, when introducing the sexual precepts Aquinas
actually repeats the Stoic formula that the natural law contains that "which nature has taught to all animals" (Quest. 94,
Art. 2). However, in doing this Aquinas is aware that he is
incorporating a distinct view of natural law. In the third
article of the same question, for example, he distinguishes
between sins which violate the nature "proper to man," in that
they contradict reason, and sins which violate the nature
"common to man and other animals"; these latter sins include
"unisexual vice" and other sexual acts opposed to procreation.
Indeed, as I noted earlier, Aquinas appears convinced that
sins of this latter sort are graver than sins against reason.
This is why he ranks masturbation as a more objectional violation of the natural law than forcible heterosexual rape (IIa-
IIae, Quest. 154, Arts. 11, 12). While rape is an inordinate
and rationally indefensible use of the sexual capacities,
masturbation is a repudiation of a pattern common to all of
nature. It is the "basicness" of the procreative drive that
seems to buttress Aquinas' view of its primacy.[34] Later
scholastics tend to follow Aquinas here, not only in distinguishing between the two different ways in which one may
violate the natural law, but in emphasizing the primacy of
sins that violate the physical and sexual component of human
nature.[35]

---

[33]The important canonist Gratian and his commentator
Rufinus, for example, refuse to accept Ulpian's definition of
the natural law. See R. W. Carlyle and A. J. Carlyle, *A
History of Medieval Political Theory*, II, pp. 102-04. Carlyle
attributes Aquinas' acceptance of Ulpian's definition to
Aquinas' Aristotelian naturalism.

[34]Janssens, *Mariage et Fécondité*, p. 46.

[35]See, for example, Francisco Suarez, "A Treatise on
Laws and God the Lawgiver," Book II, Ch. 17 in *Selections from
Three Works of Francisco Suarez*, ed. James Brown Scott (Oxford:
The Clarendon Press, 1944).

I have already said that the sexual precepts of Roman
Catholic natural law theory are unacceptable from the perspective of the contract view. It goes without saying, therefore, that the priority given these precepts is also unacceptable from a contract view perspective. But when we recognize
that these precepts represent a second, and entirely distinct,
tradition of natural law, we, are spared the necessity of
rejecting Catholic natural law theory as a whole. Indeed, we
can see that in terms of one of the two Catholic interpretations of natural law, the contract view is itself a natural
law theory. All of these awarenesses have immediate importance
for our approach to the population question. On the one hand,
since the matter of population growth is closely related to
problems of human sexuality, we might expect that an application of the contract view to this issue will yield principles
quite distinct from those suggested by Roman Catholic thinkers
on the sexual precepts of the natural law. In particular, it
is doubtful whether contract thinking would support the Roman
Catholic emphasis on the untamperable nature of the sexual
act. It is also doubtful whether it would support the
primacy of familial procreative liberty or the consistent
priority of family over society upon which some Catholic
thinkers, as we have seen, insist. On the other hand, the
affinity between the contract view and a second Catholic understanding of the natural law might lead us to expect some possibility of agreement between Catholic thinking and the contract
view in this area, especially with regard to the Catholic
insistence upon the place of economic justice for individuals
and families in considerations of population growth and the
Catholic resentment of population programs undertaken in disregard of issues of social justice. When I turn to the
contract view's implications for the matter of population
growth, I shall try to note these specific items of agreement
and disagreement.

3. *Moral Universality and the Contract View*

By understanding the contract view as a natural law
theory of ethics, however, we gain more than an insight into

Catholic population thinking. We potentially appropriate,
as well, some of the important claims made about the natural
law by its Catholic and non-Catholic defenders. Foremost
among these is the claim that the natural law represents an
authoritative moral code known to and accepted by all rational
persons. Both within the Catholic natural law tradition and
in later non-Catholic theories of natural law, there has been
consistent stress on the universality of the natural law.[36]
As I have said, this insistence has important implications for
my use of the contract view for population purposes. A view
accepted by all rational persons would not appear to require
justification. It would be a moral position capable of
eliciting immediate assent from all.

Now that we have examined the relationship between
natural law theory and the contract view, however, we are in
a position to understand the special significance of the
claim for the universality of natural law. If it is true that
"all rational persons" would accept the authority of the
natural law, this is clearly so only as they are limited to
that knowledge which they share with all other rational
persons. Aware of their own capacities and ends, they might
find the restraints imposed by moral principles detrimental
to their interests. In other words, rational persons in this
case must be understood not as real rational persons, but as
Aquinas' "essential" rational agents, or as members of the
original position. Because of this, the claim concerning
the universality of the natural law is somewhat less significant than it first appears, for no real persons are limited
in this fashion. Possessed of all their particular knowledge
and beliefs, there is no reason why real rational agents
should accept the authority of a natural law moral procedure
or of the principles it generates. The possibility, therefore,
of an immediate justification of the contract view is reduced.

Though this is true, the claim concerning the universality of the natural law is not unrelated to the justification
of the contract view. To understand this I might raise and

---

[36]See Rommen, *Natural Law,* p. 6.

try to answer two questions. First, why is it important that a moral viewpoint be universally accepted? Second, in what sense can it be said that only a position involving the kind of restriction on particular knowledge that characterizes the contract view is capable of functioning as a universal moral position?

The first of these questions has been addressed in various ways by philosophers. Perhaps the most common answer is that based upon an analysis of moral language. Within the meta-ethical literature, for example, the first-person relativism of Edward Westermarck and the cultural relativism of William Graham Sumner have both been challenged on the grounds that they do not conform to our common use of moral terms like right and good. Opponents of relativism point out that it makes sense to say that an act is right even though we do not approve of it or even though it is not approved by our culture.[37] But the difficulty with this kind of analysis is that it relies upon disputed data. Not all men use moral terms univocally, and possibly some men do use these terms in a relativistic way. Because of this, some effort has recently been made to state the concept of morality which underlies the judgment that certain uses of moral terms are inappropriate. In his work, *The Moral Rules*, for example, Bernard Gert maintains that universality is simply one of the distinguishing features of judgments or statements we call moral.[38] A moral rule differs from all our other prescriptive utterances, says Gert, precisely because it is held to apply to all rational human beings. Gert's appeal here is to a commonly intuited understanding of the moral rules. This position is perhaps less open to dispute than the linguistic defense of morality's universal extension. But it shares the difficulty of all positions which rely heavily on intuition or self-evidence.

---

[37]This kind of open-question language test of a moral utterance was pioneered by G. E. Moore in his *Principia Ethica* (Cambridge, Eng.: Cambridge University Press, 1903), p. 15.

[38]P. 66.

144

Against these kinds of linguistic or concept analyses, an effort has been made to substantiate the claim that moral principles must be universal by means of an understanding of the function of morality. Kurt Baier, for example, argues that the "moral point of view" must be understood as furnishing an impartial court of arbitration for conflicts of interest. The essence of the moral response, therefore, is that it is non-coercive. It seeks to replace force with the instrumentality of impartial reason as a means of regulating social relations.[39] Very similarly Rawls stresses the task of principles of right "in adjusting the claims that persons make on their institutions and one another." To fulfill this task, Rawls maintains, it is necessary that moral rules be capable of imposing an ordering on conflicting claims without resort to physical conflict or resort to arms (*Theory*, p. 131).

When morality is understood as a non-coercive means of settling social disputes, the basis of the claim that moral principles be universally applicable becomes clearer. While it is certainly possible for men to elaborate moral systems that apply only to their own group life, it is obvious that such particular systems render impossible the moral settlement of disputes between groups. In a world of group moralities, only physical force or more subtle forms of coercion would remain as a method of settlement between groups. If morality is to fulfill its function and is to be available as a method of settling disputes wherever possible, therefore, the moral method demands universal extension. The moral rules must finally extend to all who are capable of this means of settlement. That is, to all beings who possess reason, normal intelligence and the capacity to respect and act upon moral principles. The quality of universality thus inheres in the

---

[39]*The Moral Point of View*, Abridged edition (New York: Random House, 1965), p. xv-xvii. This understanding is reminiscent of earlier contract theory defenses of the state of civilization as against the state of nature. In *The Metaphysical Elements of Justice*, Library of Liberal Arts edition (Indianapolis: Bobbs-Merrill, 1965), p. 72, for example, Kant argues that in the state of lawlessness men cannot "wrong each other by fighting among themselves."

very concept of morality. Universality has a valid place in our intuition concerning morality. But it has a rational explanation as well. To fulfill their purpose, the rules of morality must finally extend their protection and their demands to all mankind.

This understanding of the nature of moral rules helps to explain the kind of restrictions imposed on moral choice by the contract view and suggests the answer to my second question of why a view of this sort is capable of serving as a universal moral position. Ch. Perelman notes that voluntary arbitration proceeds from the assumption that there are desires and beliefs common to the parties to the dispute, and Baier adds that settlement also requires a "higher" vantage point of arbitration free of the particular desires and beliefs which characterize each party and which serve as points of contention.[40] The contract view represents the effort to extend this understanding to a position capable of adjudicating disputes between all rational persons. The veil of ignorance allows a knowledge of all those beliefs and desires that rational human beings share in common and excludes knowledge of any belief particular to single human beings or single human groups. Contract parties are themselves rendered the kind of arbitrators required to settle disputes that may arise between all rational men, and they are able to formulate moral rules of universal applicability. Indeed, it seems the case that without this kind of restraint, there would be no agreement among men on the principles needed to settle their conflicts. Given the inequalities of power and natural ability among men, it is likely that the more advantaged would refuse to agree to any principles detrimental to their interests while the least advantaged would be similarly unwilling freely to submit to principles detrimental to their welfare. To secure any kind of universal principles, therefore, all particular knowledge must be excluded. Rawls observes that without this kind of exclusion the bargaining problem of the original position would be "hopelessly

---

[40] *Justice*, p. 74; *The Moral Point of View*, p. 96.

complicated" and we would not be able to work out any definite
theory of justice or right (*Theory*, p. 140). Referring to a
similar restriction of knowledge in his own rational moral
system, Gert has argued that there is an analytic or conceptual
link between the demand that principles be universal and the
exclusion of particular knowledge.[41] Without this exclusion
we cannot begin to speak of universal principles. Interestingly, this understanding places a slightly different interpretation on some traditional claims for the universality of the
natural law. These claims should not be interpreted in the
first place to mean that such a morality is universally
accepted. Rather these claims may be seen as hypothetical:
if there is to be one morality for all rational persons, then
it must be a natural law morality of this sort.

The very concept of morality therefore justifies the
device of the original position and the kinds of restraint it
implies. When I apply the device of the original position to
the moral issue of rapid population growth, I do so, therefore,
with the conviction that this moral methodology represents
one acceptable way of generating rules for the settlement of
a dispute of this sort, where divisions among rational persons
are so sharp and extensive. Of course, there may be other
conceptual devices which, by insuring impartiality of moral
choice, function as effectively or even more effectively than
the device of the original position in the contract view. I
am not interested in disputing this matter, and I do not wish
to contend that the contract view is the only way to generate
universal moral principles. Nevertheless, I do want to
suggest that this view meets the two criteria which any moral
position must fulfill: it takes seriously the divergent
interests of real human beings and tries to offer an impartial
vantage point for adjudicating conflicts among these interests.
Because of this, and because the idea of the original position
has been reasonably well worked out, it appears to be a valid
methodology for our purposes and one capable of generating

---

[41]*The Moral Rules*, pp. 76f. For a similar view see
Alan Gewirth, "The Justification of Egalitarian Justice,"
American Philosophical Quarterly, VIII (1971), 336.

universally acceptable moral principles.

This justification of the original position must be qualified in several ways, however. First, it is important to note that Rawls's own defense of the original position is slightly different from my own. In Rawls's view, the original position represents a series of constraints which our common sense imposes upon a conception of right. These constraints are formal and include the demand that moral principles be general in formulation, universal in application, publicly acknowledgeable, capable of ordering claims and final in their authority in settling disputes (*Theory*, pp. 130-36). The original position represents an analytic construction, expressive of these constraints and designed to produce principles conforming to them. It is a device, says Rawls,, which "best expresses the conditions that are widely thought reasonable to impose on the choice of principles" (*Theory*, p. 121). Clearly, in justifying the device of the original position solely on the basis of an understanding of morality as a non-coercive means of settling disputes, I have somewhat departed from Rawls. But I have done so because this conception of morality seems to rely less on self-evidence than do the formal constraints which Rawls would impose upon moral principles. Indeed, I would maintain that three of the formal constraints which Rawls discusses, generality, public acknowledgeability and finality, may be derived from the single constraint that principles be capable of ordering claims in a non-coercive fashion. And I have already suggested the way in which universality may be derived from this same constraint. By stressing this single constraint and its relation to the function of moral rules, therefore, it is possible, with minimum appeal to intuition or self-evidence, to derive all the constraints of right and to justify the description of the original position itself.[42]

---

[42]There is some evidence that Rawls might agree with this stress on ordering. He observes (*Theory*, p. 131) that the propriety of all the formal constraints of right "is derived from the task of principles of right in adjusting the claims that persons make upon their institutions and one another."

A second qualification concerns the extent of this justification of the original position. It should not be confused with a justification of the contract view as a whole, and particularly with the two principles of justice. Rawls notes that the justification of the two principles is complex. In addition to involving some defense of the original position, it involves demonstrating that these principles represent a rational choice for members of the original position, and once chosen, that they form a stable conception of justice for society. Justification also involves showing that these principles compare favorably with common-sense precepts of justice, either by conforming to these precepts or, where common-sense precepts conflict, by ordering and arranging their different insistences. The second and third parts of *A Theory of Justice* are devoted to this extended process of justification. Obviously, I cannot recapitulate all of Rawls's arguments here. I have sought clearly to justify the device of the original position and I have sought at least to indicate the reasoning that lies behind contract parties' choice of the two principles. Henceforth I shall assume that this moral methodology is acceptable and that the two principles at least closely express the reasoning of rational persons under conditions of moral choice.

In one sense, however, my enterprise in the following section represents a continuing effort at justifying the contract view. In what follows, I shall try to formulate a contract theory principle (or principles) of population growth. This means that I shall be striking off into areas not examined by Rawls himself. In doing so, I rely upon the adequacy of the device of the original position and its description of contract parties. I shall also draw upon the two principles and the reasoning behind them. But any population principle or principles generated in this way must be justifiable in their own right. They must accord with, and not defy common sense. And they must compare favorably with widely accepted moral principles that have been advanced with respect to this issue. For the moment, we may think of the various views of population growth we have encountered as expressing such principles. As we have seen, there exist both

Malthusian and anti-Malthusian interpretations of population growth. If the contract theory is to prove an accurate expression of our moral reasoning process, it must help us understand and arrange these different perspectives. And it must make some sense of the intense, but apparently differing moral convictions that underlie them. Just as the difference principle illuminates the many opposing concrete principles of economic justice, a contract population principle must serve to clarify the moral sense underlying antagonistic perspectives in the population debate.

In this respect, there is further importance to understanding the contract view as a natural law moral theory. If the contract view represents a structure of moral reasoning common to all rational persons insofar as they are nothing more than rational persons, we might expect few common sense moral principles in this area to accord fully with a contract principle or principles for this issue. These common-sense principles are likely to be distorted by the particular vantage points and needs of their proponents. On the other hand, insofar as these differing principles purport to be moral, we have reason to suspect that each will partly reflect truths within a more comprehensive moral understanding. If the contract view provides such an understanding, this serves as further evidence of its moral adequacy.

I might finally note that the partiality of the moral perspective of real, rational persons also places some limit on the degree to which the moral principles of a natural law position can command assent or obedience from real people. Possessed of the knowledge of their own ends and interests, men can rationalize rejection of or disobedience to the moral rules. As Aquinas puts it in more traditional terminology, all human beings possess some knowledge of the natural law, but in many individuals this knowledge is clouded by passions and continuing immoral desires (*Summa Theologica*, Ia-IIae, Quest. 94, Art. 6). Nevertheless, since it reflects the structure of our moral reason, a natural law view does command a measure of universal moral assent. Furthermore, we might expect the authority of such a view to be greatest among those groups or classes of men who, because of their social position,

150

most require the protection of moral rules and who are least
able to disregard the demands made by such rules; that is,
those groups or classes not possessing privilege or power.
This latter fact has particular bearing on the matter of population policy. Since high fertility frequently characterizes
lower-income classes or disadvantaged minority groups, there
is a special reason for population policy aimed at these
groups to have a moral foundation in a natural law position
like the contract view. For we can anticipate the moral
insistences derived from a view like this, though susceptible
to universal acknowledgement, have particular force to those
whose social position most closely approximates the conditions
of members of the original position or Aquinas' "essential
human beings," This is a matter we shall look at more closely
when we turn to the issue of population policy. For the
moment, I wish to indicate this additional reason why it is
important to understand the contract view as a natural law
position.

D. *Alterations in the Contract View Required for Population
   Purposes*

1. *The "Species Good" of Children*

My object now is to begin the process of applying the
contract view to the issue of population growth. But in
seeking to do so an immediate difficulty appears. In its
present form, the original position contains several features
which render it unsuitable for population purposes. Two
difficulties stand out. First, the theory of primary goods
tends to beg some important questions that are at issue in the
population debate. Second, Rawls's understanding of the
generational entry point of the members of the original position requires revision, or, better, explanation, if one
important population alternative, the principle of classical
utilitarianism, is not to be rejected without a fair hearing.
As presently described, the theory of primary goods
tends immediately to favor an anti-populationist point of view.
Working with this theory, which stresses income as one of the

goods which all persons desire whatever else they desire,
contract parties can be led to support efforts to maximize
income by drastically reducing population growth rates or
population size. In this respect, the theory of primary
goods is as inadequate as would be any crude economic analysis
of population growth which assumed that income is an unambiguous index of welfare on this issue. I am not suggesting that
members of the original position would not find it rational
to reduce population in order to maximize income. But if the
contract view is not simply to beg this question the original
position must not be constructed so that the good of children
is summarily dismissed from consideration.

It could be argued that provision for the good of
children is implicit in Rawls's stress on the primary good of
liberty. We have seen that liberty here is understood to
include not only political liberties, but also basic social
liberties, such as liberty of person, liberty of employment,
and the like. Now it may be Rawls's intention to include the
liberty to procreate and the liberty to have as many children
as one wishes among these liberties. Certainly, a case can
be made that the liberty to procreate, as a liberty at least
to exercise one's reproductive capacities, deserves a place
among these very basic liberties. The loss of one's reproductive capacity is commonly considered a grave evil, even by
those who may not care to have numerous offspring, or for that
matter, any offspring at all. To place this liberty among
the basic liberties does not seem unusual, therefore, and it
would amount in practice to a prohibition against state interference with one's capacity to reproduce, as, for example,
through programs of compulsory sterilization.[43]

But it may be questioned whether the liberty to try to
have as many children as one wishes is on a par with this one

---

[43]In a forthcoming volume to be published by Yale University Press and edited by Leon Kass and Daniel Callahan,
Human Rights and Population Policy, Arthur Dyck suggests
distinguishing between a "right to procreate" and a "right to
plan to have as many children as one wants." The first of
these rights, as a liberty to exercise one's reproductive
capacities, and to retain the possibility of doing so, is presumably a basic right cherished by all contract parties.

152

and whether it ought to be, or can be, included among the
basic social liberties. On reflection, it can be seen that
the liberty to try to have as many children as one wishes--the
liberty to pursue the good of children without restraint within
the limits of one's own reproductive capacities--is qualita-
tively distinct from other kinds of basic social and political
liberties. For one thing, it is not a liberty necessarily
sought by all rational persons. Whereas all desire to retain
their liberty of person in order to pursue their good, it is
not clear that all desire to retain a liberty to try to have
as many children as they wish. For another thing, the concept
of equal liberty when applied to this latter liberty is far
less clear than when applied to political and social liberties.
Equal liberty in these other areas seems capable of some kind
of reasonably clear determination. In the political sphere,
for example, equal liberty amounts to the possession of one
vote in a political process. And the equal social liberties
are usually liberties that may be fully exercised without
substantial conflict among those exercising them. The liberty
to select one's career or to move one's place of residence
are examples. But no such clear determination of an equal
liberty seems possible with respect to the liberty to try to
have as many children as one wishes. What, really, does an
equal liberty of this sort amount to? Does it mean that any
individual couple may try to have as many children as they
wish; or is their right restricted by others' right to do the
same? Obviously, answers to these questions have been
advanced. It has been argued that the liberty to have children
halts when procreation becomes physically impossible (a
standing-room only situation), or where vital resources are
exhausted, or where the ability to rear children in comfort
is impeded. But these suggestions only serve to illustrate
the difficulty of including the liberty to try to have as many
children as one wishes among the basic liberties of person.

    I can express this last difficulty another way. As
Rawls makes clear, the basic political and social liberties
take priority over the kinds of economic considerations
expressed in the difference principle. They are not liberties
which members of the original position would trade off for

economic gain. These basic liberties may be sacrificed only for the sake of their own preservation, as when conscription is needed to help wage a just war (*Theory*, p. 380), or they may be subordinated to economic development only when development is clearly needed to secure their worth. Thus Rawls qualifies the priority of the first to the second principle in those cases where an economy is so underdeveloped, and poverty so prevalent, as to render the political liberties protected by the first principle worthless (*Theory*, p. 152). But apart from this extreme instance, the basic liberties are immune to economic trade-off.

Now if the liberty to try to have as many children as one wishes is included among these basic social liberties it would seem on these grounds alone that this liberty may not be subordinated to economic considerations except, possibly, at the very lowest levels of economic development, or where population growth threatened to plunge a society into such an impoverished state. This seems to be the view of some of the more extreme Roman Catholic thinkers whose position we have examined. Thus, Anthony Zimmerman maintains that the liberty freely to have children is so fundamental that it may not be compromised except where needed to preserve its exercise. He would tolerate population limitation at the point of "absolute overpopulation," where severe hardship threatened on a world-wide scale, but no sooner.[44] Zimmerman is here partly informed by the traditional Catholic stress on the primacy of the family and the obligation to have as large a family as possible.

It may be that Zimmerman is correct and that rational members of the original position would agree upon a population principle of this kind. But such a conclusion may not legitimately be reached by assuming that the liberty to try to have as large a family as one wishes is simply one of those basic liberties cherished by all rational persons. For the fact remains that many human beings do not cherish an unfettered liberty to bear offspring. Nor do they cherish offspring

---

[44]*Catholic Viewpoint on Overpopulation* (Garden City, N.Y.: Hanover House, 1961), p. 190.

themselves (although they may cherish a right to exercise their reproductive capacity). If the device of the original position is to furnish an impartial adjudicatory panel in this case, therefore, the attitude toward children of the contract parties must reflect the different attitudes present among real, rational persons. Contract parties cannot all be said to desire offspring intensely, nor can they all be said to be willing to trade off offspring for economic gain. Children are not primary goods in the way that political liberties are, but neither can they be made completely subordinate to the primary good of income, since many rational agents would not be willing always to sacrifice children to the instrumental or primary good of income.

To express the likely place of children in the consideration of members of the original position, I would introduce a concept of my own, one not utilized by Rawls. This is the concept of a "species" good. Such a good can be understood, in the first place, as a value very widely cherished by rational persons as an end in itself apart from any consideration of its usefulness in promoting other ends. In this sense, a species good has intrinsic worth and is distinct from a primary good, which is conceived of in terms of its instrumental value. A species good would also differ from a primary good in not being an end that all human beings can be said to pursue. It is a "particular" good, although distinct from other particular goods in being widely and intensely cherished by a very large portion of mankind. Finally, there is one special sense in which a species good can be conceived of as a sort of primary good. This is the sense in which it is rational for all men to desire some quantity of this good in society, even though they may not desire this good for themselves. The species good here has an instrumental value as it is possessed by the species rather than by the individual. Without some prevalence of this good, all rational human beings would be disadvantaged in the pursuit of their own good.

Clearly, this concept is tailor-made to the good of children. Indeed, there are no other goods that precisely meet these requirements, although the liberty to engage in sexual activity perhaps comes closest. That only children are

clearly species goods is no reason for objecting to the
concept, of course, since children rightly deserve a special
place in our attention. Few other values are so intensely and
widely desired without, at the same time, being universally
pursued. Interestingly, Catholic moral theory provides an
insight into the validity of this concept. I have already
discussed Aquinas' inclusion of sexuality and the desire to
rear young as among the basic desires pertaining to the
essence of man; that is, common to all rational human beings.
This suggests that Aquinas takes seriously the prevalence and
intensity of the sexual desires and desires for offspring;
so seriously, in fact, that he sometimes appears to deny the
non-universality of these desires. But this is not entirely
true. In defending religious celibacy, Aquinas concedes that
some men's plan of the good excludes the expression of sexual
desire or procreation of the young. In conceding this Aquinas
does not fully depart from his insistence on the pertinence
of sexuality to man's basic nature. But he maintains that
this quality properly belongs to the species as a whole and
not to individuals. Thus, mankind is required to reproduce
itself, but not every man must do so.[45] Aquinas' arguments
here represent the concept of a species good expressed (perhaps
not correctly) in the form of a moral principle.

I shall soon have occasion to explore the significance
of the concept of children as species good in the reasoning
of members of the original position. But it is useful here to
spell out a bit more clearly some awarenesses that follow from
this concept. First, I might note that the non-universality
of the desire for offspring renders the species good of
children not completely symmetrical with other primary goods.
While all members of the original position desire any primary
good, not all know that they desire children or the degree to

[45]". . . the precept of procreation regards the whole
multitude of men which needs not only to multiply in body, but
also to advance spiritually. Wherefore, sufficient provision
is made for the human multitude, if some betake themselves to
carnal procreation, while others abstaining from this betake
themselves to the contemplation of Divine Things . . . ."
Summa Theologica, IIa-IIae, Quest. 152, Art. 2.

which they might desire them. I might illustrate one implication of this. If the value of children for all rational
persons who desired children could be given a standard monetary
value, and if any member of the original position could choose
between receiving (or being allowed) either an additional child
or its income equivalent, it would probably be rational for
him to choose the income equivalent. In receiving income, he
could be satisfied with his choice whether or not he desired
children, while in opting for a child he might find himself
in possession of a good for which he has no desire. This
illustration is bizarre. It is not offered as a depiction of
the contract parties' consideration with respect to population,
if for no other reason than that the assumption of a fixed
money value for children is false. The point of this illustration is to indicate a slight asymmetry in the reasoning of
impartial persons with respect to the species good of children
when this good is in conflict with the primary good of income.
All rational agents know they desire income whereas not all
have this knowledge about their desire for offspring.

The asymmetry is enhanced by a further consideration.
The species good of children cannot properly be separated from
the primary good of income. Just as additional income can
help advance anybody's plan of the good, so it can help a
representative individual further a desire for offspring, even
where the number of offspring is restricted. This is true
because the desire for offspring does not always, or even
usually, take the form of a yearning for numerous progeny.
If children are desired by rational persons, it is often very
much because of the satisfactions they provide their parents.
But these satisfactions can be intensified, without increasing
numbers, where economic resources are available.[46] The health
of children, their sound physical and mental development and
their general happiness are partly a function of parents'

[46]Cf. Judith Blake, *Family Structure in Jamaica: The Social Context of Reproduction* (Glencoe, Ill.: The Free Press, 1961), p. 189. Also, Arthur Dyck, "Population Policies and Ethical Acceptability," in *Rapid Population Growth,* National Academy of Sciences (Baltimore: Johns Hopkins Press, 1971), p. 632.

income. The implication of this is that many of those
rational persons who desire offspring have good reason for
desiring income, so long as the methods of increasing income
do not entirely eliminate the possibility of having children.
A member of the original position thus has a double reason for
preferring the primary good of income over the species good of
children. First, because a desire for children may not
characterize his own plan of the good. And second, because
even if he does desire children, he may be among the many
individuals who prefer a few, better-endowed children to
numerous but less well-endowed offspring.

So much for the asymmetry of the species and primary
goods. All these considerations serve only to suggest why
rational members of the original position might be led to
place additional weight on the primary goods and particularly
income. I might now suggest, however, some countervailing
considerations raised by the concept of the species good.
First, I should note that there seems to be a bottom limit
imposed by this concept on trade-offs between offspring and
income. Children, I have said, are to some degree cherished
by all rational human beings, if not directly for these
rational persons themselves, at least for their species.
What this means is that all rational human beings have some
desire to see the human race continue. Shortly I shall
indicate how the veil of ignorance, by obliterating contract
parties' knowledge of the generation to which they belong,
helps provide some further explanation of this desire. But
even without this consideration, rational individuals would
presumably have many reasons for not wishing the human race
to move to extinction within their lifetimes. Fellow human
beings, after all, figure importantly in the pursuit of many
plans of the good. A vanishing population can markedly disadvantage many individuals in the satisfaction of their plan
of life. This consideration is strengthened by the previous
suggestion that many rational human beings desire well-endowed
offspring. A willingness on the part of one of these individuals to trade off children for income ends when the goal
of increased income necessitates totally restricting the right
to have children. There is therefore some bottom limit on

family size below which individuals of this sort would be
reluctant to substitute income for offspring. I do not wish
to speculate on what this bottom limit might be. The point
is, simply, that a limit exists. The asymmetry between species
and primary goods should not be taken to imply their permanent
imbalance in the eyes of all rational human beings.

One further countervailing consideration deserves
mention here. I have tried to offer some tentative reasons
why rational persons might prefer income to offspring. But
this relative primacy of income over offspring may be rational
only when an individual is totally deprived of the knowledge
of his plan of the good, including knowledge of how much he
desires offspring. One implication of the concept of children
as a species good, however, is the awareness that many rational
persons intensely desire offspring. In order to estimate their
own willingness to sacrifice children to income, therefore,
contract parties must have some understanding of the intensity
of these desires as they exist in society. In addition, they
must ask whether these desires are randomly distributed among
men or whether they are clearly correlated with membership in
representative social groups or classes, especially the least-
off representative groups. If the latter is true, and the
less advantaged individuals tend to desire more children,
contract parties might be compelled to give particular attention to the way in which any principles they advance with
respect to population affect them as potential least-off
representative individuals. They must ask, for example,
whether a given approach to population or a population
principle has the effect of further eroding their position.
And they must ask how a population principle coheres with any
economic principles on which they agree. This series of
questions and problems is quite abstract. I shall look more
closely at these matters when I examine the actual reasoning
of contract parties. But for the time being, it is important
to note that the particularity of desires for children may not
dissuade members of the original position from taking these
desires very seriously, especially when these desires are con-
joined with other interests and desires they may possess as
members of identifiable and enduring social groups.

2. *Time of Entry*

Before turning to the reasoning of the contract parties, some other aspects of Rawls's description of the original
position must be considered. One of these concerns the entry
point in time of contract parties. According to Rawls, members
of the original position may be understood to be all the
living members (of the age of reason) of any single generation
in time (*Theory*, p. 139). Contract parties are living contemporaries, although the veil of ignorance deprives them of the
knowledge of the generation to which they belong, or, more
precisely, of the knowledge of which stage of advance their
generation has reached among the possible stages a generation
can attain (*Theory*, p. 287). The requirement of ignorance as
to generational stage is easily explained. It presumably
renders members of the original position impartial between
generational stages and it expresses the fact that a moral
view should be capable of settling disputes between generations. Ignorance as to generational stage is a feature of the
original position of particular importance when it comes to
producing a savings principle between generations (*Theory*, pp.
284-93); it is also, of course, relevant to the population
issue.

Less easily explained is the stipulation that members
of the original position are to be considered living members
of a present generation (whatever its stage of advance).
Rawls recognizes that this stipulation is a source of difficulty because it has a tendency to bias some of the thinking
of the contract parties and even to undercut the effect of the
veil of ignorance in obliterating knowledge of the stage of
generational advance. Knowing that they are living contemporaries, contract parties also know that they are not going to
be alive in the future. This can condition their acceptance
of a just savings principle. It is the nature of such a
principle that all generations but the first benefit from a
program of saving; the first generation must sacrifice without
the hope of direct compensation for its efforts (*Theory*, p.
288). Clearly, since they are presently alive, contract
parties have every reason to reject a savings principle. But

if they do so, their decision reflects an imperfection in the description of the original position. As described, members of the original position are not really impartial between generations on this point.

One way of correcting this difficulty is by altering the time of entry assumption for members of the original position. Members of the original position can be considered as all persons who *will* ever live at some time ("all actual persons"), or as all persons who *could* live at some time ("all possible person"). Rawls is prepared to consider these variant interpretations of the original position but he rejects them as the favored interpretation. His reason for doing so is that either variant interpretation moves the conception of the original position too far beyond the realm of common sense. "To conceive of the original position in either of these ways," he states, "is to stretch fantasy too far; the conception would cease to be a natural guide to intuition" (*Theory*, p. 139). In place of these variant interpretations, Rawls prefers to rely upon the motivational assumption that each member of the original position cares about the well-being of some of those in the next generation. Instead of being isolated individuals, contract parties are considered to represent continuing lines of claims. They are, for example, family heads and their good-will and concern extend over at least two generations. By means of this assumption, Rawls is able to offset the first generation preference of members of the original position. Concern for their offspring serves as their motivation for agreeing to a permanent savings principle, despite the fact that, as described, contract parties do not themselves profit from such a principle (*Theory*, p. 128).

Rawls's argument here may be understood as an effort to assimilate the force of the "all actual persons" description without having to accept that description itself. Concern and identification with their children has the same effect on contract parties as would concern with their own welfare as actual living persons in some future generation. Nevertheless, it must be asked whether this motivational assumption is fully appropriate with respect to the population issue and whether the "all actual persons" description, though somewhat removed

from reality, is not more fitting in this case. A special
difficulty is generated in the matter of population by the
fact that one cannot always rely upon parents' concern for
their offspring in this area. Because rational human beings
can experience many satisfactions in having and rearing children, they may possess a motivation for increasing the number
of their offspring at the expense of those very offspring.[47]
When it comes to procreation and the relationship between two
contiguous generations, in other words, there are potential
sources of conflict which Rawls's motivational assumption
obscures, and this kind of conflict fully expresses itself on
the population issue. It is possible, of course, to retain
the present time of entry description of the original position
and to insist that contract parties respect the rights of
their children. But this imports a prior moral assumption
into the description of contract parties. When dealing with
the population issue, therefore, it would seem less complex
to work with the "all actual persons" description. By means
of this, contract parties would be forced to consider the
implications of their desires and behavior for any representative individual in succeeding generations, even one of their
own children. They would have to balance their desires as
adult, procreative beings against their desires as the offspring of such beings.

One important question arises at this point. If contract parties are required to consider themselves as any
representative future human being, how far into the future
must they look? How many generations into the future may
we assume their concern extends? One possible answer to this
question is that there is a definite limit on the distance
into the future we need extend our sense of obligation. In
one of the few philosophical treatments of the issue, Martin

---

[47]Thus, in discussing reproductive motivation some
economists have advanced the concept of parental exploitation
of children. See, for example, T. Paul Schultz, "An Economic
Perspective on Population Growth," in National Academy of
Sciences, *Rapid Population Growth* (Baltimore: Johns Hopkins
Press, 1971), p. 152.

162

Golding argues that our obligations to distant future generations may be non-existent, or at least far more attenuated than
those to generations nearer our own. In Golding's view, the
fact that we do not even know which conceptions of the good
distant future men might hold relieves us of any significant
obligation to protect or promote their welfare.[48]

Expressed in terms of the contract view, this claim
may amount to limiting membership in the original position to
individuals who stand reasonably near ourselves in time, say,
the several generations that extend into the future. But is
this kind of limitation justified? And is it necessary? In
answer to the first of these questions, I might say that an
arbitrary exclusion of distant future human beings has
distinct moral disadvantages. To the degree that persons in
the future are rational, sentient, mortal beings with a plan
of the good, they can be affected by our actions and they can
raise complaint.[49] For this reason alone they deserve membership in the original position. If the contract view were a
teleological moral position which made what is right or just
depend upon the maximization of some non-moral value, it would
certainly be hard to include such future persons in our moral
considerations, since we could not know which value they
wished promoted. But members of the original position possess
only the basic interests common to all human beings. Most of
the principles they agree to, therefore, will be of use to such
beings no matter how their specific aims or ambitions might
vary. Allowing future rational human beings to participate in
the original position is a way of insuring that no principles
are agreed to which will markedly disadvantage persons of this
sort however removed they are from us in time or space.

---

[48]"What is Our Obligation to Future Generations?"
Working Paper of the Hastings Center Institute of Society,
Ethics and the Life Sciences (Hastings-on-Hudson, New York,
1971), pp. 11, 12. Also his article, "Ethical Issues in Biological Engineering," *UCLA Law Review*, XV (February 1968),
457-63.

[49]Aquinas' insistence on the unchangeability of the
primary precepts of the natural law (*Summa Theologica* Ia-IIae,
Quest. 94, Art. 5) is based on the view that this basic and
common human nature is not likely to change a great deal over
time.

Nor does it seem that excluding all future human beings
from the original position is really necessary. We may presume
that the uneasiness of Golding and others over the idea of full
obligations owed to future generations is most acute in cases
where present generations are called upon to make drastic
sacrifices in order to protect distant future persons. Somehow
we think that living human beings deserve greater concern in
such cases. But certainly we can explain this priority without
categorically diminishing our responsibility to future persons
or, what is the same thing, without excluding such persons
from the original position. In cases where drastic sacrifices
must be made by present generations in order to avoid injury
to future generations, rational agents from all generations
have reason to favor present generations. This is because
injury inflicted on those in the distant future is usually
only possible injury. Since conditions of life may change, we
cannot always be sure that acts which are presently injurious
will be so in the future. It is one thing to concede this and
qualify obligations in difficult cases, however, and another
to maintain that our obligation to people in the distant
future is not *prima facie* the same as our obligation to those
presently living. In cases where the evils inflicted on
future persons are clearly as grievous as those inflicted on
individuals in the present there would seem to be no basis for
qualifying our obligation to the future. To express this
awareness, therefore, I will assume that the original position
includes all actual human beings, with no limit on how far into
the future their generation exists.[50]

---

[50]Daniel Callahan, in his *Ethics and Population Limitation* (New York: The Population Council, 1971), p. 32, maintains that the rights of the living take clear precedence over the rights of unborn generations, but he adds that "the living have an obligation to refrain from actions which would endanger the possibility of future generations enjoying the same rights they presently enjoy." See also his article, "What Obligations Do We Have to Future Generations?" *The American Ecclesiastical Review*, CLXIV (April 1971), 265-80, for a more extensive reply to Golding's relative diminution of the rights of future generations. Callahan's viewpoint here seems assimilable to the position I have sketched. Certainly, the interests of presently living persons must be the standard from which the expectations of future beings are judged, and certainly, in cases of conflict

3. *Actual versus Possible Persons*

When I turn to the concrete reasoning of contract parties, I shall use the "all actual persons" description of the original position understood in this way. But one final question must be answered before proceeding. Both the present time of entry description and the "all actual persons" description of the original position focus upon real human beings, that is, upon persons who are alive or who will certainly be alive in the future. Since this is so, it may be asked whether either one of these interpretations renders the original position fair with respect to disputes that might be conjectured to occur between persons now alive and persons who might potentially live in the future. The claims of future *possible* persons have frequently been alluded to in the population debate. Some of those who have addressed the issue of rapid population growth, for example, have appeared to believe not only that present and future actual human beings have rights which must be respected but that possible or potential future human beings have such rights. Some of the extreme Roman Catholic opponents of population limitation that we have looked at appear to espouse this view and have sought, vicariously, to champion the rights of such possible future human beings.[51] And it seems that Engels occasionally adopted this position as have some later Marxist theorists who follow his lead.[52]

In terms of the contract theory, the idea that a moral view should be capable of heeding the claims of all persons who

---

the living take priority. But the demand that present opportunities for living persons be preserved for persons in the future suggests their *prima facie* equality. This awareness is expressed by giving future persons full entitlement within the original position.

[51]This view certainly is shared by the more extreme Catholic spokesmen such as Kelly and Zimmerman. But it seems implicit, as well, in some of the Papal admonitions to multiply physical resources rather than restrict the number of births. See above, p. 67.

[52]See the remarks by Engels, above pp. 90f.

might be born is expressed in that interpretation of the
original position which permits "all possible persons" to
participate simultaneously in the formulation of principles
of justice. If it is not to be simply concluded that the
contract view is biased against possible future persons, therefore, it must be explained why this interpretation of the
original position is not acceptable.[53] Unfortunately, when we
turn to Rawls for an explanation of why he rejects this variant
description of the original position, we are disappointed. He
nowhere provides an explanation of a decision which, for population purposes, is clearly so crucial. Apart from his
apparent rejection of this and the "all actual persons"
description as too fantastic for consideration, Rawls does
not seriously undertake to justify the neglect of future
possible beings as valid moral claimants.

The absence of a justification of this decision is
especially apparent in Rawls's treatment of classical utilitarianism. Since it is with respect to classical utilitarianism, moreover, that the population issue is most closely
joined, the absence of justification for this decision is
especially unfortunate. Classical utilitarianism is the position which holds that the right act or the just institution is
one which maximizes the absolute weighted sum of expectations
in society.[54] Classical utilitarianism evaluates an act or
institution by measuring the expectations of each representative individual. It then multiplies that level of expectations
by the number of individuals in each representative position
and sums up all the expectations involved. The implications
of this moral theory for the population issue are evident.
Other things equal, if an institution or act causes population
to double without reducing the expectations of representative

---

[53]The issue of actual versus possible persons has been
little discussed in the philosophical literature. For one
brief treatment of this matter see Robert M. Adams, "Must God
Create the Best?" *Philosophical Review*, LXXXI (July 1972),
317-32.

[54]The leading spokesman for this position is Henry
Sidgwick. See his *The Methods of Ethics* (New York: Dover
Publications, 1907, 1966), p. 415.

men, it has admirably conformed to the classical utilitarian moral demand. Indeed, within the framework of this position, it is entirely permissible for the expectations of representative persons to drop over time. As Rawls points out, for the classical utilitarian, "so long as the average utility per person falls slowly enough when the number of individuals increases, the population should be encouraged to grow indefinitely no matter how low the average has fallen" (*Theory*, p. 162f.). This means, as I noted earlier, that a society with a population twice as large at half the standard of living (if we assume this to be an expression of satisfaction), is morally equivalent from the classical utilitarian point of view to a society with half the number of people living twice as well.

Now it is because of these population implications that Rawls rejects classical utilitarianism. From the standpoint of persons in the original position, he argues, two societies like this are not morally identical. Assuming himself to be any representative individual, a contract party would find the society with half the population a superior one. Taking the role of a "hypothetical newcomer" to either society, he would find that his prospects in each society are identical with the average expectations that prevail in that society (*Theory*, pp. 164f.). Contract reasoning, in Rawls's view, thus favors an average (or per capita) form of utilitarianism over the classical form.

It should be clear, however, that this conclusion is evident only if one assumes that members of the original position are actually living persons, that is, persons who are presently alive or who will certainly be alive at some future time. Should one assume that the contract parties represent all the possible persons who could ever live, it is not clear that they would reject classical utilitarianism. **Since these parties may or may not be alive** in the future, it would seem very much in their interest to secure principles which accentuate their chances of coming into being. Other things equal, this means that they would prefer a larger future population to a smaller one. Classical utilitarianism may partly be thought of, therefore, as the moral view which

results from accepting the description of the original position
in which members represent all possible future human beings.

This being so, it is not enough to reject classical
utilitarianism and its population principle on the grounds
that it would not be accepted by members of the original
position. Rather, what must be shown is why the "all possible
persons" interpretation of the original position is unacceptable. We are brought back, in other words, to Rawls's unex-
plained reliance upon one variant interpretation of the nature
and circumstances of the contract parties. The critical
question becomes whether we should accept Rawls's favored
description of the original position at this point.[55]

One answer to this question may be suggested by a
close examination of classical utilitarianism itself. This
position, as we have just seen, permits an unceasing expansion
of population so long as average utility does not drop so fast
as to reduce the absolute weighted sum of expectations.
Expressed in terms of the original position, contract parties
considering themselves to be any possible future persons have
strong reason for wishing population to expand, even at some
cost to their own potential average prospects. It is important,
however, to ask whether there is not some bottom limit which
contract parties might place on their own prospects irrespective
of how successfully population expands. Might there not be
some level of expectations below which rational persons will
not permit themselves to fall even if it means that they
thereby deny themselves the chance to live? And if there is,
how does one determine what this level is?[56] It would seem

[55]Rawls's student, David Richards, follows Rawls on
this matter. In his *A Theory of Reasons for Action*, p. 134,
he rejects classical utilitarianism on the grounds that
rational contractors would not agree to reduce their per
capita satisfactions. Like Rawls, however, he merely assumes
that contractors are actual, as against possible, persons.

[56]In his *The Principles of Political Economy*, Sidgwick
recognizes this difficulty when, as a classical utilitarian,
he observes that population growth can, at some point,
jeopardize aggregate utility, but notes the extreme difficulty
in stipulating at what point this occurs. In his article, "On
the Concept of Optimum Population," *Review of Economic Studies*,

168

that classical utilitarianism, and the "all possible persons"
description of the original position here involves insoluble
moral difficulties, for there are probably few questions on
which rational human beings show as little agreement as the
question of at which point life is no longer worth living.[57]
Subjective and particular estimates of the value and purpose
of human life seem to inundate rational consideration at this
point and render impossible any clear determination of the
extent to which population should grow. Perhaps this is what
Rawls means when he suggests that this variant interpretation
takes us too far into the realm of fantasy to be a sound basis
for moral reasoning.

The complexity of reasoning and the incertitude which
must attend it cannot themselves be a reason for rejecting
the "all possible persons" interpretation. A view might be
unworkable and complex but nevertheless correct. What must be
shown is that there is something faulty in this interpretation
itself. Here the complexity of the reasoning process furnishes
a clue. When examined closely, it can be seen that the conception of contract parties as "all possible persons" is quite
odd. On the one hand, it is assumed that these persons are
mature, rational, self-interested beings intensely desirous
of protecting their interests when they take their places in
real society. Should principles be adopted which violate these
interests they presumably have strong grounds for dissatisfaction and for raising a moral complaint. On the other hand,
they are assumed also to be persons who might never exist.
But how can persons who do not exist raise a moral complaint
or experience dissatisfaction? It seems peculiar, in other
words, that contract parties who must be real rational persons
should put themselves in the position of beings who will not

XXXVI (July 1969), 295-318, P. S. Dasgupta notes the difficulty of specifying what he calls a "welfare subsistence"
level.

[57]Gert observes in *The Moral Rules*, p. 36, that it is
never irrational in our common judgment not to want to die. On
the other hand, it is not considered irrational to want to die
to escape various forms of suffering. Taken together these
considerations suggest the degree of variability that can exist
on the issue of the worth of living.

be at all. It seems even more peculiar that they should be
prepared to reduce their expectations as real individuals who
can experience dissatisfaction and moral resentment in order
to forestall resentment and dissatisfaction among persons who
will never be.

It is understandable that the "all possible persons"
description of the original position should involve contract
parties in peculiar reasoning like this. When this description
is employed, the original position is being used for a purpose
for which it was not intended and for which it ought not to
be intended. The original position, it will be recalled, has
its value as a device for resolving social disputes. It represents a hypothetical vantage point from which people can arrive
at moral principles regulating the various claims they make
upon scarce social resources and opportunities. Indeed, as I
have suggested, the very justification of the device of the
original position rests upon the demonstration that such a
device can effectively arbitrate real disputes among persons.
If the contract parties are assumed to be real (or actual)
rational persons, therefore, it is because it is only among
such individuals that disputes arise. When the original
position is interpreted to settle disputes between all real
persons and all possible persons it reflects a mistaken
estimate of the kind of situation which generates moral conflict. Possible persons are never in dispute with real persons.
At best, some real individuals concerned for all possible
persons are in conflict with some real individuals concerned
only with themselves or other actual human beings. But if
this is so, it is mistaken to give all possible persons a
franchise within the original position. It may be that to
render the original position fair, contract parties represent-
ing real, rational persons should be made aware that some real
people care deeply for possible future beings. But to admit
all possible persons to the original position would clearly
skew consideration in favor of those real people who harbor
this particular concern.

It must even be questioned whether any real, rational
individuals really desire to see population expand indefinitely.
Should many rational persons possess this desire, it is one

that contract parties might seriously have to consider. But
before conceding that this kind of particular desire is prevalent, it is worth asking why some individuals have displayed
vigorous concern in this direction. We have seen that some
Roman Catholic and Marxist thinkers have championed the rights
of future possible persons. The question is why they have
done so. Is this a genuine desire or is it based on mistaken
assumptions? Several explanations for their thinking in this
area might be advanced. First, one might point to the polemi-
cal context which has stimulated Catholic and Marxist reflection in this area. I have already observed that the Marxist
population position was staked out in a bitter debate with
Malthusian theory. Malthus had espoused the effort to improve
the living conditions of human beings within capitalist society
by means of a drastic curtailment of the procreation of future
human beings. In rejecting the unjust social policies and
institutions with which Malthus and Malthusianism were
associated, therefore, Engels tends to accentuate the opposite
population extreme. Whereas capitalism must rely upon a
reduction of human beings to improve material standards, he
says, communism can provide comfort for an indefinitely
expanding population. Though Catholic thinkers certainly do
not advocate communism, they share Engels' dislike for liberal
economic thought and they follow his moral logic in their
rejection of population control programs as niggardly or un-
generous. In addition, their traditional concern for family
values is responsible for a good deal of their opposition to
Malthusianism. Marxists and Catholics may reject population
limitation and favor unlimited procreation, therefore, because
of the perceived injustice and selfishness of the men and
institutions with which it is associated.

A second explanation of this concern for future persons
has to do with the moral theory employed by Catholics and
Marxists. I have noted that classical utilitarianism can lead
to this kind of populationist position. Now it may be that,
for different reasons, Catholics and Marxists have tended to
appropriate elements of classical utilitarian theory. I have
already observed that it is possible that Marx and Engels were
influenced by currents of utilitarian thought when considering

the population issue. In general, both men rejected the
utilitarian view. But on this issue, the "humanistic" implications of utilitarianism may have appealed to them. Interestingly, it is Engels, who of the two is least influenced by non-
utilitarian German philosophical thought, that is most
vehement in asserting this population position.

In the case of Roman Catholicism, the appropriation of
utilitarian awarenesses on this issue may be differently
explained. It is true that some students of Roman Catholic
moral theory have argued that there are motifs within
scholastic moral theology which lend themselves to utilitarianism. [58] One need not accept this interpretation, however, to
see the tendency to a utilitarian position in virtually any
kind of theological ethic. I have already stated that one way
of generating the classical utilitarian position is by accepting the "all possible persons" interpretation of the original
position. But Rawls suggests a different derivation, one
that proceeds without reference to an original position. In
his view, classical utilitarianism may result from utilizing
an "ideal sympathetic spectator" theory of ethics (*Theory*, pp.
184-92). According to this kind of theory, the choice of
moral principles is made by an ideal spectator who experiences
the satisfactions and dissatisfactions produced in persons by
a moral decision. [59] Such a spectator selects moral principles
much as an individual selects principles for his own life: he
determines which course of action increases his net satisfactions over time. His principles are moral principles, however,
because they harmonize the satisfactions of many discrete moral
agents. By means of the sympathetic spectator, therefore, a

---

[58] In his *Scholasticism and Welfare Economics* (Notre
Dame: University of Notre Dame Press, 1967), Stephen Worland
argues at length that the Thomist concept of the common good
is very much comprised by the concept of efficiency within
welfare economic theory.

[59] The classic expression of this position is that of
Adam Smith in *The Theory of Moral Sentiments* in *British
Moralists*, ed. L. A. Selby-Bigge (New York: Dover Books,
1965), Vol. I, 257-77. A more recent statement of this as
a meta-ethical position is that of Roderick Firth, "Ethical
Absolutism and the Ideal Observer," *Philosophy and Phenomenological Research*, XII (March 1952), pp. 317-45.

familiar deductive procedure for choosing principles (the
procedure of individual choice) is advanced, while the qualities of impartiality and universality which must attend a
moral perspective are preserved. This explains the common-
sense appeal of such a theory. According to Rawls, however,
common sense here can be misleading. One of the difficulties
with an ideal sympathetic spectator is that he represents no
real human moral agent. People to him are satisfactions which
may be aggregated as he thinks best. Just as the individual
may choose to suppress or postpone certain satisfactions in
order to maximize his long run advantage, so may the ideal
sympathetic spectator choose to disregard the needs or desires
of certain individuals in order to maximize the expectations
of the sum of representative persons. Here, then, is the link
between an ideal sympathetic spectator theory and classical
utilitarianism. If individual human beings are considered as
satisfactions experienced by an ideal sympathetic spectator,
then it can make sense to seek the numerical maximization of
these satisfactions even if individual satisfactions are
reduced.[60]

To the degree that a theistic ethical system relies
heavily upon the concept of God as the source and sustainer
of moral principles, it clearly lends itself to an ideal
sympathetic spectator viewpoint. I should point out that a
religious ideal sympathetic spectator view does not necessarily
have to lead to a classical utilitarian moral position. It is
possible, for example, for the psychology of the ideal spectator to be so described that the discreteness, integrity and
importance of individual persons are taken very seriously (as
the device of the original position tries to do).[61]

---

[60]Alternately, Rawls suggests viewing classical utilitarianism as the ethic of perfect altruists. See *Justice as
Fairness*, 1967, p. 83.

[61]Examples of this use of the ideal observer theory in
ethics may be found in the articles by Arthur Dyck, "Referent
Models of Loving: A Philosophical and Theological Analysis of
Love in Ethical Theory and Moral Practice," *Harvard Theologi-
cal Review*, LVI (October 1968), 525-45, and Charles Reynolds,
"A Proposal for Understanding the Place of Reason in Christian
Ethics," *Journal of Religion*, L (1970), 155-68.

Nevertheless, reliance upon an ideal sympathetic spectator as
the deductive basis of a moral theory can threaten to move
principles in a utilitarian direction. And this is perhaps
particularly true on the population issue. Here the choice is
not so much one of suppressing or debasing some representative
individuals for the sake of others, as one in which room is
made for new human beings at some possible expense to those
already living. A religious thinker relying upon the concept
of a moral and loving God might well shy away from the more
destructive implications of utilitarianism. But he might
easily be drawn to its creative, populationist implications.[62]

A further explanation of this kind of populationism
might be suggested. The concept of justice between generations
is obviously a peculiar one. Golding notes that it is odd to
suppose that persons who are not yet alive can make claims upon
presently living individuals.[63] Yet no moral theory can be
considered complete unless it makes some provision for the
settlement of disputes between generations. Certainly, one
generation's acts can decisively affect future generations;
and future generations have every right to be resentful when
the behavior of predecessors injures them. If a moral position
failed to provide principles for regulating behavior among
generations it would be incapable of settling some of the most
intense disputes that can occur, and it would leave individual

---

[62]I have not considered any specific religious or
moral reasons for the Catholic concern with future persons
because of consistent Catholic denials that physical procreation is a necessary part of the Christian life. See, for
example, A. J. Nevitt, *Population: Explosion or Control?
A Study With Special Reference to India* (Notre Dame, Indiana:
Fides Publishers, 1964), 201-04. For a good brief account of
Christian thinking on the duty to propagate, see William
Graham Cole, *Sex in Christianity and Psychoanalysis* (New York:
Oxford University Press, 1959), pp. 52ff. While it is true
that there is a great resonance of the Hebrew commandment to
multiply in official Catholic teaching (and probably even more
so in the thinking of the laity where it is supplemented by
folk beliefs about souls that must be born), the doctrinal
foundation of the Catholic populationist position is not to be
found here but in the vision of a generous and loving Creator
God.

[63]"What Is Our Obligation to Future Generations?" p. 4.

generations to act as they please without regard for the
implications of their behavior for persons beyond their children's generation.

No moral viewpoint, therefore, can ignore future
generations. Potential persons form part of our moral community. From the recognition that persons yet to be born can
make moral demands, however, it is a short step to the conclusion that all possible future persons can make such claims.
Indeed, it is probably this step that some Roman Catholic and
Marxist thinkers have made. Nevertheless, this step is
mistaken. The reason why no moral view can ignore future
generations is because real members of such generations can,
if neglected, raise moral complaint and have grounds for resentment. A moral view cannot make provision for those who will
never be born. To do so would be an unnecessary extension of
reasoning elaborated, in the first place, to handle real inter-
generational conflict. Thus, it may be that some thinkers
have been drawn to the "all possible persons" interpretation
because they have taken inter-generational responsibility
seriously, but perhaps too seriously. One need not go beyond
the "all actual persons" description of the original position
to handle inter-generational conflict.

One final explanation for the appeal of the "all
possible persons" description of the original position might
be advanced. If only actual persons take part in the formulation of moral rules, then it is at least hypothetically
possible that they may find it in their interests to tolerate
the extinction of the human race. Actually, I shall try to
suggest shortly why this is not a real possibility. But as a
prospect, it is of concern to rational agents. It does not
seem unjustified to say that many human beings wish to see
the human race continue. This desire may be a basic one,
defying explanation, or it may be related to our more general
affection for other human beings, a form of "love of mankind,"
as it were.[64] Or, it may be related to the self-referring

---

[64]Rawls discusses the "love of mankind" in *A Theory of
Justice*, pp. 476-79, but does not touch on the population
issue in this connection.

desires of rational agents, such as a desire to insure that
one's life plan is part of an ongoing, progressive human enterprise. Whatever the basis of this desire, it is certainly in
the interests of most rational human beings that the human
race not vanish. To prevent this, therefore, it might seem
wise to include possible future men in the original position
in order to prevent their elimination by any group of actual
human beings. But this step, with all its population implications, is not really necessary. If rational agents desire the
human race to continue, they can express this desire directly
and agree upon a moral rule enjoining the preservation of
humanity, or at least preventing its extinction. Such a rule
would necessarily be imprecise. Rather than specifying specific
population levels it would prohibit actions which eradicated
human life and culture. Indeed, it has been suggested that the
moral rule requiring recognition and respect for the "sanctity
of life" may be interpreted to prohibit extinction of the
human species.[65]   The existence, or possible existence of
such a rule, therefore, need not depend on conjecturing that
the moral rules are an outcome of a procedure in which all
possible persons take part. Rather, we can simply assume that
the great majority of rational agents have concrete reasons
for upholding a ban on species extinction and we can assume
that these reasons are strong enough to outweigh some of their
other desires within the confines of the original position.

This review of possible explanations for the appeal of
the "all possible persons" description of the original position
suggests that it may be mistaken to assume that many rational
persons are genuinely concerned with the fate of all possible
future persons. Certainly, some Roman Catholic and Marxist
thinkers have voiced concern for possible future persons. But
this does not mean that their concern is valid from the
perspective of the original position, in the sense that it is
based on a genuine desire, common among rational agents to see
future possible persons come into being. If any or all of the
explanations of this concern are correct, the desire for an

---

[65]K. Danner Clauser, "The Sanctity of Life: An Analysis
of a Concept," manuscript in the possession of this writer.

expanding population is really the outcome of a process of moral reasoning and is based upon a presumed, but mistaken, sense of moral obligation. All moral obligations, however, are subject to the test of the original position and the awarenesses that underlie it. For contract parties to take an obligation seriously, it must be one that they would agree upon, or at least share sympathy with, themselves. Our reasoning has suggested that this is not true with respect to this particular obligation. As far as contract parties are concerned, this means that they need not be seriously concerned with the prospect that they are among a group of persons intensely desirous of expanding the number of future human beings. It remains true, of course, that they may strongly desire to secure for themselves as individuals the right to try to have as many children as they wish. But this is distinct from a desire for maximum population increase.

The explanation and defense of the "all actual persons" description of the original position is now complete. As such, it provides a firm foundation for the average or per capita measure of expectations. Although it required greater explanation, Rawls's rejection of classical utilitarianism in favor of the average form is valid. Henceforth, we can assume that contract parties desire to maximize their expectations as actual living individuals and do not desire to maximize the sum of expectations of all possible persons. Moreover, while contract parties know that some rational human beings desire a maximum reproductive liberty in order to secure for themselves the species good of children, they also know that they need not consider any person's desire for an expanding population *per se*. Their possible concerns, therefore, are to maximize their per capita share of primary or species goods. Thus, we have a moral justification of the per capita measure, and our reasoning corroborates the efforts by some economists to provide a moral defense of their employment of per capita income as a welfare goal.[66] At the same time, this justification supplements discussions of the per capita measure as an

---

[66]See A. B. Wolfe, "On the Criterion of Optimum Population," *American Journal of Sociology,* XXXIX (1934), 585-99. Also, see above, pp. 41-43.

index of welfare. These discussions have the advantage for
economic science of being value-free, but, as I have noted,
they face severe difficulty when the per capita index ceases
to be a comprehensive measure of economic or social performance.
In these instances, a moral justification of the per capita
measure is called for. The contract view, and the conception
of morality which underlies it, furnish this justification.

E. *Justice Between Generations*

      1. *Permissible Growth Before Stabilization*

      The choice situation for a contract theory population
principle is now reasonably clear. Contract parties represent
those rational human beings who will be alive in any future
generation. Within the original position, their common interest is to secure for themselves as individuals the greatest
possible amount of primary social goods. Since we do not wish
to bias their consideration exclusively in this direction,
however, we assume that they know that some (or many) rational
human beings possess a desire for the species good of children
and wish to secure for themselves the maximum freedom to try
to bear and rear children. Finally, we assume that contract
parties have already agreed upon principles of justice. They
have, for example, accepted the principle of equal liberty
and the difference principle, as well as the priority rule
between them. And they have accepted a just savings principle
according to which each generation is required to add something to the stock of real capital which it hands on to its
successors (*Theory*, pp. 284-93). It is useful to assume
agreement on these principles now because they express permanent
features of the reasoning of the contract parties and will have
to be considered sooner or later. Furthermore, the assumption
that these principles have been agreed upon does not bias or
precondition the reasoning of the contract parties in any way.
They retain the ability to evaluate all of their principles
for their mutual acceptability and they are free to establish
new priority rules as they see fit.
      On the basis of this description, contract parties

proceed to propose and agree upon principles to regulate their reproductive behavior. They must do so, however, for two different contexts. On the one hand, they must determine how the liberty to procreate may be exercised by individuals within a given generation. This involves the question of how many children a representative couple may have and how the economic support of these children is to be related to the principles governing distribution of income within a generation. On the other hand, contract parties must determine how the effects of reproductive behavior across generations are to be regulated. This is the issue of population growth (or decline) itself. In other words, apart from the question of how acceptably individuals conduct their reproductive lives within a given generation vis a vis their contemporaries, there remains the question of how the aggregate reproductive behavior of their generation affects future generations.

It seems reasonable to approach this last issue first. The problems associated with reproduction are naturally distinguished by their inter-generational implications. Reproductive behavior that seems acceptable within the confines of a single generation may become intolerable when viewed over the span of several generations. By approaching the inter-generational issue first, therefore, one gains a clear idea of the parameters of choice for individuals within a single generation. Rawls's discussion of a just savings principle furnishes a parallel. According to Rawls, a generation's savings for the future are deducted from the stock of funds available for distribution within that generation. In order to determine the level at which various representative persons within a generation are to be remunerated, therefore, one must first have some idea of how much a generation is required to save (*Theory*, p. 285). This suggests that a determination of the extent of inter-generational responsibility must precede discussion of behavior within a generation.

In seeking to arrive at a principle governing the reproductive behavior of their generation, contract parties may think of themselves as assuming the vantage point of any representative individual within any possible generation. The veil of ignorance deprives them of all generational self-knowledge but this. In these circumstances, they might ask themselves whether there is a general and fixed rule governing population growth between generations upon which they would be prepared to agree. At least three options immediately present themselves. Contract parties can agree to permit population to decline constantly over time, they can permit population to grow constantly, or they can insist that population levels remain stable from generation to generation. Clearly, as permanent principles, the first two are unacceptable. Should population decline constantly over time, mankind must eventually become extinct. We do not have to assume an "all possible persons" interpretation of the original position, nor do we have to rely too heavily upon a general desire not to see the human race vanish in order to understand why such a prospect would be intolerable for contract parties. The extinction of the human race means that contract parties must face the possibility that they will be members of a drastically depopulated series of final human generations. While it is difficult to conjecture just what impact this depopulation would have on their share of any specific primary good such as income (would a normal economy be able to function in these circumstances, for example?), it seems difficult to conceive that rational human beings would choose to live in such a world. The fulfillment of most plans of the good, after all, requires the cooperation of other people with varied abilities and desires. But such people would eventually be absent from a radically depopulated world. Thus, whatever advantages earlier generations might derive from a principle allowing constant population decline would seem to be drastically offset in its final stages. Much the same could be said for the opposite principle permitting constant population growth. Here, the prospect is of a final series of generations reduced to misery and deprived of even the most basic social or personal goods. The crisis literature has sketched this prospect fully enough. Indeed, the fact that no rational individual would tolerate permitting a principle of constant growth in a finite world is the reason for the force of the crisis views and their usefulness to those who seek to stimulate concern with present growth.

It is important to explain the reasoning of members of

the original position a bit more carefully at this point.
Since contract parties are understood to be intensely
desirous of advancing their own plan of the good, I assume
that utilitarian considerations whereby one person's advantage
compensates others' disadvantage are usually ruled out. And
this is as true for generations as it is for individuals.
Indeed, Rawls suggests that utilitarian reasoning is even less
appropriate for determining issues between generations than
between individuals. From the vantage point of the original
position, the "average" form of utilitarianism may be seen as
the outcome of a willingness by contract parties to gamble
with their prospects; they may be prepared to risk lesser
expectations in one representative position in order to attain
greater expectations in another.[67] In Rawls's view, this kind
of reasoning is most suited to decisions of minor importance
or to decisions where the benefits of a policy are distributed
stochastically with each representative individual being both
a winner and loser within a reasonable period of time (*Theory*,
p. 170). Gambling becomes less rational when the decision
vitally affects the most basic interest of a contract party,
and when its effects are irreversible. In such cases, the
reasoning of a rational individual, deprived of the knowledge
of his propensity to risk, approximates a maximin solution.
According to Rawls, decisions concerning the distribution of
economic goods between generations are of this more serious
kind. Members of a particular generation are about as fated
to their prospects as human beings can be, and their placement
in that generation plays a large part in shaping their ability
to pursue and achieve their plan of life (*Theory*, p. 287;
Chapters, p. 215). For this reason, Rawls maintains that
contract parties would not agree to a utilitarian savings
principle through which one or several generations are called
upon to make great sacrifices in order to capitalize generations in the future (*Theory*, pp. 286f.). A similar rejection

---

[67]In the *Chapters on Justice* (1964-65), Ch. IV, p. 8,
Rawls characterizes contractual or "average" utilitarianism
as the principle agreed upon by "rational risk-takers."

of a utilitarian solution lies behind my claim that contract
parties would not agree to a principle allowing either constant
decline or constant increase in population. In either case,
the sacrifices made by the last in a series of generations are
not of the sort to which rational members of the original
position would agree, given the restraints of the veil of
ignorance.

The fact that contract parties would reject anything
but a fairly stable population size (or what demographers
refer to as a "stationary" population) as a permanent principle
does not mean that contract parties must categorically prohibit
population growth or decline. They can agree upon a flexible
population principle accomodated to differing stages of social
or economic advance. So long as different treatment of
specific stages could be agreed upon by all members of the
original position, no loss of objectivity or impartiality is
involved. Rawls's discussion of a just savings principle
again furnishes a parallel since he views required rates of
savings to depend upon a representative generation's ability
to save and the specific capital needs of its successors
(*Theory*, p. 287).

A flexible population principle would allow either
population growth or decline over a period of generations.
Eventually, however, size must stabilize. This is true, first,
because neither growth nor decline can permanently characterize
human population in a finite world. Second, we may assume
that in the later stages of economic development, generations
are very similar in their economic and social conditions. All
have profited by the savings of their predecessors and are in
comfortable economic circumstances. Whatever reasons contract
parties might have for permitting generations more or less
reproductive liberty (reasons presumably based on differing
economic or social conditions) vanish during this final
extensive stage and a principle of equal liberty seems demanded.
But an equal liberty to procreate in a finite world means that
population size must remain at least roughly stable from
generation to generation.

The fact that later generations can do no more than
replace themselves is important. Since the extensive series

of post-stabilization generations are represented in the
original position, arguments for growth or decline before
stabilization must have some appeal to possible representative
members of these generations. Several possibilities arise
here. It might be that population changes prior to stabilization are of unequivocal benefit to generations both before and
after the stabilization point. In this case, we might expect
ready assent to such changes. Or changes may affect pre- and
post-stabilization generations differently. If this is so, the
value of these changes to one group must be weighed against
their disvalue to another and the implications for the least-
off representative individual in each generation considered.[68]
In either case, contract parties must decide which principle
they would be prepared to put up with and they must do so with
the recognition that the implications of growth or decline are
ambiguous even over a limited series of generations.

Consider the arguments that might bear on a permission
for population growth prior to a stabilization point. One
obvious advantage of growth might draw the attention of contract
parties. With less restriction on reproduction, individual
members of the original position can anticipate a greater
liberty to secure the species good of children. Considering
themselves possibly to be among those who desire large families,
contract parties have reason to permit maximal population
growth prior to stabilization. On the other hand, as the
economists we have looked at make clear, even over the short
run, high rates of fertility can detrimentally affect the
individual's share of the primary good of income. They can do
so by reducing savings per capita, by lowering productivity in
some of the complex ways we have examined, or by increasing
the real cost of basic goods which members of the original
position are likely to desire.[69] These latter include basic
consumption goods such as environmental space and access to
nature which many individuals desire. To some degree, these
goods are particular since they are especially cherished only
by some rational persons. To some degree, they may be basic

---

[68]Cf. Leibenstein, "Long-run Welfare Criteria," p. 49.

[69]See above, pp. 48-50, 60f.

personal goods, intrinsically desired by all rational human
beings. Should the biologists who believe that open space and
access to nature are needed for health be correct, this would
be especially true. In a further sense, however, these goods
may also be thought of as primary social goods in that
rational agents desire them whatever else they desire. Freedom not to be impeded by the proximity of other human beings
and ready access to common recreational opportunities, for
example, fit into and enhance the most divergent plans of life.
Thus, increased cost of these goods represents a diminution of
real income, a basic primary good.

If this reasoning is correct, contract parties are
likely to be swayed both by a desire for more income (or the
basic goods associated with it) and a possible desire for more
offspring. Here the fact that population growth must eventually come to a halt is important. The best contract parties
can do for themselves by augmenting the liberty to procreate
is to secure a higher reproduction rate over a limited series
of generations. Also important is the relative asymmetry of
the species good of children and the primary good of income.
Since they are not aware of which particular desires are
theirs, nor of the possible intensity of their desires, members
of the original position would probably find it rational to
give priority to securing income. By permitting population
growth to consume savings or minimize productivity, contract
parties place themselves in the position of favoring one
possible desire over all the other desires they may have.
Should they, on the other hand, restrict population growth in
order to maximize savings, contract parties know that they
will be able to satisfy a wide range of possible desires.
Even if children take a large place in their plan of the good,
contract parties enhance their ability to satisfy this desire
in everything but a numerical or quantitative fashion.

It should be pointed out that contract reasoning here
serves to clarify some of the confusions that surround the
"quality-of-life" view of the population problem. I have
noted that those who argue that high fertility erodes the
quality of life have frequently excluded the good of children
from their considerations. Quality-of-life views can be seen

as arbitrary and partial in their selection of values. But
from the perspective of the original position, primary concern with a range of values other than children (values
attainable with the primary good of income) is not arbitrary.
It is a concern which makes sense when choice must be made
under conditions of uncertainty. Furthermore, a preference
for income under these conditions becomes quite rational if it
is assumed that all human beings retain some opportunity to
found a family, no matter which other values they choose to
promote. We have seen, of course, that this is the case. No
rational individual would prohibit others from at least exercising their reproductive capacity and no rational individual
would allow extinction of the human race.

The priority placed on income suggests an initial
contract principle governing population growth prior to
stabilization. Members of the original position might agree
to permit population to expand whenever it could do so without
jeopardizing savings or productivity. It is not enough that
savings or productivity keep pace with population growth, since
that would perpetuate the economic condition of contract
parties at whatever level they may be. Rather, population
growth must not diminish the highest rate of savings or growth
in income possible on a sustained basis between generations
nor must it detract from income or productivity in other ways.
At first glance, this would seem to prohibit any population
growth, since growth in numbers tends directly to diminish the
available stock of resources per capita. But, as economists
have made clear, growth can stimulate economic activity or
technological advance; and the larger population sizes growth
makes possible can facilitate economies of scale which increase
productivity per capita. This initial contract population
principle, therefore, need not prohibit growth when the
positive income effects of growth outweigh the negative. Not
surprisingly, this principle amounts to a restatement of the
population rule of economic optimum theory.

Mention of optimum theory, however, suggests a qualification of this initial contract population principle. In
surveying optimum theory I observed the uncertainty concerning
the time period over which the optimum is to be

measured.[70] But this kind of uncertainty does not characterize
contract parties. They are assumed to belong to any representative future generation, and their concern extends indefinitely
into the future. This means that a contract theory optimum
must be considered over the longest possible future time period.
When this perspective is taken, however, the simple optimum
formula is called into question. It is no longer adequate to
determine whether the economic effects of population growth
are positive over a series of generations. Equally important
is the question of whether the larger population sizes produced
by growth are themselves acceptable from the vantage point of
the original position. Indeed, we have seen that long term
concerns have moved some economists to review their focus on
optimum growth rates alone and have forced a reconsideration of
the role of population size in optimum theory.[71] Contract
reasoning supports this reconsideration.

When the matter of population size is looked at in terms
of its implications over a long period of time, the permissibility of growth is further qualified. Once population has
reached that permanent size which will be desired in the extensive series of post-stabilization generations, contract
parties have strong reasons for not wishing growth to continue.
For one thing, larger population sizes can require later
generations to trim back their populations and force members
of those generations further to restrict their liberty to procreate. Knowing that they may be among those individuals who
desire children, contract parties have reason to object to this
prospect. Second, whenever population size moves above a
permanently desired level, the cumulative drain upon the
environment and fixed stock of natural resources is accentuated.
Larger pre-stabilization population sizes can delay the time
when future generations need no longer save in order to bring

---

[70]See above, pp. 45-47.

[71]Paul Demeny, "The Economics of Population Control,"
in National Academy of Sciences, *Rapid Population Growth*
(Baltimore: Johns Hopkins Press, 1971), p. 208.

their successors to a comfortable level. And larger population
sizes can force post-stabilization generations to devote a
disproportionate part of their labor simply to restoring or
maintaining the resource base. Energies which could be directed
out of the economic sphere into other satisfying lines of
endeavor would have to be exerted merely to prevent a negative
savings rate.[72]

2. *Stable Population Size*

These considerations suggest a *prima facie* case against
population growth once a population has reached a permanently
desired size. The post-stabilization population size, therefore, functions as a kind of norm or standard against which all
prior growth must be measured. Since this is so, it is important to have some idea of what this size might be for a representative society. Unfortunately, few questions are more
difficult to answer using the contract view or any other moral
theory. This is so for both moral and factual reasons. The
differing preferences of rational agents on matters of population density, for example, prohibit an absolutely clear moral
determination of optimum population size.[73] Also, an answer
must be tentative because the geographical, social, political
and technological conditions of post-stabilization societies
cannot now be known with certainty by rational agents. Optimum
population size for any given future society differs, for
example, depending on whether the society is autarkic or
whether it participates in economic communities beyond its

---

[72]Rawls assumes that generations living after the point
where savings cease will still be required to keep up and maintain their material inheritance (*Theory*, p. 287). It would be
odd to understand them as preoccupied with this task, however.

[73]For a recent series of discussions of the various
ways in which optimum population may be determined, see S.
Fred Singer, ed., *Is There an Optimum Level of Population?*
(New York: McGraw-Hill, 1971).

borders.[74] Similarly, technological developments can affect
the specific optimum size. If contract theory is to be of any
use on this matter, therefore, it is not by giving any concrete
determination of ideal population density, but rather by
locating the concerns of most importance to impartial rational
persons on this issue. In particular, contract thinking enables
certain economic, political and social considerations to stand
out and suggests that post-stabilization population sizes might
not be very large.

Several economic considerations limit the size of post-
stabilization generations. First, there is the fact that per
capita income during this period is assumed to be high. While
the last stage at which savings is required is not one of
great abundance, a level of comfort is reached at which all
members of these generations are sufficiently free of economic
concerns to devote themselves to meaningful work and activities
which they deem rewarding in their own right (*Theory*, p. 290).
This may suggest at least a standard of living already
characteristic of the middle classes in the developed nations,
but a standard to be enjoyed by *all* members of post-stabilization generations. As economists and ecologists have pointed
out, however, it is just this level of living that poses the
most acute problems for environmental and resource maintenance.
Should this standard become the universal one, therefore, a
great deal of the energy of post-stabilization generations will
be devoted merely to sustaining the standard itself and this
is truer if populations are large. Contract parties may have
reason, therefore, to desire populations at this stage which
are smaller in size and density than those that presently
characterize many of the industrialized nations. The same conclusion is supported, secondly, by anticipating the high demand

---

[74]I purposely neglect to consider the issue of a
military optimum population in this connection. This consideration, which greatly concerned many earlier optimum
population theorists, seems of little concern in an era in
which technology, and particularly nuclear weaponry, serve
largely to compensate for national variations in manpower
available for military service. If anything, the issue of a
military optimum is one largely subsumed under that of the
economic optimum.

for the goods of open space and ready access to nature at
this stage of economic development. Economists have spoken of
the high income elasticity for these goods at upper income
ranges. Certainly, if we consider that such goods are often
freely available to those who live at lower stages of economic
development, it seems reasonable to suppose that contract
parties desire a like measure of such goods at the end of the
savings process. If such goods had to be sacrificed to economic advance, the savings process would represent not only
progress but retrogression.

Finally, I might point to the likely future direction
of technological advance. While technological progress during
the early stages of industrialization seems to call for larger,
rather than smaller, population sizes, the reverse seems true
once industrialization is well underway. Here developments
in communication and transport render a smaller population
spread out over a large geographical area as capable of sustaining economic and cultural activity as a larger population
during an earlier era. Indeed, the very sophistication of
transport and communications in a developed economy and the
increased toll on the environment that these represent furnish
another argument for reduced population.

In addition to these by now familiar economic considerations, there are several political and social reasons why
contract parties might favor smaller rather than larger post-
stabilization population sizes. Arguments in favor of smaller
political units, direct political participation and minimal
reliance upon representative politics have a hallowed place in
the population literature.[75] They have also re-emerged, as we
have seen, in the course of recent population discussion.[76]
But when viewed in terms of the contract theory, these arguments

---

[75]See the brief review of these arguments in the
United Nations document, *The Determinants and Consequences
of Population Growth* (New York: United Nations, 1953), pp.
21-24, and the article by Myron Weiner, "Political Demography:
An Inquiry into the Political Consequences of Population
Change," in *Rapid Population Growth*, II, 567-617.

[76]See above, pp. 33f.

assume new importance. Contract parties, as Rawls states, place a general priority on political liberty over economic gain. So long as their political liberties have worth, that is, so long as they are not rendered meaningless by low states of economic development, contract parties would refuse to trade off these liberties for economic rewards. Now, while it is not necessarily true that larger population sizes jeopardize political liberty, as some crisis writers have maintained, it does seem reasonable to assume that larger political units afford the individual less say in the political process. As units grow in size, a single vote dwindles in importance, representation replaces direct participation and those stages of the process where participation is retained become less important in shaping the outcome of the process as a whole. During the early stages of economic development, where so much time and energy is devoted to overcoming scarcity, this prospect may be relatively unimportant. But at the more affluent stages, the political sphere may be assumed to grow in importance. Political life becomes one area where the individual expresses his own sense of equal worth and dignity, and it becomes an important point where the individual makes his unique contribution on the affairs of his community. In view of this, contract parties have good reason for seeing that the population size which characterizes post-stabilization generations not be so large as to preclude direct participation at meaningful stages of the political process.

The same reasoning applies to non-political groups and organizations. Rawls notes that as the level of well-being in a community rises, the economic needs satisfied by labor are likely to dwindle in importance to rational persons. I have already noted that contract parties need not require economic growth to continue once a level of material comfort is reached. More important is the opportunity for meaningful work and significant personal control over the institutions through which one's labor is channeled. Increasingly, at this stage, says Rawls,

> it becomes more important to secure the free internal
> life of the various communities of interest in which
> persons and groups seek to achieve, in modes of
> social union consistent with liberty, the ends and

> excellences to which they are drawn. In addition
> men come to aspire to some control over the laws
> and rules that regulate their association, either
> by directly taking part in its affairs or indirectly
> through representatives with whom they are affiliated
> by ties of culture and social situation. (*Theory*,
> p. 543)

These aims, too, seem more secure in a less populated society,
with smaller rather than larger social and economic institutions.

Finally, I might note that this concern for a larger
degree of individual participation in social and political
groups is of more than personal importance to contract parties.
They desire to maximize individual participation and authority
in these groups not only because they believe it to be to
their immediate advantage, but also because they have reason
to believe that such participation enhances the stability of
the just institutions they establish. A vital interest of
contract parties is seeing to it that all real members of
society do their part in maintaining just institutions. One
way of guaranteeing that they will do so is by seeing that
they develop a psychological propensity to act in a morally
principled way. This is the propensity which, when it is
applied to just institutions and fair schemes of cooperation,
Rawls terms a "sense of justice." Following Piaget, Kohlberg
and others, he believes this propensity to be the outcome of
a life-long process of moral learning.[77] Family relationships
contribute to its development by stimulating attitudes of love
and trust in the individual (*Theory*, pp. 462-67). Social cooperation which engenders friendly feelings and mutual confidence among participants plays an important part (*Theory*,
pp. 467-72). Finally, just institutions, by benefitting the
individual and those for whom he cares, elicit the developed
sense of justice itself. Rawls does not believe that the sense

---

[77]Jean Piaget, *The Moral Judgment of the Child* (London:
Kegan Paul, Trench, Trubner, 1932); Lawrence Kohlberg, "The
Development of Children's Orientation toward a Moral Order:
1. Sequence in the Development of Moral Thought," *Vita Humana*,
VI (1963), 11-33, and "The Child as Moral Philosopher,"
Psychology Today, II (September 1968), 25-30.

of justice, or any principled respect for moral rules,
requires personal contact between members of a community. On
the contrary, he argues that the fact that a political scheme
or institution is just is sufficient reason for it to stimulate
the sense of justice in its participants (*Theory*, p. 474).
However, Rawls does add that where natural ties of friendship
and mutual concern are present, the propensity to respect just
institutions is enhanced (*Theory*, p. 475). Person to person
contact, in other words, can strengthen compliance with a just
scheme and increase its stability.

Applied to the institutions of a just society, this
reasoning would indicate, other things being equal, that contract parties have very strong reasons for preferring a
political order and social and economic institutions in which
the opportunity for real personal contact and a developing
sense of mutual regard among participants is greatest. Where-
ever possible, for example, contract parties would prefer
direct rather than representative governance over the institutions, or levels of institutions, that markedly affect their
lives. Or, where representative governance is unavoidable,
contract parties prefer schemes permitting personal participation during important stages of the representative selection
process, and among the delegates to representative assemblies.
Face to face contact, permitting the development of sustained
ties of mutual regard, therefore, constitutes the ideal to
which contract parties would wish their institutions to
conform.

Obviously, this ideal can be realized by means other
than the regulation of population size. The degree of individual authority and participation in a political process is
very much a function of the way that process is organized. If
this were not so then all smaller nations would be uniformly
more democratic than larger nations, which is patently false.
Nevertheless, the fact that organization is an important consideration does not mean that contract parties would neglect
the matter of population size. Existing achievements in the
area of political organization can be jeopardized or weakened
by population size and future advances in organization can be
made more difficult by demographic pressure. Other things

being equal, therefore, smaller population sizes help promote the ideal of participatory democracy within meaningful political units. Furthermore, given the priority that contract parties would place upon their political and institutional life, the burden of proof rests on those who would justify population sizes that markedly diminish the prospect for personal participation in the life of these institutions.

All these considerations work together to suggest that post-stabilization population sizes need not be great. In terms of the contract reasoning, this means that any growth of population above these levels during the pre-stabilization period is *prima facie* unacceptable. Once this size is reached, contract parties have strong reasons, as we have seen, for wishing population not to grow. This does not mean, however, that contract parties must categorically prohibit population growth past this size. Since they may stand in any representative generation, contract parties are prepared to balance the needs and claims of earlier generations against later generations. In this respect, the strongest case can be made for population growth during the early stages of economic advance if population growth is the only viable way of promoting development out of states of backwardness. As we have seen, the contract view disallows strict utilitarian reasoning, whereby the immiseration of one or several generations is permitted for the sake of other generations' prosperity. Thus, contract parties may permit some growth above a permanently desirable level if this is needed in order to remedy markedly backward economic conditions. But this appears to be the only instance where growth is permissible, and it is a hypothetical permission contingent upon the proved necessity of growth. As economic development proceeds, and moderate levels of physical comfort are reached, contract parties have less and less reason to permit growth. From this point onward, growth must halt and moderate population decline is demanded until permanent stable population levels are reached.

The fact that some later generations must have negative growth rates in order to compensate for the overly large populations of their predecessors is one of the reasons, as we have seen, why contract parties are reluctant to permit

higher growth rates in the first place. But if larger earlier
populations are justifiable in extreme cases, contract parties
must be prepared to tolerate the burden of population decline.
As far as required population decline is concerned, all of the
contract theory awarenesses we have explored to this point
seem applicable. Thus, negative growth rates are justifiable
in terms of the long range view of contract parties. Though
they are reluctant to diminish their possible liberty to have
children, they recognize that this liberty may be compromised
for permanent economic and political advantage. Furthermore,
in view of the fact that population growth must eventually
cease, negative growth rates represent only an accentuation of
an inevitable restriction on this liberty.

The anti-utilitarian quality of contract reasoning
bears on this issue as well, however. Though prepared to
submit to a period of population decline, we may assume that
contract parties generally would be unwilling to inflict the
full burden of this decline upon one or several generations.
If possible, they would prefer that the negative growth rates
be shared by a series of generations in order to minimize the
toll taken on each one. This seems especially true during the
period when per capita income has achieved a moderate level
and when the urgency to increase income has somewhat slackened.
It is less true at those very low states of economic development where populations are both larger than permanently
desired and where decline in growth rates and population size
would promote economic development. Here, the desire to move
rapidly out of backwardness, coupled with their objection to
large sizes, might lead contract parties to demand a sharper
rate of population reduction and more precipitous lowering of
fertility rates. But whether or not it is feasible to suggest
that sizes be reduced at such a stage, population growth which
consumes or reduces savings at such stages or which traps a
society in chronic backwardness is intolerable in every way,
as many economists have assumed. And contract parties would
demand a dramatic reduction of fertility in such cases. The
relatively great sacrifice of procreative liberty demanded of
one or several generations at such stages would be more than
compensated by the dramatic improvement in living standards

194

enjoyed by successor generations.

However, the requirement that reduction in population
growth or size be sharpest at these stages must also be
qualified. Since infant mortality is high during early stages
of development, the reproductive sacrifice demanded of these
early generations is particularly severe. In some cases,
parents might be compelled to forego the satisfactions associated with having surviving offspring. This does not mean that
contract parties would not demand drastic population decline
at this stage. They certainly do not wish to perpetuate their
condition as the possible offspring of these parents. But
they might choose to soften this burden in various ways, such
as by insuring that an added priority be placed on medical
and public health investment during this period. Investment
of this sort not only improves the life prospects of all members of these early generations, but enables them to make the
reproductive sacrifices which contract parties have reason to
demand. The stress placed upon health care as a major component of population policy by some students of the population
problem of the underdeveloped nations, therefore, has moral as
well as practical importance.[78] It is needed not only to
motivate fertility reduction, but to satisfy the moral
priorities of impartial rational persons.

3. *The Inter-Generational Principle*

I am now in a position to state a complete contract
theory principle governing population growth. This principle
would prohibit population growth once a society's size and
density reaches a point consistent with the maintenance of

---

[78]See, for example, Roger Revelle, "International
Cooperation in Food and Population," *International Organiza-
tion,* XXII (1968), 363, and "Population," in *The Survival
Equation,* eds. Roger Revelle, Ashok Khosla and Maris Vinovskis,
eds. (New York: Houghton Mifflin, 1971), pp. 1-24. Carl
Taylor also stresses the importance of reduced infant mortality
for population limitation in his article, "Five Stages in a
Practical Population Policy," *International Development
Review,* X (1968), 2-7.

moderately high living standards over an unlimited series of
generations. A "moderately high living standard" is presumed
to include not only the goods of environmental space and access
to nature, but the time and opportunity for personal participation in the governance of those political, social and economic
institutions that directly affect each individual's life.
Prior to reaching this size, population growth is permitted,
except where too rapid growth impedes fair savings between
generations. However, once this size is reached, growth is
prima facie prohibited, except in cases where it represents
the only viable way of improving standards of living from very
low levels. Finally, wherever population is unjustifiably in
excess of this permanent size or where growth rates are too
high, reduction is called for, with the most drastic reductions
demanded where population is a contributing factor to severe
or chronic economic underdevelopment.

Obviously, this contract population principle is not
very precise. Many concrete questions must remain unanswered.
But the value of this principle must be understood to lie not
in its specificity but in the way it illuminates, or expresses,
the major parameters of decision on this issue. Thus, the
relative primacy of income over procreation places a limit on
reproductive freedom and rules out constant population growth.
In addition, the long term goal of a society characterized by
"moderately high living standards" also prohibits population
growth in the name of economic productivity alone. The long
term goal is not an economy of abundance, but one in which
primary emphasis is placed on freedom of movement, freedom
from determination by economic needs and freedom to participate within and control the major institutions of society.
This places the burden of proof on those who would argue for
larger, rather than smaller, permanent population sizes. What
those who argue this way must show is that such sizes make a
real contribution not only, say, to economic efficiency, but
to the kind of economic and social life sketched out by the
contract view.

Finally, contract reasoning betrays a general opposition
to utilitarian modes of calculation. Whenever possible, single
generations are not to carry the burden of policies which

advantage many other generations besides themselves. And this is true not only of economic policies but of population policies as well. Thus, where population reduction is called for, a contract perspective suggests that this responsibility be spread out over a series of generations to ease the burden on each. The priority placed on income, especially at the lower stages of economic development qualifies even this rule, of course, since drastic reduction may be called for to move an economy out of backwardness and to help it escape a demographic trap. But this does not undercut the contract opposition to utilitarian calculations. With respect to each separate issue, be it economic advancement or procreative liberty, contract reasoning always militates against the sacrifice, where avoidable, of any one participant in a cooperative enterprise for the advantage of others, whether that participant is an individual or a generation. Where severe sacrifices are called for, ameliorating policies are thus demanded. Careful attention to medical care investment for underdeveloped societies that must dramatically limit growth rates is an example.

All these awarenesses are expressed by the contract inter-generational population principle. But in a sense, the awarenesses are more important than the principle itself. One of the advantages of the contract view, as against intuitionist theories of justice, is that it provides some insight into the deductive process that leads to moral rules. Since the circumstances which generate rules may change, the deductive procedures associated with an issue may be more useful than the concrete rules it generates. This means that the primary value of the contract population principle lies in the way it reveals the modes of reasoning of contract parties on the population issue.

F. *Justice within Generations and Population Policy*

   1. *The Need for a Distributive Principle*

With the matter of inter-generational responsibility reasonably clear, I can begin to address the issue of the

reproductive responsibility of individuals within any given
generation. It is important at this point, however, to underscore the importance of considering inter-generational
responsibility first. Apart from the fact that only the cross-
generational perspective affords a proper understanding of the
behavior required of a specific generation, there is the fact
that responsibility in this area must be understood as first
of all incumbent upon generations. It is easy to assume that
the moral aim of stabilizing population growth requires
individual couples to restrict their families roughly to
replacement size, and this may be the final rule for individuals upon which all rational persons would agree. But it is
mistaken to move directly from the norm incumbent upon a
generation to behavior required of a family. Strictly speaking,
population growth is a concern for generations. Generations,
not individuals, have responsibility to the future. The
question of how this responsibility affects the behavior of the
many individuals who make up a generation is subject to
separate moral determination.

In seeking to generate norms for individual behavior
within a representative generation, it is important to be clear
about the choice situation. We may assume that some degree of
reproductive restraint is called for: that an entire generation is called upon to lower its natural growth rate in order
to halt population increase or to reduce an excessively large
present population. We need not consider the question, less
urgent today, raised by too low rates of natural increase.[79]
The situation, then, involves a distributive problem. Contract
parties are asked to consider how they shall distribute the
right to have children where this right cannot be exercised
freely by all members of society. What is desired first is a
general principle specifying each individual's entitlement to

[79]Presumably, whatever principles or policies apply to
restraining natural increase also apply, in reverse, to promoting it. In this respect, it is useful to note that Roman
Catholic thinking has generally interpreted the obligation
incumbent on families to maintain the race as part of the
natural law. See, for example, Aquinas, *Summa Theologica*,
IIa-IIae, Quest. 152, Art. 2.

198

have children. Such a principle precedes, but is not identical with, the question of population policy. Population policies involve a determination of how compliance with this kind of intra-generational distributive principle is to be effected. Programs enabling or compelling couples to have families of a morally demanded size belong to the question of population policy. Obviously, the questions of a population principle and population policy for generations cannot be separated. Policies possess distributive implications and certain distributive principles necessitate policy considerations. But I shall try, as we proceed, somewhat to separate these issues. In the first place, we need a principle determining the just distribution of the scarce right to have children.

2. *A Eugenic Principle*

As was true with the inter-generational principles, contract parties can be imagined to propose, consider and vote upon various alternate distributive principles. One obvious candidate immediately presents itself. Since the veil of ignorance renders all contract parties effectively identical, it seems logical for them to agree upon a principle of equal reproductive liberty. According to this principle, each representative family in society could have as many children as any other family within the number allotted to the entire generation. Where the allotted number involved a fraction, each family would possess an equal right to participate in some fair lottery procedure through which the right to the additional children was distributed. Since contract parties know only that they may be among those who intensely desire offspring, this seems a rational method of protecting their vital interest.

Although it is an appealing first principle, the principle of equal liberty has its disadvantages. Most of these have to do with its neglect of the differing needs, desires and capacities of real rational human beings. Not all persons desire children, after all, and the children of all

are not equally desired. Thus, we might suppose that a
series of alternate principles could be advanced which each
contract party might feel better advantaged him on his return
to society. One candidate which deserves consideration is a
"eugenic" distributive principle. Since contract parties are
aware of the general facts of society, they know that individuals differ widely in their share of natural talents and
failings. Many of the qualities possessed by real persons are
also recognized and rewarded by the difference principle,
because the exercise of these qualities is to the advantage of
all rational persons. To stimulate entrepreneurial activity
or the exercise of other talents useful in promoting economic
development, for example, contract parties are prepared to
allow those who possess these qualities a disproportionate
share of income or authority. Now, since they value such
qualities anyway, it might be rational for contract parties
directly to insure their prevalence in society by permitting
individuals who possess them to have larger families. Whether
these qualities are genetically determined or shaped in the
rearing process, the net effect of this means of distribution
is to raise the proportion of individuals possessing these
desired qualities. Contract parties would benefit by the
increased productivity of their society and by the fact that
as actual future persons, they might be recipients of this
better genetic or family inheritance. Since they do not know
how much they value children themselves, it would seem
rational to prefer these other goods.

Although this principle too seems initially reasonable,
it deserves closer examination. There are certain obvious
difficulties. Many of the qualities rewarded by the difference principle are of the sort that would not be elicited at
a given stage of economic advance without incentives. Entrepreneurial activity is a good example. But many of these
qualities also have a time-bound character. They are useful
at one stage of economic activity, but may not be so at a
different stage. If a eugenic policy were to be keyed in some
way to the difference principle, therefore, rational agents
would find themselves in the peculiar position of irreversibly
promoting traits which they might no longer desire after a

200

short period of time.

This difficulty can perhaps be mitigated by identifying and designating qualities useful in a variety of different stages of social advance. What Rawls calls the "natural goods" of intelligence, creativity, physical health and resiliency may be qualities of this sort. A eugenic distributive principle would thus require that society establish objective ways of identifying the presence of these qualities in individuals and then allow parents who possess them to have a right to a larger share of children. Merely to contemplate this kind of procedure, of course, creates anxiety. The abuses of eugenic policies and the past inadequacies of intelligence testing procedures are notorious. Apart from this, there is the fear that has bothered men since Plato and which has recently arisen in literature critical of "meritocracy," of whether a society organized in this way might not be both impersonal and inhuman. [80] The question, therefore, is whether this fear has any basis or whether properly administered eugenic policies cannot meet the approval of all rational agents.

To illuminate this question, I might compare the reasoning behind a eugenic principle with that which supports the difference principle. Earlier, I noted that the difference principle represents a qualified maximin solution to the economic distributive problem. Contract parties conceive of themselves as either winners or losers in the natural lottery of birth. They possess or do not possess qualities desired by many people (intelligence, creativity, etc.). Because many of these qualities are correlated with qualities useful at various stages of economic and cultural development, all rational agents have reason to permit differential payments (or disproportionate grants of privilege and authority) which tend to reward those who have won in the lottery of birth. However, rational agents also have good reason for not permitting such payments. To do so can, over the short run, diminish one's self-respect. Permitting extra payments or authority to those who possess the desired qualities one lacks

---

[80]See Michael Young, *The Rise of Meritocracy* (London: Thames and Hudson, 1958).

further undermines one's status in real society. If the difference principle is finally accepted, as Rawls maintains, it is because these negative considerations are not great enough to outweigh the principle's advantages. For one thing, the difference principle permits the least-off representative persons markedly to improve their material circumstances over time. For another thing, the loss to self-respect is not that great. Differential payments and rewards are only loosely related to the individual's basic sense of self-respect. Many of the qualities which are economically valued during one epoch may not be so in the future. Indeed, Rawls has suggested that for a variety of reasons, as economic circumstances improve, capacities which during an earlier era were markedly disesteemed and unrewarded may become singled out for economic reward. In addition, by permitting economic growth, the difference principle facilitates a level of material comfort which can help ease many of the circumstances that perpetuate particular qualities or which render them especially onerous. Better family circumstances, for example, can help to elicit latent talents and abilities in the individual without necessitating any basic change in his talents or failings. This means that any individual who is not among those rewarded during early stages of the difference principle, need not resent or despise his given nature. He can console himself with the prospect that his basic capacities might someday be esteemed or at least not disesteemed. To summarize these awarenesses, we might say that the difference principle represents a reasonably stable principle for society. Taking into consideration what Rawls calls the "strains of commitment" (*Theory*, pp. 176ff.), contract parties have reason to believe they can abide by this principle even if they prove to be one of the least-off representative persons.

Can the same be said of a eugenic distributive principle? It is true that all rational agents may stand to gain by such a principle. From the vantage point of future generations, they have good reason to desire the best possible genetic endowment and family background. It might be argued, however, that it is impossible to say in advance exactly which basic qualities possessed by men will be cherished at some future

point. Even if qualities like intelligence, imagination and
the like are of general value, it is difficult to say in what
particular mix they will be useful in the future, or whether
there are not other basic skills that may be of greater value.
More troubling, perhaps, is the fact that many qualities today
disesteemed may be possessed by an individual with other
genetic traits of unknown usefulness in the future. This had
led some population geneticists to argue that the wisest
genetic policy is one which sustains all the variety in the
human gene pool.[81]

   But even without becoming involved in these issues, we
can see the difficulty in this kind of eugenic procedure. Unlike the difference principle, it seems markedly corrosive of
the individual's self-respect. What is involved here, after
all, is a decision, enforced by society, not only that the
individual's basic endowment is deficient but so deficient that
it ought not to be perpetuated.[82] The sense that this judgment
is time bound and historically conditioned is undercut and
even the individual's hope of vindication through his
descendants is eliminated.

   This difficulty with a eugenic principle may be viewed
in a different way. I have just suggested that this principle
can directly undermine an individual's sense of self-respect
by calling his basic endowment into question. But it can also
diminish his self-respect in a more complex way by undermining
the social basis of self-esteem. I touched on the matter of
self-respect earlier, but it is important to note that Rawls
defines self-respect (or self-esteem) as having two aspects.
It includes, in the first place, a person's "own sense of

---

[81]See Robert F. Murray, "Ethical Aspects of Population
Policy from the Perspective of the Population Geneticist,"
Documentary study prepared for the Commission on Population
Growth and the American Future (Hastings-on-Hudson, N.Y.:
Institute of Society, Ethics and the Life Sciences, 1971).

[82]In his article, "The Idea of Equality," in *Philosophy,
Politics and Society*, eds. Peter Laslett and W. G. Runciman,
Series II (London: Basil Blackwell, 1962), p. 127, Bernard
A.O. Williams makes a similar point in arguing that the social
goal of absolute genetic equality can finally undercut the idea
of the essentially equal dignity of all men.

value, his secure conviction that his conception of the good,
his plan of life, is worth carrying out." In the second
place, it implies "a confidence in one's ability, so far as it
is within one's power, to fulfill one's intentions" (*Theory*,
p. 440). A lack of self-respect, according to Rawls, can
decisively impede the satisfaction of one's plan of life.
"When we feel that our plans are of little value, we cannot
pursue them with pleasure or take delight in their execution.
Nor, plagued by failure and self-doubt, can we continue in our
endeavors" (*Theory*, p. 440). For this reason, self-respect
is rightly included among the primary goods and is even to be
considered the most important of these goods.

Among the circumstances which support self-respect,
and particularly its first aspect, the sense of our own worth,
Rawls includes the experience of finding "our person and deeds
appreciated and confirmed by others who are likewise esteemed
and their association enjoyed" (*Theory*, p. 440). This means
that the individual, as an adult maintains and enhances his
self-respect by participating in an association of shared ends
and purposes in which both he and his contributions are
appreciated. Following von Humboldt, Rawls terms this kind of
association a "social union."[83] As against a "private
society," where individuals are joined only by common external
aims and take no pleasure in their mutual cooperation, the
purpose of a social union is both external and internal. Its
members participate very much for the mutual edification and
support that their cooperation generates. Social unions may
range in size from large cultural or scientific associations
to simple relationships among friends. But in many ways, the
family is a paradigmatic social union. In no other institution
are the ties that join members so close, the sense of common
purpose so clear or the function of mutual enhancement so
explicit.

Conceiving of the family as a social union, we can
properly appreciate its importance in maintaining the stability

---

[83]Wilhelm von Humboldt, *The Limits of State Action*, ed.
J. W. Burrow (Cambridge, England: Cambridge University Press,
1969), pp. 16f.

of a just society. All social unions contribute to the self-respect of their participants. But the family does so to an extraordinary degree, both because it is such a common form of association and because the mutual affirmation of its members is so intense. To the degree that an individual is able to build and support a family he is able to enhance his self-esteem, even if he is denied the opportunity to participate in other social unions with this effect. The concern with the family implicit in the family-planning view of the population problem is thus supported by an understanding of the place of the family in a just society.

In view of this, we can gain some additional idea why contract parties might resist a eugenic principle for distributing children. To proceed rationally, they must consider the implications of any principle for all representative persons in society. Should they be among those who have lost in the natural lottery of birth, or who lack the qualities esteemed by their peers, their sense of worth is already shaky. Though they may participate in a social union or unions outside the family, it is likely that these unions are themselves disesteemed. This is especially true at the lower stages of economic advance where the opportunity to develop one's capacities within a meaningful association of labor remains small. Thus, the family becomes the primary association in which the individual can establish the self-respect that is so important for any of the ventures he undertakes. Now it is true that a eugenic principle of distribution need not interfere with the individual's opportunity to raise a family. No such extreme limitation on the right to procreate need be considered. Nevertheless, the mere fact that the society's estimate of the individual is carried into the confines of the family can itself undermine the individual's self-esteem. Instead of his offspring being a source of joy and self-confidence, they become a product scorned by the society as a whole. In his own quota of children, the individual is vividly reminded of his peers' estimate of his worth.

This account of the reasoning of a representative individual is largely speculative. It has some support in

discussions of the value of children to low-income families.[84]
But if this account is correct, it suggests that contract
parties have reason to believe a eugenic principle could not
withstand the strains of commitment once put into effect in
real society. And they probably would reject it on that ground.
Of course, there are limits even to the validity of this
reasoning. In cases where serious defects of a genetic sort
are involved, contract parties might be prepared to agree to
some kind of eugenic principle.[85] Here, their concern over
substantial possible injury, as the future recipients of these
defects, might offset their reluctance to expose themselves to
the workings of such a principle. But this exceptional case
reveals just how extreme the circumstances must be to lead to
a clear approbation of this principle. Certainly a eugenic
principle to the disadvantage of large numbers of presumably
less endowed individuals does not elicit ready approval.

[84]Robert F. Murray stresses the importance of the
family unit as the locus of creativity and self-confidence
among low-income black Americans. See his article, "The
Ethical and Moral Values of Black Americans and Population
Policy," Documentary Study Prepared for the Commission on
Population Growth and the American Future (Hastings-on-Hudson,
New York: Institute of Society, Ethics and the Life Sciences,
1971), p. 3. A similar point is made by Judith Blake in her
Family Structure in Jamaica (Glencoe, Illinois: The Free
Press, 1961), 188; also, Robert Coles, Children of Crisis
(Boston: Atlantic-Little Brown, 1964), pp. 368f.

[85]Rawls believes that contract parties would adopt
"reasonable policies" in order to insure their descendants the
best genetic endowment, but he specifies only that a society
is "to take steps at least to preserve the general level of
natural abilities and to prevent the diffusion of serious
defects" (Theory, p. 108). My reasoning supports this kind of
policy, but questions whether contract parties would agree
to any stronger policy than this, especially prior to the
period when self-respect is solidly assured by just social
arrangements. Here I differ with David Richards' contention
in his A Theory of Reasons for Action, p. 135, that contractors
would adopt a positive eugenics policy in hopes of improving
their genetic quality over time. Richards does state that
contractors would not adopt policies that "lower the life
prospects or desire satisfaction of the lowest standard
class." But he does not seriously consider whether any
positive eugenics policy can meet this test.

3. Income-Based Allocations and the Unjust Society

Contract parties' rejection of a eugenics principle
conditions their response to another alternative principle
which might draw their attention. This principle would key
the right to have children to one's share of income as determined by the economic institutions of a just society. Within
the limits of one's income, it would be permitted to spend as
much as one wished on the good of offspring. Of course, such
a principle could be seriously abused to the detriment of those
in future generations. Parents might choose to have a larger
number of children at the expense of each individual child.
To prevent this, we can assume that children are to be supported at some standard level (which could be adjusted to
achieve a just generational reproductive rate).[86] The real
aim of this principle, therefore, is not to facilitate the
abuse of future beings or excess population but to permit
parents, within the range of their income, to select among
their expenditures.

Since contract parties know that rational agents differ
in their desire for offspring, this kind of income-based
allocation is appealing. It permits those who value children
highly to devote as much of their income as they like to this
good. And it frees those who do not desire children to use
their income in ways more to their advantage. The very flexi-
bility of this principle recommends it. Nevertheless, when
looked at closely, it becomes apparent that this principle
shares all the difficulties of the eugenic principle. If we
assume that income in a fully just society is distributed in
keeping with the difference principle, the individual's right
to have children is as thoroughly related to society's
estimate of his basic qualities as is the case with the eugenic
principle. Indeed, since the difference principle rewards

---

[86]A proposal like that of Kenneth Boulding for market-
able licenses in babies would have the effect of an income
allocation without permitting parental exploitation of offspring. See his *The Meaning of the 20th Century* (New York:
Harper & Row, 1964), pp. 135f.

capacities of present economic or social value, this income
principle represents the eugenic principle at its worst.
Qualities that may be of only fleeting value are rewarded and
diffused. Apart from its usefulness in proportioning the
right to have children to the desire to have them, therefore,
this kind of income principle is at least as faulty as the
eugenic principle. This does not mean that the virtues of
the income principle cannot be separated from its defects. I
shall look in a short while at a more acceptable form of this
principle. Before doing that, however, it is important to
digress in order to explore an important set of issues raised
by this initial income principle itself.

In arguing for an income-based allocation of children
I assumed that the distribution of income in a society is just.
The hypothetical society has already been made to conform to
the two principles of justice. Even under these circumstances
it seems that an income-based allocation would not be accepted
by contract parties. But what can be said of this principle
in a society in which income is not fairly distributed and in
which the economic and political institutions in no way conform to the two principles of justice? Imagine, for example,
a society organized according to some kind of utilitarian rule,
in which the continued inferior position of some representative
persons is justified in terms of the increased advantages
accruing to other individuals, identified by means of their
race, class background or possession of some particular
character traits or skill. Clearly those who are in the least-
off position have reason to resent this kind of social arrangement; they can know that it would not be agreed upon by all
rational persons in the original position. Should they prove
to be one of the least-off individuals, therefore, contract
parties know they would have valid grounds for resentment.
But how might they react to an income-based allocation of offspring in these circumstances? Again, it seems clear that
they would not accept this kind of principle. Once put into
effect, such a principle would serve further to demean the
individual without affording him any tangible benefit. Even
the improved circumstances of future generations, in whose

208

name a limitation of reproduction is demanded, have no value
to the least-off representative individual since he knows that
the bulk of increased income will go to the offspring of the
better-off representative persons and that his own children
or descendants will be further disadvantaged.[87]

In view of this reasoning, we are now in a better
position to understand the Marxist and Roman Catholic objections
to Malthusian population theory, as well as the logic of more
recent radical or minority group opposition to population control programs. Such programs violate the norms of justice in
several important ways. In the first place, even the most
voluntary of them (e.g. family-planning programs) usually
amount to income based allocations of offspring in societies
where the economic institutions in the eyes of many individuals
lack justice, or where the justice of these institutions, at
least, is not seriously scrutinized. In terms of what has
just been said about such allocations, this clearly violates
the wishes of contract parties.

In the second place, such programs involve a deep moral
contradiction. On the one hand, population restraint is a
part--indeed, one of the more important parts--of a total program of justice. A population principle, and corresponding
population policy, aim at bringing one generation's reproductive
behavior into conformity with behavior that could be agreed
upon by all generations, and they aim at fairly distributing
the burden of procreative restraint among all members of a
given generation. As we have seen, Malthus himself was clear
to recognize that procreative restraint is at least hypothetically a responsibility of justice. On the other hand, when
separated from discussion of the larger context of justice--
as is often the case in Malthusian treatments--population
control assumes very curious form: it becomes a demand of
justice made of those who are or may be victims of injustice.

---

[87]Murray, in "The Ethical and Moral Values of Black
Americans and Population Policy," p. 5, observes that ghetto-
dwelling black Americans have little reason to be concerned
with preserving the quality of the environment since their own
environment has consistently been of the lowest quality.

And it is a demand frequently made by the very ruling groups
responsible for injustice in the first place.

Resentment at this kind of contradiction is compounded
when procreative irresponsibility is used as an excuse for
existing distributive difficulties. Here also Malthus established a pattern that has been followed by many later thinkers.
Recognizing the need for population restraint in a justly
organized society, one in which wealth is equitably distributed,
he argued that continued population growth in such a society
must eventually diminish everyone's share of wealth, or, if a
system of private property is instituted and each individual
is made to suffer the penalty of his own irresponsibility,
continued population growth must plunge those who are responsible for it into poverty and misery. But from this valid moral
argument Malthus moved, as we noted, to the conclusion that
the existing social and economic inequities of English society
were the result of rapid population growth.[88] He nowhere
demonstrated that anything like an equal base-point of distribution had been established in the past from which irresponsible
procreation had caused society to err. Nor did he demonstrate,
or even try to demonstrate, that the poverty of the lower
social classes was the result of their past high fertility.
It is true that he pointed to the high fertility of the poor,
but he did not undertake to prove that this fertility was a
cause, rather than a consequence of their economic status.
Thus, Malthus employed valid moral reasoning about population
wrongly to justify existing economic inequities. And, to
make matters worse, he then advocated that these "justified"
inequities be made the basis of future allocations of the
right to have children.

These violations of the norms of justice explain much
of the resentment felt by underprivileged groups at the demand
for population restraint and they explain the particular
resentment of Marxist and Roman Catholic thinkers at population
programs. Both intellectual traditions have a strong commitment to distributive justice. Indeed, the moral foundations

[88]See above, pp. 35-38.

of these traditions are virtually identical since both
derive from a common natural law methodology. I have discussed the natural law roots of Catholic thinking. And I can
suggest Marx's rootage in this same tradition via his debt to
Kantian moral theory.[89] It is partly because of this similar
moral background and commitment, therefore, that Marxists and
Catholics have been able to perceive contradictions and hypo-
crisies in population control programs which often escape even
the well-intentioned proponents of these programs.

I might add that the perceived hypocrisy of those who
advocate birth limitation is not the only reason why least-off
members of an unjust society might resent any effort to limit
their right to procreate. In addition, there are many concrete
reasons, whose force depends upon particular social circumstances, why impartial persons might find it rational to object
to or resent population control programs. Population growth,
for example, can be one means by which an oppressed minority
accumulates the physical or political power to throw off an
unjust social system. Against this, population control can be
a means used by unjust regimes to diminish the power and ward
off the threat posed by disadvantaged groups. This perhaps
explains why groups who believe themselves to be treated unjustly frequently oppose birth limitation programs. Such
opposition forms a constant theme in radical and minority group
literature opposed to birth control. And it can have a valid
moral basis.

---

[89]For an account of Marx's intellectual debt to Kant,
via Hegel, see Eugene Kamenka, *Marxism and Ethics* (London:
Macmillan, 1969), p. 9, and Herbert Marcuse, "Ethical Tenets,"
in *Soviet Marxism* (New York: Vintage Books, 1961), p. 184.
Contract theory represents a contemporary restatement of
Kantian moral theory (*Theory*, section 40). As my remarks
concerning contract theory and natural law indicate, however,
this general position, and therefore Kant's moral theory
clearly stand within the natural law tradition. For Kant's
own identification of his position with the natural law tradition see *The Metaphysical Elements of Justice*, pp. 26, 33, 65.
In his article, "The Primitive Ethic of Karl Marx," *The
Australasian Journal of Philosophy*, XXXV (August 1957), pp.
84f. Kamenka maintains that in his early writings Marx
employed concepts and terms clearly borrowed from the Kantian
and natural law tradition.

Another reason why disadvantaged individuals might resent population control programs arises in circumstances where the members of a society enjoy some kind of income transfer program by which funds are distributed on a per capita basis. Where such programs exist, and where the society is not fully just, population control can mean that least-off representative individuals with large families are further deprived of income which they believe is rightly theirs. The historic opposition of Marxists to Malthusianism, I noted, was patly generated by Malthus' opposition to the English Poor Law system. The more recent opposition of radical and minority group spokesmen to birth control, abortion and sterilization programs is also based on a reading of the importance of these programs to those who wish to reduce welfare payments.[90] And Roman Catholic opposition to Western birth control programs in underdeveloped nations has roots in the strong commitment of Catholic moral theory to international justice and economic assistance. Where transfer programs are operative, objections to population restraint by low-income groups, while not always justified by the facts of the situation, nevertheless have a valid moral basis.

The timing of population control programs may also breed resentment. Within an unjust society, population growth can occasionally work to the advantage of groups that dominate the social order. Where they are sure of their power and authority, these groups can use burgeoning populations to reduce the income shares of the least-off men and to pit these men against one another in a struggle for survival. Also, population growth can increase the value of fixed possessions such as land and capital goods in the hands of dominating

---

[90]J. Mayone Stycos, "Some Minority Opinions on Birth Control: Blacks, Women's Liberation, and the New Left," Documentary Study Prepared for the Commission on Population Growth and the American Future (Hastings-on-Hudson, New York: Institute of Society, Ethics and the Life Sciences, 1971), p. f-9, documents the response of minority groups to those efforts to link contraception or sterilization with welfare programs in the United States.

groups.[91]   Sudden reversals in population policy, therefore,
may be particularly resented by least-off groups. They can
indicate to these groups that their oppressors have esteemed
continued growth threatening enough to outweigh its continued
advantages. For no other reason than to confound those who
oppress them, therefore, the least-off groups have reason to
resist further manipulation and resent the demands of birth
limitation.

Finally, population control programs can directly disadvantage the least-off representative persons in a society
by denying them the offspring which serve as a source of
economic assistance and security. It is a commonplace of the
population literature that children are economically useful
during early stages of development and among lower-income
groups in agriculturally based societies.[92]   Where no provision
is made by a developing society for the financial security of
the less advantaged segment of the population, the demand that
families be limited strikes hardest at the least-off representative individuals. Not only do these individuals most
need the support and assistance of their offspring, but because
of their higher rates of mortality, they require larger
families to achieve this security. Disassociated from just
programs of redistribution and social reform, therefore,
demands for population limitation, even if imposed equally on
all citizens, inadmissibly disadvantage the lowest income
groups and for that reason would not be accepted by impartial
rational agents. Furthermore, resistance to population control

---

[91]This effect of population growth was noted by
Ricardo. It has recently been discussed as a problem of the
sociology of population growth by Neil Chamberlin in *Beyond
Malthus: Population and Power* (New York: Basic Books, 1970),
p. 160.

[92]See, for example, John B. Wyon and John E. Gordon,
The Khanna Study; Population Problems in the Rural Punjab
(Cambridge, Mass.: Harvard University Press, 1971), p. 231.
Also, Laila Shukry El-Hamamsy, "Belief Systems and Family
Planning in Peasant Societies," in *Are Our Descendants
Doomed?*, eds. Harrison Brown and Edward Hutchings, Jr. (New
York: The Viking Press, 1972), pp. 352ff.

is to be expected from low-income groups and is both understandable and justifiable.

4. *Positive Incentive Policies*

In order to overcome this kind of resistance, some
students of the population problems of underdeveloped nations
have advocated the use of incentive programs to induce low-
income parents to limit their family size. Though these programs differ in detail, all seek to compensate parents for the
economic losses entailed by birth limitation. Bonuses are
paid either directly to parents who succeed in restricting
births in their family over a given period of time or are
awarded as old age pensions at the completion of the reproductive period.[93] Certainly, these incentive policies are
morally appealing on first inspection. They reduce the amount
of coercion employed in lowering population growth rates and
they eliminate the injustice involved in depriving low income
families of the economic support of offspring.[94]

---

[93]An extensive literature exists on proposals for incentive schemes. For some of the leading discussions and
proposed programs see Stephen Enke, "The Economics of Government Payments to Limit Population," *Economic Development and
Cultural Change*, VIII (1960), 339-48; Oliver D. Finnigan III
and T. H. Sun, "Planning, Starting, and Operating an Educational Incentives Project," *Studies in Family Planning*, III
(1972), 1-7; Lenni W. Kangas, "Integrated Incentives for Fertility Control," *Science*, CLXIX (September 1970), 1278-83;
Edward Pohlman, *Incentives and Compensations in Birth Planning*,
Carolina Population Center, Monograph 11 (Chapel Hill: Uni-
versity of North Carolina, 1971); Ronald G. Ridker, "Synopsis
of a Proposal for a Family Planning Bond," *Studies in Family
Planning*, I (June 1969), 11-16, and "Savings Accounts for
Family Planning: An Illustration from the Tea Estates of
India," *Studies in Family Planning*, II, No. 7 (1971), 150-52.
For a recent evaluation of some of these programs see Everett
M. Rogers, "Incentives in the Diffusion of Family Planning
Innovations," *Studies in Family Planning*, II, No. 12 (1971),
241-48.

[94]Joseph J. Spengler defends one such incentive proposal
on the grounds that it "entails as little interference as possible with individual freedom of choice," in his "Population
Problem: In Search of a Solution," *Science*, CLXVI (December
5, 1969), 1238. For a similar view see M. Brewster Smith,

Nevertheless, when viewed in terms of the complete theory of justice I have been elaborating, such programs appear markedly deficient. This is so, first, because they involve society in paying for behavior which is demanded of its citizens on the grounds of justice alone. When a generation exceeds its fair population size, it is morally required in justice to reduce that size. Similarly, individual members of a generation are morally required not to exceed their fair share of offspring. No society need pay its members to fulfill their basic moral obligations, any more than an individual need pay a thief to prevent himself from being robbed.[95] Indeed, the general moral difficulty with this kind of incentive payment becomes clear when it is applied to an extreme degree. Should the members of a given generation have a natural growth rate far in excess of what inter-generational justice allows, incentive programs might reduce this growth rate only by siphoning off that share of income which was set aside for savings. Either way, future generations are the victims of this procedure. As Warren Robinson has noted, what is efficient when only a single generation is considered may not be so when several generations are taken into account.[96]

But this is not the only serious difficulty with these incentive schemes. Equally troubling is the neglect by those who advocate them of the larger context of justice in which a population control program stands. Proponents of these programs seem rarely to consider whether income and opportunities are fairly distributed in a given society and they commonly fail to explore the links between these programs and existing injustices. It may be that these proponents believe that by

---

"Ethical Implications of Population Policies: A Psychologist's View," *The American Psychologist*, XXVII (January 1972), 31-36.

[95] A similar point is made by Edwin G. Dolan in relation to the use of incentives for pollution abatement, although Dolan finally does not favor punitive measures in this particular area. See his *Tanstaafl; The Economic Strategy for Environmental Crisis* (New York: Holt, Rinehart and Winston, 1969), p. 42.

[96] "Population Growth and Economic Welfare," *Reports on Population/Family Planning*, No. 6 (February 1971), 32.

allowing lower-income parents freely to choose income over
children, the issue of justice can be bracketed since no lower-
income individual is made worse-off by having this option
available. Furthermore, some who have defended incentive
schemes have even viewed them as a valid means of redistribut-
ing income and of correcting inequities in a social system.
By taking income from low-fertility upper income groups and
distributing it to high-fertility lower income groups such
programs can be said to ease the plight of the worse-off.[97]
But what must be asked is whether neglect of this larger context is acceptable and whether, if the social system is unjust,
incentive schemes really represent a valid way of correcting
the injustices. Expressed in terms of the contract view, we
might ask whether members of the original position would themselves be prepared to tolerate incentive schemes in an unjust
society and whether they would view these schemes as an acceptable method of reforming a social order.

A fully satisfactory answer to these questions would
require something I have not and here cannot elaborate, a
complete theory of compensatory justice.[98] Nevertheless, with
some confidence I think I can at least suggest the reasoning
of contract parties on this one issue. If my earlier remarks
about the relationship between self-respect and family life
among the least-advantaged are correct, contract parties might
have reason to believe they would resent the presence of
incentive schemes in an unjust society. Such programs are
clearly aimed at reducing the fertility of the lower-income
groups, since this is the social stratum most attracted by the

---

[97]Boulding, *The Meaning of the Twentieth Century*, p.
136, stresses this redistributive effect as a positive feature
of these programs.

[98]With some exceptions, the contract view, as presently
formulated, does not include a theory of partial compliance
covering such matters as retributory or compensatory justice.
Rawls rightly insists on the priority of full compliance theory
(*Theory*, p. 8). Partial compliance theory would involve contract parties' asking what kinds of principles they would
advocate to respond to infractions of their full compliance
principles. In essence, that is the approach I adopt with
respect to the evaluation of incentive schemes as measures of
compensatory justice.

monetary incentive.[99] But if this is true, incentive schemes
have much the same psychological effect as a eugenic distributive principle. Lower income groups may easily perceive in
these programs an indication that society does not value them
or their children. Indeed, the money payment of an avoided
child, though rational from the perspective of an economic
planner, can easily be interpreted by a member of a lower-
income group as concrete evidence of the lengths to which the
leaders of society are prepared to go in order to halt the
proliferation of the poor.[100] Thus a program advanced on
behalf of and in the name of the less-advantaged can, with
reason, be interpreted by these individuals as a direct assault
on their position. In addition, if this program is the only
one undertaken to redress economic and social inequities, all
the other sources for resentment which we have discussed can
make their presence felt. Thus, lower-income groups can view
these incentive schemes as a means of limiting their political
power, or even as a nefarious plot to halt a long-term welfare
drain.

---

[99]Rogers, "Incentives in the Diffusion of Family Planning Innovations," p. 244, reports that in test programs among
factory workers, incentives are most effective among those in
the lower-income range. He maintains that at higher levels,
incentives are without effect. This observation is further
confirmed by examinations of the socio-economic status of
individuals submitting to sterilization in mass vasectomy programs in India, where monetary incentives are used. See S.
Krishnakumar, "Kerala's Pioneering Experiment in Massive
Vasectory Camps," and V. H. Thakor and Vinod M. Patel, "The
Gujarat State Massive Vasectomy Camp," both in *Studies in
Family Planning*, III (August 1972), pp. 180, 189, 191.

[100]It is noteworthy that the issue of resentment is
virtually neglected in the treatments of incentive programs.
Moral analysis of these programs by their advocates seems
limited to the question of whether they are coercive of parents
or whether they might have undesirable side effects on family
values, such as promoting the monetization of childbearing or
even encouraging infanticide. Where programs are purposely
designed to be free of these sorts of difficulties, however,
the moral issue of justice seems not to be at all perceived.
Thus, Finnigan and Sun state of their own educational savings
incentive program in Taiwan that it is "morally acceptable"
("Planning, Starting and Operating an Educational Incentives
Project," p. 2).

If all these grounds for resentment exist when such programs are initiated in an unjust context, we might assume that impartial rational agents would prefer other means of remedying economic inequities. Incentive schemes are a suspect instrumentality because they too closely link aims which may be just in themselves with the sensitive issue of birth control in an unjust context. If a society is in fact intent on rectifying injustices and conforming its institutions to the two principles of justice, there is no reason why direct steps cannot be taken to that end, steps such as land reform, just taxation, employment opportunity programs, and the like. If society is intent upon limiting population out of a sense of obligation to its present and future members, it can demand procreative restraint of all its citizens without inducements. By bringing these two different but morally demanded aims together in one program, however, the integrity of each is compromised. The poor are likely to see the funds transferred to them for limiting their children not as their fair share of the cooperative social product, but as direct payments for limiting their families, payments which in an unjust society serve only further to humiliate those who receive them.

This prolonged excursion into the significance of an income allocation principle or any population restriction in the context of an unjust society has definite policy implications. It suggests that virtually any program of birth limitation, however non-coercive, is likely to breed resentment if it is not related to obvious efforts to render the society as a whole more just. The presence of resentment, of course, does not mean that a given policy will not be successful. The less advantaged might bitterly dislike an incentive scheme and nevertheless avail themselves of the opportunity to improve their circumstances. Indeed, the same can be said even of notably unfair und coercive programs employed to reduce birth rates. Compulsory abortion programs for certain groups, for example, might occasion vehement resistance but still prove successful in inducing members of these groups to lower the sizes of their families. The primary ground of opposition to

such policies is not pragmatic but moral.[101] They are
policies to which no rational individual in an original position would consent. As true as this is, it might also be
argued that policies which breed resentment are also likely,
over time, to prove ineffective. By forcing an individual to
behave in a way he could not agree to and by subjecting him to
ends which are not to his advantage, these policies encourage
deception and evasion. In addition, since such policies
accustom the individual to injustice, they lay the foundation
for further future disobedience to the norms of justice. They
accustom individuals not only to a "monetization" of child-
bearing, feared by some population writers, but, more seriously, to the monetization of basic social responsibility.[102]
What this means in terms of population growth is that the
achievements of unjust population control programs (or policies
undertaken in a context of injustice) may be short lived.
Instead of cultivating permanent habits of procreative restraint, based on a sense of justice, these policies may
encourage each family to place its interest first with the
result that when income or circumstances allow birth rates may
again spiral upward.[103]

---

[101]This kind of moral priority is not commonly stressed
in the literature of family planning and population control.
One exception is the article by Daniel Callahan, *Ethics and
Population Limitation*, p. 39, where Callahan insists on the
responsibility, in justice, of organizations involved in family
planning to inquire into the social and moral implications of
their programs within the societies where they are maintained.

[102]For a brief discussion of the issue of the "monetization" of childbearing, see Bernard Berelson, "Beyond Family
Planning," *Science*, CLXIII (February 7, 1969), 538.

[103]In his review of incentive programs, Rogers reflects
a concern with the "low quality" of many of the decisions to
adopt sterilization in some of these programs. He refers to
the tendency of some adopters to undergo sterilization without
their wives' consent, or to be motivated primarily by pecuniary
gain; and he believes that these poor quality decisions can
lead to a "plateau effect" whereby adoptions drop off in the
future ("Incentives in the Diffusion of Family Planning Innovations," p. 246). Characteristically, Rogers neglects to
inquire whether many of the adoptions undertaken in this
program of sterilization or contraception may not be of "low
quality" simply because they are induced by a degrading kind

5. *The Priority of Social Reform*

If population limitation programs can meet such
resistance when severed from a context of social justice, it
is also reasonable to suppose that a context of justice can
facilitate these programs. Indeed, in view of these prior
considerations, it may even be suggested that programs of
social reform are the logical first step in any population
policy. According to Rawls, any effort to make members of a
society comply with the principles of justice is most likely
to succeed when pursued on a board front. Efforts to correct
the violation of a single rule of justice may fail because,
within a larger context of injustice, that violation serves
to compensate for other violations.[104] Since rapid population
growth represents a single violation of this sort, and one
that in many ways can be seen as compensating for other
injustices, the reduction of birth rates is most likely to
succeed where other major aspects of a society are rendered
just.

This is true first because social reform diminishes
resentment and stimulates the sense of justice.[105] As such it

---

of monetary incentive. And he neglects to inquire into the
long-term effect for birth limitation generally of programs
of this sort.

[104]See *Justice as Fairness* (1967), p. 24, for a discussion of compensating injustices within a social system.

[105]The importance of a sense of justice in stimulating
cooperation with population control schemes is perhaps
implicitly recognized by Wyon and Gordon in their favorance of
community-based programs in the less developed regions (*The
Khanna Study*, pp. 247-55, 282). Presumably members of communities have a stronger sense of principled concern with their
local society than their nation. A further support of the
importance of a sense of justice in this context is derived
from a distinct, and in many ways, contradictory area of
experience. Rainwater has shown that one reason for the large
family size of lower income working class families is the conviction on the part of these parents that large families fulfill a moral obligation. See Lee Rainwater, *Family Design*
(Chicago: Aldine, 1965), p. 165. This evidences the force of
the sense of justice in the area of sexuality and population,
a force presumably subject to proper moral regulation.

elicits the adherence of the masses to the goals and strategies of development, of which population restraint is a necessary part.[106] But it is also true because reform makes procreative restraint possible.[107] When a society is organized to improve the prospects of the least-off representative individuals, the economic and social reasons for having children dwindle (especially when a priority is placed on investment in medical programs of aid to the poor). Equal political liberty and enhanced employment prospects furnish a basis for self-respect which can reduce the compelling importance of the family in the lives of the less advantaged. And efforts to insure fair equality of opportunity through educational programs, if nothing else, can have direct impact on the citizen's ability and willingness to employ contraception. Many students of the development and population problems of poorer nations have come to believe that the former problem is causally related to the latter. High fertility is seen as one aspect of the general problem of underdevelopment so that modernization becomes a prerequisite for substantial reduction in birth rate.[108] To the degree that social reform alleviates the harshest aspects of underdevelopment for those groups with the highest fertility, it can facilitate the modernization process and birth limitation. Of course, the common objection to this stress on the importance of modernization is that population control is itself required to generate the savings which make modernization possible. One answer to this is that social and economic reform is an international, as well as national, concern. Rectified trade relationships, development aid and

---

[106] For a discussion of the importance of mass acceptance of development goals, see Denis Goulet, "That Third World" in *World Development; An Introductory Reader*, ed. Hélène Castel (New York: The Macmillan Co., 1971), p. 21.

[107] See Arthur Dyck, "Population Policies and Ethical Acceptability," in *Rapid Population Growth*, p. 623.

[108] See, for example, Simon Kuznets, "Population and Economic Growth," *Proceedings of the American Philosophical Society*, CXI (June 1967), 189. Also, Harry Raulet, "Family Planning and Population Control in Developing Countries," *Demography*, VII (May 1970), 231ff.

the like can furnish the preconditions of development. I have
noted how heavily Catholic population thought has stressed
programs of social justice on the international level. And,
although I have not elaborated a contract theory view of
international justice, as Rawls himself has not, I can suggest
that this view would sanction many of the kinds of demands made
by Catholic thinkers, especially where extremely underdeveloped
nations are involved. But even confining attention to the
national level, it is important to stress that social reform
and modernization are not the same thing. Even in those circumstances where savings are limited, reforms can be made in
tenancy institutions, political and other institutions which
can bring some of the benefits of modernization to the least-
off groups and facilitate population limitation.[109]

This does not mean that modernization and its population
benefits cannot be effected without social reform. Experience
over the past several centuries has shown that development and
consequent fertility decline have come about in social circumstances marked by widely differing degrees of conformity to
the principles of justice. But social reform can represent
a short-cut to modernization. Furthermore, it can help
eliminate fertility-increasing pressures that sometimes
accompany modernization.[110] Finally, social reform can provide

---

[109]See Gunnar Myrdal, *Asian Drama* (New York: Pantheon
Books, 1968), III, p. 2068, for a discussion of the independent
importance of social reform in modernizing underdeveloped
nations. Similarly, Judith Blake, referring specifically to
the issue of female employment, notes that this kind of
fertility-reducing social reform does not entirely depend upon
prior economic development. See her article, "Demographic
Science and the Redirection of Public Policy," in *Public
Health and Population Change*, eds. Mindel C. Sheps and Jeanne
Clare Ridley (Pittsburgh: University of Pittsburgh Press,
1965), p. 68.

[110]In his *Population Theories and Economic Interpretation* (London: Routledge & Kegan Paul, 1957), pp. 173ff., the
Marxian economist Sidney Coontz maintains that the unregulated
industrialization process in the 19th century England was a
major cause of that nation's unprecedented population growth.
More recently, some students of the "Green Revolution" in India
and Pakistan have noted that agricultural development
unaccompanied by tenancy reform can serve to worsen the situation of the lowest income groups and thereby sustain or

a firm foundation, first, for sustained and even population
decline, and eventually for population stabilization. Very
commonly, discussions of the relationship between fertility
and per capita income treat the latter measure as an aggregate
and ignore distributive issues.[111] Such discussions perhaps
accurately record the general fertility tendencies of societies
undergoing modernization (such as the inverse relationship
between income and fertility). But it may be asked whether
underneath these general tendencies there are not wide variations between representative social groups and classes which
may continue to plague a society even when modernization is
well underway.[112] The relatively high fertility of lower-
income and minority groups in some of the developed nations
is an example. Neglect of distributive issues in the modernization process may thus create fertility imbalances which keep
aggregate growth rates high and which further threaten constantly to de-stabilize broad cooperation with population
restraint between generations.[113] In any case, conformity to

---

accentuate the conditions leading to high fertility. See,
for example, Wolf Ladejinsky, "Ironies of India's Green Revolution," *Foreign Affairs*, XLVIII (July 1970), 758-68.

[111]For one example of such stress on the population
implications of the per capita income measure see Harvey
Leibenstein, *Economic Backwardness and Economic Growth*
(New York: John Wiley & Sons, 1957), pp. 162ff.

[112]In this vein, Harry Raulet notes in his article,
"Family Planning and Population Control in Developing
Countries," 225, that one must observe the class basis of
mortality in estimating the value of this and other income-
related developments in reducing fertility. He observes that
in (then) West Pakistan mortality remains highest precisely
among lower-income, high-fertility rural families.

[113]Carl Taylor, in his article, "Five Stages in a
Practical Population Policy," p. 6, argues that conflict
between economic and political groups presently impedes cooperation on population restraint at the village level in
India and Pakistan. Growing inequities might exacerbate this
problem.

the two principles of justice may help eliminate this kind of difficulty.[114]

6. *Population Growth in the Well-Ordered Society*

The suggestion of a cause and effect relationship between the existence of just institutions and sustained fertility restraint raises an important question. To this point I have been examining various principles for distributing the right to have children (a matter still not fully resolved). In the course of this examination I have also had occasion to touch upon various policy proposals connected with the implementation of one or another alternate principle. But it is useful to speculate now upon whether a justly organized and stable society, what Rawls calls a "well-ordered" society (*Theory*, pp. 453f.), may not render the whole issue of distributing the right to have children moot. Any question of justice, it will be recalled, involves competing claims made upon scarce goods or opportunities. The question, therefore, is whether the right to have children will remain scarce in a society whose basic structure is fully regulated by the two principles of justice. This is not only the question of whether a well-ordered society will have to enforce, with appropriate sanctions, a principle distributing the right to have children, although that question is involved. In addition, it is the question of whether such a society will be characterized by excessive population growth from generation to generation. Or, will growth rates in a well-ordered society eventually stabilize of their own accord at or near replacement levels? Would members of a fully just society even have to concern themselves with just population size? I

[114] It is interesting to note that recent treatments of development which stress the importance of encouraging rational modes of orientation as a prerequisite for modernization rarely discuss the function of moral reason in this context. Yet the extension and application of moral reason (through programs of social and political reform) has been very much a part of the experience of the developed nations.

224

have already noted that there is a tendency among some Marxist
population theoriests to reinterpret Marx and Engels' thinking
to provide a negative answer to this last question. Just as
communist society may be a society "beyond justice" with
respect to political and economic problems, so it may be beyond
the circumstances of justice with respect to population and
reproduction; here, as elsewhere a natural harmony will
characterize the behavior of its members.[115] In such a fully
just society none of the circumstances which presently compel
population growth are presumed to exist.

If we consider the circumstances of at least an
economically developed well-ordered society these claims have
some merit. For one thing, by providing a secure material
foundation and educational opportunity such a society eventually removes the economic reasons for having large families.
For another, improved material circumstances and a developed
sense of justice are likely to stimulate greater concern for
the quality of family life and child-rearing. Rawls notes
that persons who have developed a sense of justice are the
offspring of good homes; for this and other reasons they "are
confident in their self-esteem and are more likely to care for
their children with manifest intention" (*Theory*, p. 498).
Apart from the question of whether persons in such a society
are led morally to consider the welfare of those outside the
family in regulating their reproductive life, therefore, it is
possible that the sense of justice might directly lead to
smaller family sizes.

But the consideration of perhaps greatest importance
concerns the place of women in the well-ordered society. The
contract view may help to illuminate the circumstances of
women once the principles of justice are fully effected. There
are, for example, the implications of the requirement of fair
equality of opportunity. Rawls nowhere explores the significance of this requirement for female participation in social
and economic institutions. It is reasonably clear, of course,

---

[115]See above, pp. 150f. For an interpretation of full
communist society as "beyond justice" see R. C. Tucker, *The
Marxian Revolutionary Idea* (New York: W. W. Norton, 1969),
Chs. I and II.

that this requirement forbids discrimination based on sex.
But it may be asked whether it does not go beyond this. Since
women must take years out of their productive life to fulfill
the socially demanded task of bearing and rearing children,
fair equality of opportunity might imply, at least above the
stage of economic hardship, that, despite these interruptions
and delays, society has a responsibility to equip women for
careers equal to those pursued by men and to make room within
social and economic institutions for women so equipped.
Interpreted this way, of course, fair equality of opportunity
can as easily stimulate as restrain population growth. Female
participation in the labor force is not necessarily inimical
to the bearing of large families, as the experience of the
United States during the 1940's and 1950's reveals.[116] And a
greater opportunity for combining careers with motherhood
might accentuate fertility.

Nevertheless, female participation in the labor force
must not be interpreted only in a quantitative sense. Rawls
himself assumes a basic principle of motivation which he terms
the "Aristotelian principle" (*Theory*, pp. 424-33). According
to this, human beings are assumed to enjoy the exercise of
their realized capacities, and other things equal, to desire
those activities which call upon "a larger repertoire of more
intricate and subtle discriminations" (*Theory*, p. 429). In
terms of labor, this principle means that individuals, where
possible, desire career opportunities that elicit their highest
excellences. The fully just society aims at providing these
opportunities. Such a society is a "social union of social
unions" (*Theory*, p. 527), because within a common framework of
mutual cooperation and respect, it supports numerous associations of work and culture through which individuals can express
their highest realized capacities.

Applied to the matter of female participation in
associations outside the home, the Aristotelian principle
suggests that as a just society progresses many women will

---

[116]Stycos, "Some Minority Opinions . . .", p. f-33,
notes the correlation between female employment and fertility
during this period.

choose to develop their special excellences through careers.
Even if they choose to raise families, as might be expected,
there is reason to believe that their family sizes will not be
large. Considering their presumed desire, as persons with a
sense of justice, to "care for their children with manifest
intention" (*Theory*, p. 498) and their desire to excel in a
career, it is difficult to see how many women would be capable
of rearing large families, even if they are aided by child-
care institutions. Of course, it is true that the family
itself is a "social union" and one in which women might perceive the opportunity to develop their own special excellences.
But it is to be questioned whether, in the presence of numerous
fair equal opportunities for personal development outside the
home and in the absence of an artificial and pervasive maternal
career ethos, there would be enough women selecting this
opportunity to create high fertility rates. Here the experience of an advanced economy like that of the United States
during the 1940's and 1950's is not illuminating since the
popularity of the maternal role among middle- and upper-income
women during this period has been partly related to the absence
of genuine fair equality of opportunity in employment.[117]

All these considerations are, of course, highly speculative. For that reason, it would be inappropriate to utilize
them as a basis for ignoring the issue of reproductive
restraint and population policy, as some Marxist and radical
thinkers have tried to do. Indeed, there are at least two
reasons why even the fully just society may have to rely upon
its citizens' knowledge and respect for a principle distributing the right to have children and why it may even have to

---

[117]See Lois W. Hoffman and Frederick Wyatt, "Social
Change and Motivations for Having Larger Families: Some Theoretical Considerations," *Merrill-Palmer Quarterly*, VI (1960),
235-44. Richard F. Tomasson contrasts the Swedish with the
American experience in this regard. The continuing low fertility of Swedish women during the 1940's, 1950's and 1960's, he
maintains is related not so much to the proportion of women
employed, which is not as high in Sweden as in the United
States, as to the proportion of women in the professions and
traditional male occupations. Swedish fertility remained low
during this period, he argues, partly because these high
status acceptable role possibilities for women helped eclipse

develop a policy to enforce this principle. First, because
the kind of circumstances just sketched in which fertility
would effectively regulate itself can only be assumed to prevail once the process of development is well underway, and
once the attitudes and sentiments which linger from a period
of underdevelopment or injustice have vanished. During a
long transition period, therefore, many of the opportunities
afforded by a just society may serve to actually stimulate
population growth.

In the second place, it is not clear that even in a
fully developed just society a matter as important as population growth can be left entirely to the discretion of individual couples. Rawls observes that fair social arrangements can
be unstable in two ways (*Theory*, p. 336). They can be unstable if an individual is tempted to shirk doing his part
while still being able to benefit from the fruits of others'
cooperation or restraint. This is the famous "free-rider"
problem.[118] However, this form of instability may not be a
great problem with respect to reproduction in a well-ordered
society, since fertility restraint may be spontaneous and the
public good it secures not the sort that tempts many individuals to shirk. But institutions or practices can also be
unstable if individuals have reason to believe that by stick-
ing to a practice they disadvantage themselves relative to
other people. Now, since reproductive restraint when not
practiced by all can diminish over time an individual's or a
family line's place in a social order, rational individuals,
even in a just society, may have reason to fear the persistent
higher fertility of certain groups of families. This in turn
might prompt them to exceed having the number of children they
wish. To prevent this kind of possibility, members of a just

---

the maternal career ethos. See his *Sweden: Prototype of
Modern Society* (New York: Random House, 1970), pp. 188-93.

[118]See J. M. Buchanan, *The Demand and Supply of Public
Goods* (Chicago: Rand McNally, 1968), Ch. V, for a discussion
of this problem. Mancur Olson also furnishes an excellent
account of the difficulties associated with public or collective goods in his *The Logic of Collective Action*
(Cambridge, Mass.: Harvard University Press, 1965), Ch. 1.

society might desire some kind of public rule specifying the fair limits of individual family size. And they might even desire that reasonable sanctions be attached to this rule. As Rawls points out, the presence of sanctions need not be a sign that members of a society are unwilling to cooperate with a fair scheme or practice. Such santions can serve the purpose of their making known to one another their good intentions. Thus, the sanctions need not be severe and once a society has moved past a transition period they need never be applied. But their presence can serve to assure each participant that his cooperation will not be an occasion for others' abuse.

7. *A Contract Intra-Generational Principle and Policy*

This reasoning returns us to the question of a principle for distributing the right to have children and the policies appropriate to enforcing that principle. My lengthy digression from this issue, however, has not been purposeless. If there is reason to believe that fertility will eventually be self-regulating in a just society, this conditions the kinds of principle and policies adopted for that society during the transition period when population growth remains a problem. The aim, after all, is to establish an approach to fertility which can facilitate a natural progression to circumstances where the matter regulates itself and where couples have the fullest measure of freedom. Policies which undermine this possibility are therefore suspect, no matter how reasonable they may appear. Conversely, policies which accord with this goal may be desirable even if they are deficient in other ways.

The examination of alternate principles and policies for distributing children, it will be recalled, did not advance us beyond a principle of equal liberty. But two related difficulties with this principle must be mentioned. First, there is the fact, already noted, that this principle ignores human beings' varying desires for children. Those individuals who greatly desire children will chafe against this restriction, while those who care little for offspring will find themselves in possession of a right they do not wish to exercise. It was to correct this difficulty that contract parties initially considered the otherwise unacceptable income-based principle. Second, a principle of strict equality might develop an inappropriate psychological foundation for an advanced state of society, where, within reasonable limits, family size can again be left to the discretion of individual couples. It may be supposed that within a developed just society, there will be individuals for whom the family is the particular social union where they can display their own highest realized capacities in the role of parents. So long as these individuals do not use the liberty to procreate for the purpose of founding disruptive and burgeoning family lines, they may be considered an asset to society. Their excellence as parents will be reflected in the quality of their offspring. By establishing the equal liberty to have children as the normative principle for a just society, however, contract parties threaten to instill such parents with an unnecessary sense of guilt. There is no reason why every couple in an advanced just society should feel compelled to limit their families if they are convinced they can best contribute to society as parents.

One solution to both these difficulties is some kind of income-based allocation avoiding the difficulty of the income schemes we examined earlier. For example, an allocation might attach a price to children by means of tax measures, but it might make this price progressive with the parents' income. Those parents who are beneficiaries of higher income through the difference principle would be required to pay proportionately more, through direct fees or taxes, for the right to have a child. Schemes of this sort have been suggested by Senator Robert Packwood and Robert Veatch.[119]

[119]Senator Robert Packwood, S 3632, 91st Congress, 2nd Session, "A Bill . . . to Limit the Number of Personal Exemptions Allowable for Children of Taxpayers Who Are Born After 1972;" and Robert Veatch, "A Proposal for Taxing Child-Bearing: Can It Be Just?" Hastings Center Institute for Society, Ethics and the Life Sciences, Working Paper, No. 4 (Hastings-on-Hudson, New York, 1971); also Veatch's paper "An Ethical Analysis of Population Policy Proposals," Documentary Study Prepared for the Commission on Population Growth and the American Future (Hastings-on-Hudson, N.Y.: Institute of Society, Ethics and the Life Sciences, 1971).

Packwood's proposal removes income tax deductions for children after the second child. Presumably parents with higher income would pay heavier taxes for each succeeding child. Veatch's proposal is less tied to any specific existing tax scheme and is more directly progressive. He would base economic penalties for having children on a percentage of some just form of the income tax.

From the perspective of contract parties, a child tax keyed progressively to parents' income has several advantages. First, it circumvents the difficulty of the flat-rate income allocations I mentioned earlier. By permitting inequalities in income and authority the difference principle, although acceptable to contract parties, moves perilously close to undermining the self-respect of least-off representative individuals. Any flat-rate fee on children serves further to destabilize this arrangement by augmenting the reasons why unequal economic distribution can jeopardize self-respect. But a progressive fee on children nullifies this tendency. It insures that differences in income are not readily translated into differences in permissible family size since the offspring of better-off families cost more.[120] Thus a progressive tax cuts the link between income and offspring and restores the basic equal liberty of families to have children whatever their income. At the same time it permits representative families to allocate their income as they wish. In this way it expresses a principle of equal opportunity, which seems a rational choice for contract parties. Indeed, I might term this "equal opportunity rule" the contract theory intra-generational population principle. It is the basic principle with which contract parties would approach the distribution of the

---

[120] I neglect here any discussion of the intrinsic justness of this kind of tax in terms of the claim that upper income families and children effect a heavier toll on the environment. For a brief discussion of this issue see Wayne Davis, "Overpopulated America," *New Republic*, January 10, 1970, pp. 13-15, and Veatch, "A Proposal . . .," p. 9. From the perspective of contract theory this issue is immaterial since all economic distribution is initially considered just when in keeping with the difference principle and may be spent as parents please. Impermissible expenditures are established by separate public policy and are regulated by considerations such as the just savings principle.

right to have children and it is the principle that would
condition any policy they would accept.

A further advantage of these particular schemes is
that they involve penalties for excess childbearing. By their
nature, penalties or punishments are more appropriate than
are rewards for insuring compliance with moral rules. If
nothing else, they are more workable, since in cases of violation one need only increase the penalty with no injury to
compliant individuals. Increasing rewards to insure compliance,
however, can directly penalize those who obey the rules by
siphoning off income or goods which are rightly theirs.[121] Of
course, it may be objected that in the special case of reproduction penalties are inappropriate since they can affect the
offspring of non-compliant parents. Certainly this is one of
the more difficult problems of any population policy, especially in connection with income-transfer policies.[122] Nevertheless, in the circumstances of a just society this problem
need not be severe. It will be recalled that all my remarks
assume a society organized in keeping with the two principles
of justice. In the absence of justice any population policy
is unjust, not only to offspring but to the parents themselves.
Where the two principles regulate the basic structure of a
society, however, the most grievous effects of sanctions
against child-bearing are eliminated. This society seeks over
time to improve the lot of the least-off representative
individuals. In cases of extreme hardship during early stages
of the development process, efforts are made to insure that
the least-off are not victimized for future generations. And
particular concern is directed at the children of the least-
off, since, in a sense, they are the most disadvantaged
individuals of all. What this means is that even during an
early stage of development priority is placed upon medical and

---

[121]For a good discussion of the moral advantages of
penalties over rewards, see Gert, *The Moral Rules*, Ch. 3.

[122]For a discussion of the difficulty of uniting a
punitive population policy with an income-transfer policy
see John Williamson, "Urban Policy and Population Policy:
A Conflict in Goals?" *Urban and Social Change Review*, IV
(Fall 1970), 21-23.

educational programs for the children of the poor. These
programs place an income floor under children, irrespective
of whatever penalties their parents might incur for excessive
breeding. Indeed, in extreme cases transfers aimed directly
at children may permit their circumstances to improve even as
the economic circumstances of their irresponsible parents
stand still or, if possible, decline.[123]

It may seem peculiar that a population policy has this
result. On the one hand, in the name of justice irresponsible parents are penalized and deprived of income while, on the
other hand, society seeks at the same time to improve the circumstances of their young. Yet such a policy would seem to be
demanded not only out of basic moral respect for the innocent
children but in the name of justice. This policy is an expression of the rational demand that a society separate its income
policy from the matter of family size. The separation, of
course, cannot be complete so long as disincentive economic
penalties are used. But by seeing that these disincentives
are keyed progressively to income and by insuring that the
children of the least-advantaged minimally suffer because of
their parents' behavior, a society can, without compromising
its demand for procreative responsibility, tangibly express
its commitment to the equal dignity of the families and
children of all its members.

This policy raises one further question concerning the
manner in which taxes or penalties are to be levied. Should
taxes be applied only after a family has exceeded its fair
size (after the "nth child") or should such taxes be levied on
all offspring? Several arguments have been advanced both for
and against nth child taxes.[124] On the one hand, these taxes
are sensitive to the fact that it is only excess children who
pose a moral problem. If all parents were to limit their

---

[123]Without basing it on a full theory of justice, Guido
Calabrisi has advocated such an "income floor" population tax.
For an account of his position see the Law Note, "Legal Analy-
sis and Population Control: The Problem of Coercion,"
Harvard Law Review, LXXXIV (June 1971), 1904.

[124]See Veatch, "A Proposal . . . ," p. 11.

families to the size needed to meet their generation's population responsibility, no taxes need be levied at all. By
taxing families once they have exceeded this size, therefore,
the burden is placed on the most acute offenders. In addition,
we have seen that all persons have an interest in insuring the
continuance of mankind. It seems unfair, therefore, to
penalize parents who fulfill, but do not exceed their
responsibility in this regard.

On the other hand, taxes levied after the nth child may
inflict an unfair psychological penalty on siblings born after
the nth child. Also, by establishing a social policy dis-
criminating against families above a certain size, this policy
can provide an inappropriate psychological foundation for
family life in a developed just society. The expectation, or
hope, for such a society is that family size can be left to
the discretion of individuals, with those who think they can
make a unique contribution as parents feeling free to do so.
Established policies penalizing larger family sizes can erode
the confidence of such parents as the need for family limitation recedes.

More troubling, however, is the significance of an nth
child policy during the transition period out of low states of
economic development. Since it is the lower income classes in
underdeveloped societies that traditionally have larger
families, members of these classes can interpret this policy
as ingenuously rigged against themselves. Existing upper income groups, the most likely initial recipients of higher
income through the difference principle, have usually learned
procreative restraint and they may not be affected at all by
the taxes levied under an nth child policy. The poor, on the
other hand, might find themselves sorely penalized for behavior to which they have long been accustomed. This alone might
render them hostile to the policy and undercut its efficacy.
For the variety of reasons I have sketched, population control
is one of the more sensitive aspects of a program of justice
and is the aspect most likely to breed resentment among the
least advantaged. Any policies which furnish further grounds
for resentment are, therefore, suspect.

A policy which taxes all children can help avoid these
difficulties. It is true that the larger families of the

poor are disproportionately penalized by this policy as well.
But the public knowledge that the children of all members of
society are subject to taxation can ease resentment. This
policy can also help convey the basic awareness that procreative responsibility is incumbent not upon individuals, in the
first place, but upon the entire generation to which they
belong. Linked together in time, all the members of a generation are the victims or beneficiaries of their predecessors'
actions. It seems fitting, therefore, when sacrifice is
demanded that all share this sacrifice to some degree, even if
they are among those who naturally prefer smaller families.
It remains true that parents who exercise some responsibility
and keep their families within the size roughly demanded of
all members of a generation may judge this policy to be unfair.
But policies which are unfair need not be unjust. So long as
rational members of an original position have good reason for
tolerating an unfair distribution of goods or liberties, that
distribution is just. One example is the exemption from
military service permitted those who conscientiously refuse to
participate in what they believe to be an unjust war (*Theory*,
pp. 377-82). Such exemptions are unfair to those who must
carry the additional burden of the war effort. But they need
not be unjust since impartial rational persons have many
reasons for allowing the exemptions in the first place.[125]

   I have tried to suggest that the same may be true

---

[125] I have not discussed the possibility of a complete
right of conscientious objection and immunity from penalties
for a couple whose religious convictions prohibit them from
using effective means of birth control or who are motivated,
on religious grounds, to have large families. For a proposal
for a right of conscientious objection to population programs
see Arthur Dyck, "Population Policies . . .," p. 269. Should
permanent procreative restraint be demanded in a society, a
full right of conscientious objection would probably be
unacceptable to contract parties, since they have good reason
to fear the burgeoning family lines of sects lacking a sense
of justice in this regard. On the other hand, progressive
all-child taxes, minimized in a developed fully just society,
function very much to permit liberty for objectors of this
sort. And the justice of such a society might eventually lead
members of these religious groups to comply with the just
population policies of the society. For a parallel discussion
on the level of religious freedom see Rawls' section, "Tolera-
tion of the Intolerant," in *Theory*, pp. 216-21.

concerning policies that tax all children in a given generation. These policies help avoid resentment during the transition period and prepare the way for procreative freedom at a
developed stage of society (taxes would presumably be diminished to nothing as such a stage was approached). Of course,
if either of these reasons are not valid the case for this
policy is weakened and that for an nth child policy strengthened. It may be, for example, that an nth child policy does
not breed resentment during a transition period in a given
society. Should the latter prove true, all-child taxes may
themselves be a source of resentment, since those who
voluntarily restrict their families roughly to replacement
size may feel persistently exploited by those who do not. In
any case, since we cannot know in advance how parents will
behave in such a society and since it does seem likely that
nth child proposals will particularly disadvantage lower income
groups in the present, a reasoned choice would favor a policy
taxing parents for each child they have whenever a generation
is called upon to lower or reduce its population size or
growth rates.

This completes my analysis of a contract view intra-
generational population principle and policy. It will be noted
that I have failed to examine the specifics of the many policy
proposals that have been set forth, as well as the precise
way in which an all-child policy is to be put into effect
(for example, the rate at which taxes are to be levied,
exactly how and when they are to be paid, and so on).[126] But
my intention was not to engage in an extensive discussion of
this issue so much as to indicate the broad outlines of a
policy demanded by justice. If this discussion is substantially correct, it remains for policy-makers and legislators to
flesh in the details on the basis of additional factual and
moral considerations, although the device of the original
position and the issues I have tried to bring to it remain a
fundamental tool for further investigation in this area.

One omission, however, deserves mention. I have
obviously neglected to discuss the more radical policy

---

[126]For a discussion of these issues, see Bernard
Berelson, "Beyond Family Planning," pp. 533-43. Also,
Veatch, "A Proposal . . .," pp. 6ff.

proposals advanced by some contributors to the population
debate. These range from proposals for compulsory sterilization and abortion to proposals for disseminating fertility
control agents against the will of populations through drink-
ing water or basic food commodities.[127] As some commentators
have noted, these proposals are fraught with technical difficulties.[128] My failure to discuss them, however, has nothing
to do with their unfeasibility. Nor do I simply assume that
such policies are unworthy of moral consideration. The contract view is not an absolutist moral position. In the face
of grievous necessity, contract parties can allow forms of
behavior which depart markedly from what they would permit
under ideal conditions. In doing so they would still insist,
of course, that all such behavior meet the test of the original position.

If I have not considered these more radical proposals,
it is because I consider them the very last step in a response
to the population problem. The first step in any population
policy, I have tried to say, must be the reform of a society
so that its basic structure conforms to the two principles of

---

[127]See, for example, Melvin M. Ketchel, "Fertility
Control Agents as a Possible Solution to the World Population
Problem," *Perspectives in Biology and Medicine*, XI (1968),
687-703; also Kingsley Davis, "Population Policy: Will
Current Programs Succeed?" *Science*, CLVIII (1967), p. 738;
and Edgar Chasteen, "The Case for Compulsory Birth Control,"
in Daniel Callahan, ed., *The American Population Debate*
(Garden City, N.Y.: Doubleday, 1971), pp. 274-78. It is
interesting to note that Ketchel's proposal, as well as
related proposals for the mass dissemination of contraceptive
agents, have the moral advantage, from a contract perspective,
of at least distributing the opportunity to have children
in a fashion free of genetic, cultural or class considerations. A grave defect in these proposals, however, is that
they distribute not the opportunity to have children equally,
but only the opportunity to have the opportunity to have
children. Through such proposals and programs some couples
that intensely desire children can have their fertility so
reduced as to be unable to reproduce. All stand equally
exposed to this prospect in a statistical fashion, it is true.
But losers under such programs can definitely lose their
opportunity to reproduce.

[128]See, for example, Carl Djerassi, "Birth Control
After 1984: A Realistic Appraisal of Future Contraceptive
Developments," in *Are Our Descendants Doomed?*, eds. Harrison
Brown and Edward Hutchings, Jr., pp. 122-63.

justice. Borrowing a term from Rawls, I might say that
programs of social reform have a "lexical priority" to any
specific population policy. Only when such programs have
been effected and have failed to lower birth rates may population policies begin. These presumably would take the form of
disincentives for child-bearing. The weight of such disincentives might be increased as needed. Without prior social
reform these policies, even at their mildest, are unjust, and
this injustice grows as the coerciveness of policies increases.
Those who advocate compulsory policies of this sort must show
far more clearly than they already have that the proper steps
have been taken and have failed to halt population growth.
Without evidence to this effect, compulsory population
policies only compound and intensify injustice.

CONCLUSION

This concludes my inductive and deductive approach to the issue of population growth. In an effort to coordinate and arrange the various views of the issue first examined and the various distributive preferences they reflect, I have assumed the standpoint of the original position and have asked how impartial rational agents would respond to population growth. The result of this inquiry is a principle regulating population growth between generations, a principle distributing the right to have children within generations (the principle of equal reproductive opportunity) and elements of a policy for putting the latter principle into effect. These principles and policy recommendations are obviously very general. Though derived from a full range of basic interests manifested in this area, they are abstracted from the real conditions of human communities affected by population growth. As is true of any moral principles they are meant to serve as ideal guides and restraints to conduct. Within specific social and historical contexts they must certainly undergo application and be supplemented by knowledge of the valid exceptions they allow.

I have already stated that in the process of applying these principles the methodology elaborated in this thesis may be more important than the principles or policy themselves. Specifically, I refer to the conceptual device of the original position and the constraints it imposes on the choice of moral principles. It is the standpoint of the original position that furnishes the court of arbitration for all consideration of concrete issues raised by population growth. By facilitating universality of concern and impartiality of judgment this device seeks to preserve the notion of fairness which, as Rawls suggests, is at the heart of our understanding of morality (*Theory*, p. 12). Indeed, it is probably correct to say that this idea of fairness is even more fundamental to our moral reasoning process and even more pertinent to the adjudication of conflicts having to do with population or any other issue than is the device of the original position itself. Certainly one of the major tasks of this thesis has been the alteration of the original position for population

240

purposes. We saw, for example, that in several instances, Rawls's favored description of the original position is inadequate to adjudicate disputes in this area. By excluding individuals not yet alive or by neglecting the series of desires and needs associated with human sexuality, Rawls's description of the original position proved unfair to real interests likely to manifest themselves in disputes over population. In adjusting the original position to include these interests, I have tried to preserve the essential idea of fairness with which contract theory begins. The same idea of fairness, as the inclusion and impartial consideration of real interests, would presumably be the guide as these population principles and policies are embodied in concrete circumstances.

In their basic content the principles and policy I have arrived at represent a view combining elements of both Malthusian and anti-Malthusian interpretations of population growth, of interpretations which affirm that growth poses a moral problem and of those which deny that it does so. With Malthus and his various intellectual descendants I agree that population growth is of moral concern and that population restraint is a moral obligation. All rational agents can suffer evil because of population growth. Neither future generations nor members of present generations need tolerate irresponsible procreation. Nor does justice permit the well-being of living human beings to be sacrificed to facilitate population growth. Even without the prospect of famine, plague or environmental crisis, procreative restraint is demanded both of individuals and generations. The quality of life, defined specifically in terms of material goods, environmental space, social and political liberty, takes priority over an unchecked right to reproduce or the absolute freedom of individual families. In this respect, my conclusions go against the family-planning position and the views of some Marxist and Roman Catholic thinkers.

But we have also seen that these demands are made in the name of justice. Population growth poses a moral problem because it violates the norms of distributive justice; population restraint is a requirement of justice and principles governing population are part of a total theory of justice. In this respect, my conclusions support the objections of

Catholic, Marxist and other radical thinkers to Malthusian population theory and to the views of many of those concerned with the population problem. Malthus and those who follow him have sought to abstract the population issue from the larger moral context in which it belongs. They have neglected the valid interests of whole classes and groups of persons and they have frequently abandoned the impartial and universal perspective, the stance of fairness, which morality demands. The just demand for procreative restraint has been made of lower-income groups in both developed and underdeveloped societies, but it has been made for the sake of narrow and often unjustly privileged interest groups. Moreover, no corresponding effort has been made to address or remedy the social injustices experienced by these groups, injustices which very often play a part in raising their fertility. In some cases, these demands have worsened the conditions of these groups. This is particularly true of policy directed against the family life of the less-advantaged since the family functions as one of the few institutions where individuals are able to resist the incursions of an unjust social order. Here, those who have tried to understand the population problem in terms of its impact on the family have rightly sensed a deeply important issue. Whether or not demands for procreative restraint have actually disadvantaged lower-income groups, however, these demands have tended to generate valid resentment. Many of the critics of Malthus have been sensitive to this resentment and have served as its articulate publicists. Their position, though partly mistaken in denying that high fertility can pose a moral problem, has therefore contained a truth of enormous importance. And this truth has often eluded those who have failed to set the population issue within the confines of a complete discussion of social and economic justice, where it properly belongs.

This combined Malthusian and anti-Malthusian position undergirds my concrete policy proposals and explains the "lexical priority" of programs of justice in any effort to control population growth. One reason for this priority is pragmatic and involves the belief that without just reform, valid resentment may vitiate any effort at sustained population control. But a second and more important reason is moral.

The aim of social policy goes beyond insuring continued human survival or material comfort. In addition to these, social policy should have as its goal the cooperative human society which Rawls calls a "social union of social unions." This society is not constructed overnight. It is the outcome of many generations' cooperation. When earlier generations restrain their population sizes, they help establish the material foundation for this society. But they establish its moral foundation when they structure their institutions to reflect a commitment to the equal dignity of all persons and when they see that these institutions especially respect the interests of those least favored by the circumstances of birth.

BIBLIOGRAPHY

A. *General Discussions of Population and "The Population Problem"*

Allison, Anthony, ed. Population Control. Middlesex, England: Penguin, 1970.

American Assembly. Overcoming World Hunger. Englewood Cliffs, N.J.: Prentice-Hall, 1969.

American Friends Service Committee. Who Shall Live? Man's Control over Birth and Death. New York: Hill and Wang, 1970.

Appleman, Philip. The Silent Explosion. Boston: Beacon Press, 1965.

Barnett, Harold J. "Population Problems -- Myths and Realities," Economic Development and Cultural Change, XIX (July 1971), 545-59.

Bates, Marston. The Prevalence of People. New York: Charles Scribner's Sons, 1955.

_____. A Jungle in the House. New York: Walker & Co., 1970.

Bauman, Karl and J. Richard Udry. "Powerlessness and Regularity of Contraception in an Urban Negro Male Sample: A Research Note," Journal of Marriage and the Family, XXXIV (February 1972), 112-14.

Behrman, S.J., Leslie Corsa and Ronald Freedman, eds. Fertility and Family Planning: A World View. Ann Arbor: University of Michigan Press, 1969.

Berelson, Bernard, et al., eds. Family Planning and Population Programs. Chicago: University of Chicago Press, 1966.

_____. "The Present State of Family Planning Programs," Studies in Family Planning, No. 57 (September 1970), 1-11.

Beshers, James M. Population Processes in Social Systems. New York: The Free Press, 1967.

Blake, Judith. "Demographic Science and the Redirection of Public Policy," in Public Health and Population Change, eds. Mindel C. Sheps and Jeanne C. Ridley. Pittsburgh: University of Pittsburgh Press, 1965, pp. 41-69.

_____. Family Structure in Jamaica. New York: The Free Press, 1961.

243

244

Bogue, Donald J. "The End of the Population Explosion," The
Public Interest, No. 7 (Spring 1967), 11-20.

Brown, Harrison and Edward Hutchings, Jr. eds. Are Our
Descendants Doomed? New York: The Viking Press, 1972.

Brown, L. R. Man, Land and Food. Washington, D.C.: Government Printing Office, 1963.

_____. Seeds of Change. New York: Praeger Publishers,
1970.

Callahan, Daniel, ed. The American Population Debate. Garden
City, N.Y.: Doubleday & Company, 1971.

Cépède, M., F. Houtart and L. Grond. Population and Food.
New York: Sheed and Ward, 1964.

Chamberlin, Neil W. Beyond Malthus. New York: Basic Books,
1970.

Coale, Ansley J. "Should the United States Start a Campaign
for Fewer Births?" Population Index, XXXIV (Oct.-Dec.
1968), 467-74.

Cochrane, W. The World Food Problem. New York: Crowell,
1969.

Coles, Robert. Children of Crisis. Boston: Atlantic-Little
Brown, 1964.

Commission on Population Growth and the American Future.
Population and the American Future. New York: New
American Library, 1972.

Commoner, Barry. The Closing Circle. New York: Alfred A.
Knopf, 1971.

Cook, Robert. Population and Food Supply. New York: United
Nations, 1962.

Cutler, Donald, ed. Updating Life and Death. Boston:
Beacon Press, 1969.

Davis, Wayne. "Overpopulated America," New Republic,
January 10, 1970, 13-15.

Dumont, René. The Hungry Future. New York: Praeger Publishers, 1969.

Dyck, Arthur J. "Religious Factors in the Population Problem,"
in The Religious Situation, ed. Donald Cutler. Boston:
Beacon Press, 1968.

_____. "Technological Parochialism and the Popula-
tion Problem," Christianity and Crisis, XXVII (Dec.
11, 1967), 289-92.

Fagley, R. M. The Population Explosion and Christian Responsibility. New York: Oxford University Press, 1960.

Frederiksen, Harald. "Feedbacks in Economic and Demographic Transition," Science, CLXVI (November 14, 1969), 837-47.

Freedman, Ronald, ed. Population: The Vital Revolution. Garden City, New York: Doubleday & Company, 1964.

Frejka, Tomas. "United States: The Implications of Zero Population Growth," Studies in Family Planning, No. 60 (December 1970), 1-4.

Gardner, Richard N. Population Growth, A World Problem: Statement of U. S. Policy. Washington, D.C.: Government Printing Office, 1963.

Gonnard, René. Histoire des Doctrines de la Population. Paris: Nouvelle Librairie Nationale, 1923.

Goulet, Denis. "Ethical Issues in Development," Review of Social Economy, XXVI (September 1948), 97-117.

_____. "That Third World," in World Development: An Introductory Reader, ed. Hélène Castel. New York: The Macmillan Company, 1971, pp. 1-24.

Greep, Roy O. Human Fertility and Population Problems. Cambridge, Mass.: Schenkman Publishing Company, 1963.

Gregg, Alan. "A Medical Aspect of the Population Problem," Science, CXXI (May 13, 1955), 681-82.

Handler, Philip, ed. Biology and the Future of Man. New York: Oxford University Press, 1970.

Hardin, Garrett. "Multiple Paths to Population Control," Family Planning Perspectives, II (June 1970), 24-26.

_____. "Parenthood: Right or Privilege?" Science, CLXIX (July 31, 1970), 427.

_____, ed. Population, Evolution and Birth Control. 2nd ed. San Francisco: W. H. Freeman & Co., 1969.

_____. "The Tragedy of the Commons," Science, CLXII (December 13, 1968), 1243-48.

Harkavy, O., F. S. Jaffe and S. M. Wishik. "Family Planning and Public Policy: Who Is Misleading Whom?" Science, CLXV (July 25, 1969), 367-73.

Hauser, Philip M., ed. Population and World Politics. Glencoe, Illinois: The Free Press, 1958.

_____, ed. The Population Dilemma, 2nd ed. Englewood Cliffs, N.J.: Prentice-Hall, 1968.

Heer, David M., ed. Readings on Population. Englewood Cliffs, N.J.: Prentice-Hall, 1968.

_____. Society and Population. Englewood Cliffs, N.J.: Prentice-Hall, 1968.

Hertzler, Joyce O. The Crisis in World Population: A Socio-
    logical Examination, with Special Reference to the
    Underdeveloped Areas. Lincoln, Nebraska: University
    of Nebraska Press, 1956.

Hoffman, L. W. and F. Wyatt. "Social Change and Motivations
    for Having Larger Families: Some Theoretical Consider-
    ations," Merrill-Palmer Quarterly, VI (1960), 235-44.

Hopcraft, Arthur. Born to Hunger. Boston: Houghton Mifflin
    Co., 1968.
Hulett, H. R. "Optimum World Population," BioScience, XX
    (February 1, 1970), 160-61.

Institute of Society, Ethics and the Life Sciences. Ethics,
    Population and the American Tradition, A Report to the
    Commission on Population Growth and the American Future.
    Hastings-on-Hudson, N.Y., 1971.

Kay, David and Eugene B. Skolnikoff, eds. World Eco-Crisis:
    International Organizations in Response. Madison:
    University of Wisconsin Press, 1972.

Keyfitz, Nathan. "National Population and the Technological
    Watershed," Journal of Social Issues, XXIII (1967),
    62-78.

Ladejinsky, Wolf. "Ironies of India's Green Revolution,"
    Foreign Affairs, XLVIII (July 1970), 758-68.

Lapham, Robert J. and W. Parker Mauldin. "National Family
    Planning Programs: Review and Evaluation," Studies in
    Family Planning, III (March 1972), 29-52.

Maury, Marian, ed. Birth Rate and Birth Right. New York:
    Macfadden-Bartell Corp., 1963.

Mayer, Jean. "Food and Population: The Wrong Problem?"
    Daedalus, XCIII (Summer 1964), 830-44.

_____. "Toward a Non-Malthusian Population Policy,"
    Columbia Forum, XII (Summer 1969), 5-15.

Meadows, Donella H., Dennis L. Meadows, Jorgen Randers and
    William W. Behrens III. The Limits to Growth. New
    York: Universe Books, 1972.

Mudd, Stuart, ed. The Population Crisis and the Use of World
    Resources. The Hague: Dr. W. Junk Publishers, 1964.

Nam, Charles B., ed. Population and Society. Boston:
    Houghton Mifflin Co., 1968.

National Academy of Sciences. Rapid Population Growth: Con-
    sequences and Policy Implications. Baltimore: Johns
    Hopkins Press, 1971.

Ng, Larry K. Y. and Stuart Mudd, eds. The Population Crisis.
    Bloomington, Indiana: Indiana University Press, 1965.

Norman, Dorothy. _Population and Family Planning Programs:_
A Factbook. New York: Population Council, 1969.

Notestein, Frank W. "Zero Population Growth: What Is It?"
Family Planning Perspectives, II (June 1970), 20-24.

Organski, Katherine F. and A. F. K. Organski. _Population_
and World Power. New York: Alfred A. Knopf, 1961.

Osborn, Fairfield, ed. _Our Crowded Planet: Essays on the_
Pressure of Population. Garden City, N.Y.: Doubleday
& Company, 1962.

Parkes, A. S. "The Right to Reproduce in an Overcrowded
World," in _Biology and Ethics: Symposia of the_
Institute of Biology, No. 18. London: Academic
Press, 1969, pp. 109-16.

Petersen, William. _Population._ 2nd ed. New York: Macmillan
Co., 1962.

Pohlman, Edward. _The Psychology of Birth Planning._ Cambridge, Mass.: Schenkman Publishing Co., 1969.

Population Reference Bureau. "The First National Congress
on Optimum Population and Environment," _Population_
Bulletin, XXVI (November 1970), 2-18.

Potter, Ralph B. "Religion, Politics and Population -- Time
for a Change," _Harvard Medical Alumni Bulletin_, XLI
(Spring 1967), 14-21.

_____. "The Simple Structure of the Population
Debate: The Logic of the Ecology Movement," Docu-
mentary Study Prepared for the Commission on Population
Growth and the American Future. Hastings-on-Hudson,
N.Y.: Institute of Society, Ethics and the Life
Sciences, 1971.

President's Science Advisory Committee, Panel on the World
Food Supply. _The World Food Problem._ 3 vols.
Washington, D.C.: Government Printing Office, 1967.

Quinn, F. X., ed. _Population Ethics._ Washington, D.C.:
Corpus Books, 1968.

Rainwater, Lee. _And the Poor Get Children._ Chicago:
Quadrangle Books, 1960.

_____. _Family Design._ Chicago: Aldine Publishing
Co., 1965.

Revelle, Roger. "International Cooperation in Food and Population," _International Organization_, XXII (1968),
362-91.

_____. "Population," _Science Journal_, II (October
1967), 113-19.

_____. "Population and Food Supplies: The Edge of
the Knife," _Proceedings of the National Academy of_
Sciences, LVI (August 15, 1966), 328-51.

Revelle, Roger. "Testimony," Effects of Population Growth
on Natural Resources and the Environment. Hearing
before the Reuss Subcommittee on Conservation and
Natural Resources. Washington, D.C.: U.S. Government
Printing Office, 1969.

_____, Ashok Khosla and Maris Vinovskis, eds.
The Survival Equation. Boston: Houghton Mifflin Co.,
1971.

Singer, S. Fred, ed. Is There an Optimum Level of Population? New York: McGraw-Hill, 1971.

Sorokin, Pitirim, ed. Contemporary Sociological Theories.
New York: Harper & Brothers, 1928.

Spengler, Joseph J. "Values and Fertility Analysis,"
Demography, III, 109-30.

_____. "The World's Hunger -- Malthus, 1948,"
in Food: Proceedings of the Academy of Political
Science, XXIII (January 1949), 53-72.

Spengler, Joseph J. and Otis Dudley Duncan. Population
Theory and Policy. Glencoe, Illinois: The Free Press,
1956.

Stern, Curt. "Qualitative Aspects of the Population Problem,"
Science, CXXI (May 13, 1955), 683-86.

Taylor, Carl E. "Five Stages in a Practical Population
Policy," International Development Review, X (December
1968), 2-7.

Thompson, Warren S. and David T. Lewis. 5th ed. Population
Problems. New York: McGraw-Hill, 1965.

Tomasson, Richard F. "Why is Swedish Fertility So Low?"
in Sweden: Prototype of Modern Society. New York:
Random House, 1970, pp. 188-93.

United Nations, Department of Economic and Social Affairs.
Proceedings of the World Population Conference, 1965.
4 vols. New York: United Nations, 1966-1967.

United Nations, Department of Social Affairs. Determinants
and Consequences of Population Trends, Population
Studies, No. 17. New York: United Nations, 1953.

United States Congress, House of Representatives, Sub-com-
mittee on Government Operations. Effects of Population
Growth on Natural Resources and the Environment.
Washington, D.C.: Government Printing Office, 1969.

United States Congress, Senate, Committee on Government
Operations, Subcommittee on Foreign Aid Expenditures.
Population Crisis (The Gruening Hearings). 14 vols.
Washington, D.C.: Government Printing Office, 1965-
1968.

Wagar, J. Alan. "Growth versus the Quality of Life,"
    Science, CLXVIII (June 5, 1970), 1179-84.

Wattenberg, Ben. "The Nonsense Explosion," The New Republic,
    April 4 and 11, 1970, 18-23.

Weller, Robert H. "Role Conflict and Fertility," Social and
    Economic Studies (Jamaica), XVIII (September 1969),
    263-72.

Westoff, Leslie A. and Charles F. Westoff. From Now to Zero;
    Fertility, Contraception and Abortion in America.
    Boston: Little, Brown and Co., 1971.

Wharton, Clifton. "The Green Revolution: Cornucopia or
    Pandora's Box," Foreign Affairs, XLVII (April 1969),
    464-76.

Winsborough, Halliman H. "The Social Consequences of High
    Population Density," Law and Contemporary Problems,
    XXX (Winter 1965), 120-26.

Wrong, Dennis. Population and Society. 3rd ed. New York:
    Random House, 1967.

Wyatt, Frederick. "Clinical Notes on the Motives of Repro-
    duction," Journal of Social Issues, XXIII (1967),
    29-56.

Wyon, John B. and John E. Gordon. The Khanna Study: Popula-
    tion Problems in the Rural Punjab. Cambridge, Mass.:
    Harvard University Press, 1971.

B. *Malthusian Population Theory*

Bonar, James. Malthus and His Work. New York: The Mac-
    millan Company, 1924.

Buer, M. C. "The Historical Setting of the Malthusian Con-
    troversy," in London Essays in Economics: In Honour
    of Edwin Cannan, eds. T. E. Gregory and Hugh Dalton.
    London: George Routledge & Sons, 1927, pp. 137-53.

Eversley, David. Social Theories of Fertility and the
    Malthusian Debate. Oxford: The Clarendon Press, 1959.

Flew, Antony. "The Structure of Malthus's Population Theory,"
    Australasian Journal of Philosophy, XXXV (May 1957),
    1-20.

Glass, David V. Introduction to Malthus. New York: John
    Wiley & Sons, 1953.

_____. "Population Controversy in Eighteenth-
    Century England, Part I. The Background," Population
    Studies, VI (July 1962), 69-91.

250

Hutchinson, E. P. The Population Debate: The Development of
Conflicting Theories up to 1900. Boston: Houghton
Mifflin Co., 1967.

Levin, Samuel. Malthus and the Conduct of Life. New York:
Astra Books, 1967.

_____. "Malthus and the Idea of Progress," Journal
of the History of Ideas, XXVII (January-March 1966),
92-108.

Malthus, Thomas Robert. An Essay on the Principle of Popula-
tion, as It Affects the Future Improvement of Society,
With Remarks on the Speculations of Mr. Godwin, M.
Condorcet, and Other Writers (1798) and An Essay on
the Principle of Population, 7th ed. (1872) in Gertrude
Himmelfarb, ed. On Population. New York: The Modern
Library, 1960.

_____. "A Summary View of the Principle of
Population," in Three Essays on Population. New York:
Mentor Books, 1960.

_____. Principles of Political Economy.
London: W. Pickering, 1836.

_____. Thomas Robert Malthus on the Nature
and Progress of Rent, 1815. Baltimore: Johns Hopkins
Press, 1903.

Marshall, T. H. "The Population of England and Wales from
the Industrial Revolution to the World War," Economic
History Review, V (1935), 65-78.

Sowell, Thomas. "Malthus and the Utilitarians," Canadian
Journal of Economics and Political Science, XXVIII
(May 1962), 268-74.

Spengler, Joseph J. "Malthus's Total Population Theory: A
Restatement and Reappraisal," Canadian Journal of
Economics and Political Science, XI (1945), 83-110,
234-64.

_____. "Was Malthus Right?" Southern Economic
Journal, XXXIII (July 1966), 17-34.

C. *The Family-Planning View*

Banks, J. A. and Olive Banks. Feminism and Family Planning
in Victorian England. New York: Schocken Books, 1964.

Calderone, Mary S. "Family Planning" in Foundations for
Christian Family Policy, ed. E. S. Gennie. New York:
National Council of Churches of Christ in U.S.A.,
1961, pp. 191-99.

_____. "What I Do DOES Matter," Harvard Medical
Alumni Bulletin, XLI (Spring 1967), 22-23.

Campbell, A. A. "The Role of Family Planning in the Reduction
    of Poverty," Journal of Marriage and the Family, XXX
    (May 1968), 236-44.

Fryer, Peter. The Birth Controllers. London: Secker &
    Warburg, 1965.

Hankinson, R. K. B. and Nani Doewondon, eds. Family Planning
    and National Development. International Planned
    Parenthood Federation, 1969.

Kennedy, David M. Birth Control in America: The Career of
    Margaret Sanger. New Haven: Yale University Press,
    1970.

Kiser, Clyde V., ed. Research in Family Planning. Prince-
    ton, N.J.: Princeton University Press, 1962.

Lader, Lawrence. The Margaret Sanger Story and the Fight for
    Birth Control. Garden City, N.Y.: Doubleday &
    Company, 1955.

Sanger, Margaret. An Autobiography. London: Victor
    Gollancz, 1939.

_____. Motherhood in Bondage. New York:
    Brentano's, 1928.

_____, ed. The Sixth International Neo-Malthusian
    and Birth Control Conference. Vol. 4: Religious and
    Ethical Aspects of Birth Control. New York: American
    Birth Control League, 1926.

D. Crisis Views

Archer, E. James. "Can We Prepare for Famine?" BioScience,
    XVIII (July 1968), 685-90.

Baade, Fritz. The Race to the Year 2000; Our Future: A
    Paradise or the Suicide of Mankind. Garden City, N.Y.:
    Doubleday & Company, 1962.

Benedict, M. R. "Population and Food: Precarious Balance,"
    Foreign Policy Bulletin, August 1, 1959.

Borgstrom, Georg. The Hungry Planet. New York: Collier
    Books, 1967.

_____. Too Many: A Study of the Earth's Biologi-
    cal Limitations. New York: Macmillan Co., 1969.

Boyd-Orr, John. The White Man's Dilemma: Food and the
    Future. London: Allen and Unwin, 1953.

Brown, Harrison. The Challenge of Man's Future. New York:
    The Viking Press, 1954.

Brown, Lester R. Man, Land and Food: Looking Ahead at World
    Food Needs. Washington, D.C.: Government Printing
    Office, 1963.

Burch, Guy Irving and Elmer Pendell. Population Roads to
    Peace and War. Washington, D.C.: Population Refer-
    ence Bureau, 1945.

Cole, Lamont. "Can the World Be Saved?" BioScience, XVIII
    (July 1968), 679-83.

Darwin, Sir Charles Galton. The Problems of World Population.
    Cambridge: The University Press, 1958.

Ehrlich, Paul. "Coming Famine," Natural History, LXXVII
    (May 1968), 6-8.

_____. "Eco-Catastrophe," Ramparts, VIII (September
    1969), 24-28.

_____. "Overcrowding and Us," National Parks
    Magazine, XLIII (April, 1969), 10-12.

_____. The Population Bomb. New York: Ballantine
    Books, 1968.

Ehrlich, Paul and Anne H. Ehrlich. Population, Resources,
    Environment. San Francisco: W. H. Freeman, 1970.

Ehrlich, Paul and Richard L. Harriman. How to Be a Survivor.
    New York: Ballantine Books, 1971.

Ehrlich, Paul and John P. Holdren. "The People Problem,"
    "Hidden Effects of Overpopulation," and "Deceptive
    Birth Rates," Saturday Review (July 4, August 1 and
    October 3, 1970), pp. 42-43, 52, 58.

_____. "Population and Panaceas:
    A Technological Perspective," BioScience, XIX (Decem-
    ber 1969), 1065-71.

Fisher, Todd. "The Food-Population Dilemma," Population
    Bulletin, XXIV (December 1968), 4-9.

Greep, Roy O. "Prevalence of People," Perspectives in
    Biology and Medicine, XII (Spring 1969), 332-43.

Heilbroner, Robert L. "Ecological Armageddon," New York
    Review of Books, April 23, 1970, 3-9.

Howard, Walter E. "The Population Crisis Is Here Now,"
    BioScience, XIX (September 1969), 779-84.

Huxley, Sir Julian. "The Crowded World," in Sir Julian
    Huxley, Essays of a Humanist. London: Chatto &
    Windus, 1964, pp. 241-50.

_____. The Human Crisis. Seattle: University
    of Washington Press, 1963.

Johnson, Gale D. The Struggle Against World Hunger. New York: Foreign Policy Association, 1967.

Kiefer, David M. "Population -- Technology's Desperate Race with Fertility," Parts I and II, Chemical and Engineering News, XLVI (October 1968), 90-107, 118-44.

Lader, Lawrence. Breeding Ourselves to Death. New York: Ballantine, 1971.

Laffin, John. The Hunger to Come. London: Abelard-Schuman, 1966.

Lenica, Jan and Alfred Sauvy. Population Explosion: Abundance or Famine. New York: Dell Publishing Co., 1962.

Miles, Rufus E. "Three Ways to Solve the Population Crisis," The Futurist, October 1971, 200-04.

Nicol, Hugh. The Limits of Man: An Enquiry into the Scientific Bases of Human Population. London: Constable, 1967.

Osborn, Fairfield. Our Plundered Planet. Boston: Little, Brown and Company, 1948.

Oser, Jacob. Must Men Starve? The Malthusian Controversy. London: Jonathan Cape, 1956.

Paddock, William and Paul Paddock. Famine -- 1975! Boston: Little, Brown and Company, 1967.

_____. Hungry Nations. Boston: Little, Brown and Company, 1964.

Population Reference Bureau. "Spaceship Earth in Peril," Population Bulletin, XXV (March 1969), 1-2.

Price, Daniel O., ed. The 99th Hour: The Population Crisis in the United States. Chapel Hill: University of North Carolina Press, 1967.

Robbins, John. Too Many Asians. New York: Doubleday and Company, 1959.

Sax, Karl. The Population Explosion. New York: Foreign Policy Association, 1956.

_____. Standing Room Only: The World's Exploding Population. Boston: Beacon Press, 1960.

Schimm, Melvin. Population Control, The Imminent World Crisis. New York: Oceana Publications, 1961.

Snow, C. P. The State of Siege. New York: Charles Scribner's Sons, 1969.

Tydings, Joseph. Born to Starve. New York: William Morrow and Company, 1970.

Vogt, William. _People! Challenge to Survival_. New York:
William Sloane Associates, 1960.

_____. _Road to Survival_. New York: William Sloane
Associates, 1948.

E. _Quality-of-Life Views Emphasizing the Physical and
Institutional Environment_

Calhoun, John B. "Population Density and Social Pathology,"
Scientific American, CCVI (February 1962), 139-48.

_____. "Social Welfare as a Variable in Population
Dynamics," _Cold Spring Harbor Symposia on Quantitative
Biology_, XXII (1957), 339-56.

Dasmann, Raymond F. _A Different Kind of Country_. New York:
Macmillan Co., 1968.

Day, Lincoln H. and Alice Taylor Day. _Too Many Americans_.
New York: Delta Press, 1965.

Dubos, René. _Man Adapting_. New Haven: Yale University
Press, 1965.

Greep, Roy O. "The Population Crisis is Here," _The Pharos_,
XXXI (July 1968), 94-100.

_____. "Prevalence of People," _Perspectives in
Biology and Medicine_, XII (Spring 1969), 332-43.

Lucas, F. L. "The Greatest Problem of To-day," in F. L.
Lucas, _The Greatest Problem and Other Essays_. New
York: Macmillan Co., 1961.

Miles, Rufus E., Jr. "Whose Baby Is the Population Problem?"
Population Bulletin, XXVI (1970), 3-14.

Park, Charles F., Jr. _Affluence in Jeopardy_. San Francisco:
W. H. Freeman, Cooper & Co., 1968.

Spengler, Joseph J. "The Aesthetics of Population," _Popula-
tion Bulletin_, XIII (1957), 61-75.

_____. "Population and Freedom," _Population
Review_, VI (July 1962), 74-82.

_____. "Population Pressure, Housing and Habi-
tat," _Law and Contemporary Problems_, XXXII (Spring
1967), 191-208.

Udall, Stewart. _The Quiet Crisis_. New York: Holt, Rinehart
and Winston, 1963.

Viel, Benjamin. "The Social Consequences of Population
Growth," _Population Reference Bureau_, No. 30, October
1969.

F. *Economic Views, Welfare and Optimum Theory*

Arrow, Kenneth. <u>Social Choice and Individual Values</u>. New
     York: John Wiley & Sons, 1963.

Barnett, Harold J. and Chandler Morse. <u>Scarcity and Growth:
     The Economics of Natural Resource Availability</u>. Balti-
     more: Johns Hopkins Press, 1963.

Baumol, William J. <u>Economic Theory and Operations Analysis</u>.
     2nd ed. Englewood Cliffs, N.J.: Prentice-Hall, 1965.

_____. <u>Welfare Economics and the Theory of the
     State</u>. London: G. Bell & Sons, 1965.

Becker, Gary S. "An Economic Analysis of Fertility," in
     <u>Demographic and Economic Change in Developed Countries</u>,
     National Bureau of Economic Research. Princeton, N.J.:
     Princeton University Press, 1960, pp. 209-40.

Belshaw, Horace. <u>Population Growth and Levels of Consumption,
     with Special Reference to Countries in Asia</u>. New
     York: Institute of Pacific Relations, 1956.

Boserup, Ester. <u>The Conditions of Agricultural Growth: The
     Economics of Agrarian Change under Population Pressure</u>.
     London: G. Allen & Unwin, 1965.

Boulding, Kenneth E. "The Economics of the Coming Spaceship
     Earth," in <u>Environmental Quality in a Growing Economy</u>,
     ed. H. Jarrett. Baltimore: Johns Hopkins, 1966, pp.
     3-14.

Cannan, Edwin. <u>A Review of Economic Theory</u>. London: P. S.
     King and Son, 1929.

Chen, Kuan-I. <u>World Population Growth and Living Standards</u>.
     New York: Bookman Associates, 1960.

Clark, Colin. <u>The Conditions of Economic Progress</u>. New York:
     Macmillan Co., 1940.

_____. <u>Population Growth and Land Use</u>. London: St.
     Martin's Press, 1967.

_____. "World Population," <u>Nature</u>, CLXXXI (May 3,
     1958), 1235-36.

Coale, A. J. "The Economic Effects of Fertility Control in
     Underdeveloped Areas," in <u>Human Fertility and Popula-
     tion Problems</u>, ed. Roy O. Greep. Cambridge, Mass.:
     Schenkman Publishing Co., 1963, pp. 143-73.

Coale, A. J. and Edgar Hoover. <u>Population Growth and Economic
     Development in Low Income Countries</u>. Princeton, N.J.:
     Princeton University Press, 1958.

Dalton, Hugh. "The Theory of Population," <u>Economica</u>, VIII
     (1928), 23-50.

Dasgupta, P. S. "On the Concept of Optimum Population," Review of Economic Studies, XXXVI (July 1969), 295-318.

David, Abraham S. and Ching-Ju Huang. "Population Theory and the Concept of Optimum Population," Socio-Economic Planning Sciences, III (1969), 191-217.

Dolan, Edwin. Tanstaafl; The Economic Strategy for Environmental Crisis. New York: Holt, Rinehart & Winston, 1971.

Easterline, Richard A. "Towards a Socioeconomic Theory of Fertility: Survey of Recent Research in Economic Factors in American Fertility," in Fertility and Family Planning, A World View, eds. S. J. Behrman, Leslie Corsa, Jr., and Ronald Freedman. Ann Arbor, Michigan: University of Michigan Press, 1969, pp. 127-56.

Enke, Stephen. "Birth Control for Economic Development," Science, CLXIV (May 16, 1969), 798-802.

_____. "The Economic Aspects of Slowing Population Growth," Economic Journal, LXXVI (March 1966), 44-56.

_____. Economics for Development. Englewood Cliffs, N.J.: Prentice-Hall, 1963.

Ferenczi, Imre. The Synthetic Optimum of Population. Budapest: International Institute of Intellectual Cooperation, 1938.

Frankel, S. H. The Economic Impact on Underdeveloped Societies; Essays in International Investment and Social Change. Cambridge, Mass.: Harvard University Press, 1953.

Gottlieb, Manuel. "The Theory of Optimum Population for a Closed Economy," The Journal of Political Economy, LIII (December 1945), 289-316.

Hagen, E. E. "Population and Economic Growth," American Economic Review, XLIX (June 1959), 310-27.

Hicks, John R. "Foundations of Welfare Economics," Economic Journal, XLIX (1939), 696-712.

Hirschman, Albert O. The Strategy of Economic Development. New Haven: Yale University Press, 1958.

Jones, Gavin. The Economic Effect of Declining Fertility in Less Developed Countries. New York: Population Council, 1969.

Kaldor, Nicolas. "Welfare Propositions of Economics and Interpersonal Comparisons of Utility," Economic Journal, XLIX (September 1939), 549-52.

Kuznets, Simon. Modern Economic Growth. New Haven: Yale University Press, 1966.

Kuznets, Simon. "Population and Economic Growth," Proceedings of the American Philosophical Society, CXI (June 22, 1967), 170-93.

Leibenstein, Harvey. "The Consequences of Population Growth -- The Impact of Non-Traditional Inputs," Manuscript in the possession of this writer.

_____. Economic Backwardness and Economic Growth. New York: John Wiley & Sons, 1957.

_____. "Entrepreneurship and Development," American Economic Review, LVIII (May 1968), 72-83.

_____. "Long-run Welfare Criteria," The Public Economy of Urban Communities, ed. Julius Margolis. Washington, D.C.: Resources for the Future, Inc., 1965, pp. 39-51.

_____. "Notes on Welfare Economics and the Theory of Democracy," Economical Journal, LXXII (June 1962), 299-319.

_____. "Pitfalls in Benefit-Cost Analysis of Birth Prevention," Population Studies, XXIII (July 1969), 161-70.

_____. "Population Growth and Development of Underdeveloped Countries," Harvard Medical Alumni Bulletin, XLI (Spring 1967), 29-33.

_____. A Theory of Economic-Demographic Development. Princeton, N.J.: Princeton University Press, 1954.

Little, I. M. D. A Critique of Welfare Economics. 2nd ed. Oxford: The Clarendon Press, 1957.

Meade, J. E. "Population Explosion, The Standard of Living and Social Conflict," Economic Journal, LXXVII (June 1967), 235-55.

_____. Trade and Welfare. London: Oxford University Press, 1955.

Mill, John Stuart. Principles of Political Economy, ed. W. J. Ashley. New edition. London: Longmans, Green and Co., 1923.

Mishan, Ezra. The Costs of Economic Growth. New York: Frederick A. Praeger, 1967.

Myrdal, Gunner. Asian Drama. 3 vols. New York: Pantheon Books, 1968.

_____. The Political Element in the Development of Economic Theory. London: Routledge & Kegan Paul, 1953.

Ohlin, Goran. Population Control and Economic Development. Paris: Development Centre of the Organization for Economic Cooperation and Development, 1967.

Penrose, E. F. Population Theories and Their Application. Stanford, California: Stanford University Food Research Institute, 1934.

Pigou, Arthur C. Economics of Welfare, 4th ed. London: Macmillan and Co., 1950.

Raulet, Harry M. "Family Planning and Population Control in Developing Countries," Demography, VII (May 1970), 211-34.

Reder, Melvin. Studies in the Theory of Welfare Economics. New York: Columbia University Press, 1947.

Robbins, Lionel. "The Optimum Theory of Population," in London Essays in Economics: In Honour of Edwin Cannan, eds. T. E. Gregory and Hugh Dalton. London: Routledge & Sons, 1927, pp. 103-34.

Robinson, Warren C. "Population Growth and Economic Welfare," Reports on Population/Family Planning, No. 6, February 1971.

Schultz, T. Paul. "An Economic Model of Family Planning and Fertility," Journal of Political Economy, LXXVII (March-April 1969), 153-80.

Sidgwick, Henry. The Principles of Political Economy. London: Macmillan and Co., 1883.

Simon, Julian L. "The Effect of Income on Fertility," Population Studies, XXIII (November 1969), 327-41.

_____. "The Per-Capita-Income Criterion and Natality Policies in Poor Countries," Demography, VII (August 1970), 369-78.

Spengler, Joseph J. "Aspects of the Economics of Population Growth," Southern Economic Journal, XIV (1947-48), 123-47, 233-65.

_____. "Economic Factors in the Development of Densely Populated Areas," Proceedings of the American Philosophical Society, XCV (February 1951), 20-53.

_____. "The Economist and the Population Question," American Economic Review, LVI (March 1966), 1-24.

_____. "Measures of Population Maladjustment," in Proceedings of the XIVth International Conference of Sociology, Rome (1951), pp. 336-64.

_____. "Optimum Population Theory," International Encyclopedia of the Social Sciences. New York: Macmillan and The Free Press, 1968, vol. XII, pp. 358-62.

Spengler, Joseph J. "Pareto on Population," Quarterly Journal of Economics, LVIII-LIX (1943-44, 1944-45), 571-601, 107-33.

_____. "Population and Per Capita Income," Annals of the American Academy of Political and Social Science, CCXXXVII (January 1945), 182-92.

_____. "Population and World Economic Development," Science, CXXXI (May 20, 1960), 1497-1502.

_____. "Welfare Economics and the Problem of Overpopulation," Scientia, LXXXIX (1954), 1-21.

Votey, Harold L., Jr. "The Optimum Population and Growth: A New Look. A Modification to Include a Preference for Children in the Welfare Function," Journal of Economic Theory, I (October 1969), 273-90.

Wolfe, A. B. "On the Criterion of Optimum Population," American Journal of Sociology, XXXIX (1934), 585-99.

_____. "The Theory of Optimum Population," Annals of the American Academy of Political and Social Science, CLXXXVIII (1936), 243-49.

G. *Roman Catholic Views of Population Growth*

Abbot, Walter. The Documents of Vatican II. New York: Guild Press, 1966.

Anciaux, Paul. "Ethical Aspects of Demographic Policy," World Justice, V (1963-1964), 5-20.

Bailey, Derrick S. The Man-Woman Relation in Christian Thought. London: Longmans, 1959.

Baker, Jeffrey J. W. "Science, Birth Control, and the Roman Church," BioScience, XX (February 1, 1970), 143-51.

Barrett, Donald N., ed. The Problem of Population. 3 vols. Notre Dame, Ind.: University of Notre Dame Press, 1964, 1965.

Birmingham, William. What Modern Catholics Think About Birth Control. New York: The New American Library, 1964.

Blake, Judith. "The Americanization of Catholic Reproductive Ideals," Population Studies, XX (July 1966), 27-43.

Burch, Thomas K. "Facts and Fallacies About World Population Growth," Catholic World, CXC (March 1960), 345-51.

Callahan, Daniel, ed. The Catholic Case for Contraception. London: Macmillan Co., 1969.

Calvez, Jean-Yves and Jacques Perrin. The Church and Social Justice. Chicago: Henry Regnery Co., 1961.

260

Camp, Richard. The Papal Ideology of Social Reform. Leiden:
E. J. Brill, 1969.

Chakerian, Charles G. and Louis Dupré. Two Theological Views
of Population Control. Population Reference Bureau,
Selection No. 21, 1968.

Cole, William G. Sex in Christianity and Psychoanalysis.
New York: Oxford University Press, 1959.

Cook, Robert C. "The Vatican and the Population Crisis,"
Population Bulletin, XXI (February 1965), 1-3.

Drinkwater, F. H. Birth Control and Natural Law. Baltimore:
Helicon Press, 1965.

Dunne, George H., S.J. "World Peace and the Population
Crisis," Population Bulletin, XXI (February 1965),
12-15.

Ederer, Rupert J. "Overpopulation: A Study in Relativity,"
World Justice, IX (1967-1968), 48-62.

Fogarty, Michael P. "Is Starvation Inevitable?" The Common-
weal, LXII (June 3, 1955), 223-26.

Gibbons, William. "The Catholic Value System in Relation to
Human Fertility," in Studies in Population, ed. G. F.
Mair. Princeton, N.J.: Princeton University Press,
1949, pp. 107-34.

Griese, O. The Morality of Periodic Continence. Washington:
The Catholic University of America Press, 1942.

Horne, Herbert H., Jr. "World Population Problems and the
Catholic Point of View," International Journal of
Fertility, VIII (January-March 1963), 415-18.

Janssens, Louis. "Catholics and Non-Catholics: Their Collaboration in Family Planning," World Justice, V
(1963-1964), 21-40.

_____. Mariage et Fécondité; De "Casti Connubii"
a "Gaudium et Spes". Gembloux: Editions J. Duculot,
1967.

Pope John XXIII. Encyclical Letter Mater et Magistra.
Providence, Rhode Island: Providence Visitors Society,
1961.

Kelly, George. Overpopulation: A Catholic View. Glen Rock,
N.J.: Paulist Press, 1960.

Kelly, Gerald, S.J. "The Common Good and the Socio-Economic
Order," Proceedings of the Catholic Theological
Society of America, VII (1952), 83-110.

_____. Medico-Moral Problems. St. Louis:
Catholic Hospital Association of the United States and
Canada, 1959.

Kelly, Gerald, S.J. "Periodic Continence," Theological Studies, XXIII (December 1962), 590-624.

deLestapis, Stanislas. Family Planning and Modern Problems. New York: Herder and Herder, 1961.

McCormack, Arthur, ed. Christian Responsibility and World Poverty. London: Burns and Oates, 1963.

_____. "The Church and the Population Explosion," in War, Poverty, Freedom; Concilium 15. Glen Rock, N.J.: Paulist Press, 1966, pp. 145-60.

_____. Pius XII and Overpopulation. Liverpool: Catholic Social Guild, 1960.

_____. The Population Problem. New York: Crowell, 1970.

_____. Poverty and the Christian; The Catholic Doctrine of International Responsibility. Hincley, Leics: Samuel Walker, 1963.

_____. World Poverty and the Christian. New York: Hawthorn Books, 1963.

McKernan, C. S. P. "Population in a Changing World," The Catholic World, CXC (February 1960), 286-93.

Marshall, John. Catholics, Marriage and Contraception. Baltimore: Helicon Press, 1965.

Moran, William E., Jr. Population Growth -- Threat to Peace? New York: P. J. Kennedy & Sons, 1965.

Nevett, Albert. Population: Explosion or Control? A Study With Special Reference to India. Notre Dame, Ind.: Fides Publishers, 1964.

Noonan, John T. Contraception: A History of Its Treatment by the Catholic Theologians and Canonists. Cambridge, Mass.: Harvard University Press, 1965.

Nugent, Vincent J., ed. Christian Marriage: Some Contemporary Problems. Jamaica, New York: St. John's University Press, 1961.

O'Brien, John Anthony. Family Planning in an Exploding Population. New York: Hawthorne Books, 1968.

Pope Paul VI. "Address to the General Assembly of the United Nations, 1965," Acta Apostolicae Sedis, The Fourth Session: The Debates and Decrees of Vatican Council II, September 14 to December 8, 1965, ed. Xavier Rynne. New York: Farrar, Straus and Giroux, 1966.

_____. Encyclical Letter Populorum Progressio, "On the Development of Peoples." New York: Paulist Press, 1967.

Pope Paul VI. Statement on Population, November 17, 1970. *New York Times*, November 18, 1970.

Pope Pius XII. Encyclical Letter *Exsul Familia*. 1952. Staten Island, N.Y.: St. Charles Seminary, 1962.

_____. *Major Addresses of Pius XII*, ed. V. A. Yzermans, 2 vols. St. Paul, Minnesota: North Central Publishing Co., 1961.

Population Reference Bureau. "The Vatican and the Population Crisis," *Population Bulletin*, XXI (February 1964), 1-15.

Pyle, Leo, ed. *Pope and Pill: More Documentation on the Birth Regulation Debate*. Baltimore: Helicon Press, 1969.

Ransil, Bernard. *Abortion*. New York: Paulist Press, 1969.

Rock, John. *The Time Has Come*. New York: Alfred A. Knopf, 1963.

Ryan, John A. "Population," *The Catholic Encyclopedia*. New York: Encyclopedia Press, 1907-1912, XII, 276-78.

St. John-Stevas, Norman. *The Agonising Choice; Birth Control, Religion and the Law*. Bloomington, Ind.: Indiana University Press, 1971.

_____. *Birth Control and Public Policy*. Santa Barbara, Cal.: Center for the Study of Democratic Institutions, 1961.

_____. "A Roman Catholic View of Population Control," *Law and Contemporary Problems*, XXV (Summer 1960), 445-69.

Schall, J. V. "Christian Political Approaches to Population Problems," *World Justice*, VIII (1966-1967), 301-23.

Shannon, William H. *The Lively Debate; Response to Humanae Vitae*. New York: Sheed & Ward, 1970.

Snoek, C. Jaime. "The Third World, Revolution and Christianity," *War, Poverty, Freedom, Concilium 15*. Glen Rock, N.J.: Paulist Press, 1966, pp. 31-48.

Sulloway, Alvah W. *Birth Control and Catholic Doctrine*. Boston: Beacon Press, 1959.

Thomas, John L., S.J. *Catholic Viewpoint on Marriage and the Family*. Garden City, N.Y.: Doubleday & Company, 1958.

Valsecchi, Ambrogio. *Controversy: The Birth Control Debate, 1958-68*. Washington, D.C.: Corpus Books, 1968.

Von Hildebrand, Dietrich. *The Encyclical Humanae Vitae; A Sign of Contradiction*. Chicago: Franciscan Herald Press, 1969.

Von Hildebrand, Dietrich. "Marriage and Overpopulation," Thought, XXXVI (1961), 81-100.

Zeegers, G. H. L. "The Meaning of the Population Problem of the World," Cross Currents, VIII (1958), 19-23.

Zimmerman, Anthony F. "Birth Control in Japan," World Justice, V (September 1963), 41-55.

_____. Catholic Viewpoint on Overpopulation. Garden City, N.Y.: Hanover House, 1961.

_____. "Morality and the Problem of Overpopulation," Proceedings of the Catholic Theological Society of America, 1959.

_____. Overpopulation: A Study of Papal Teaching on the Problem with Special Reference to Japan. Washington, D.C.: Catholic University of America Press, 1957.

H. *Marxist and Radical Views of Population Growth*

Aird, John S. "Population Policy in Mainland China," Population Studies, XVI (July 1962), 38-57.

Arab-Ogly, E. "Russia: Facing the Facts," translated from Literaturnaya Gazeta in Atlas, XII (September 1966), 24-26.

Barber, William J. A History of Economic Thought. Hamondsworth, England: Penguin, 1967.

Bebel, August. Die Frau und der Sozialismus. Stuttgart: J. H. W. Dietz Nachfolger, 1904.

Beshers, James M. Population Processes in Social Systems. New York: The Free Press of Glencoe, 1967.

Brackett, James W. "The Evolution of Marxist Theories of Population: Marxism Recognizes the Population Problem," Demography, V (1968), 158-73.

Brand, Salvador O. "La Falacia del Malthusianismo," Economía Salvadoreña, XI (January-December 1962), 37-44.

Consuegra, Jose. "El Pensamiento Económico y el Crecimiento de la Populacion," Economía Salvadorena, XVI (July-December 1967), 55-76.

Cook, Robert C. "Soviet Population Theory from Marx to Kosygin: A Demographic Turning Point?" Population Bulletin, XXIII (October 1967), 85-115.

Coontz, Sidney H. Population Theories and the Economic Interpretation. London: Routledge & Kegan Paul, 1957.

264

Daly, Herman E. "A Marxian-Malthusian View of Poverty and Development," Population Studies, XXV (March 1971), 25-37.

_____. "Toward a New Economics: Questioning Growth," Yale Alumni Magazine, XXXIII (May 1970), 47-52.

David, Henry P. Family Planning and Abortion in the Socialist Countries of Central and Eastern Europe. New York: Population Council, 1972.

Dumas, L. Le Socialisme et le principe de la population. Paris, 1908.

Economist. "Malthusians & Marxists," CLXXXIII (June 1, 1957), 764-66.

Engels, Frederick. Dialectics of Nature. New York: International Publishers, 1940.

_____. The Origins of the Family, Private Property, and the State. New York: International Publishers, 1942.

Faundes, Anibal and Tapani Luukkainen. "Health and Family Planning Services in the Chinese People's Republic," Studies in Family Planning, III (July 1972), 1965-76.

Fetscher, Irving. "Marx's Concretization of the Concept of Freedom," in Socialist Humanism; An International Symposium, ed. Erich Fromm. Anchor Books edition. New York: Doubleday & Company, 1965, pp. 260-72.

Freville, J. L'Epouvantail malthusien. Paris: Editions Sociales, 1956.

Fuchs, Sandor. "Population, Pollution and Natural Resources; Ecology Movement Exposed," Progressive Labor Party, September 1970, 50-63.

Geiger, H. Kent. The Family in Soviet Russia. Cambridge, Mass.: Harvard University Press, 1968.

Guzevaty, Y. "Population Problems in Developing Countries," International Affairs, No. 9 (September 1966), 52-58.

Heer, David M. "Abortion, Contraception, and Population Policy in the Soviet Union," Soviet Studies, XVII (July 1965), 76-83.

Heer, David M. and Judith Bryden. "Family Allowances and Population Policy in the U.S.S.R.," Journal of Marriage and the Family, XXVIII (November 1966), 514-19.

Hyde, Gordon. "Abortion and the Birth Rate in the U.S.S.R.," Journal of Biosocial Science, II (July 1970), 283-92.

Kamenka, Eugene. Marxism and Ethics. London: Macmillan Co., 1969.

Kamenka, Eugene. "The Primitive Ethic of Karl Marx," The
    Australasian Journal of Philosophy, XXXV (August
    1957), 76-96.

Kautsky, Karl. Der Einfluss der Volksmehrung auf den Fort-
    schritt der Gesellschaft. Vienna: Bloch and Hasbach,
    1880.

Khalatbari, Parvis. Übervölkerung in den Entwicklungslän-
    dern; Ein Beitrag zur Marxistischen Bevölkerungs-
    theorie. Berlin: Akademie-Verlag, 1968.

Lal, Amrit. "China's Population Policy," China Report, I
    (August 1965), 25-28.

Lenin, V. I. Collected Works, Vol. XIX. Moscow: Foreign
    Languages Publishing House, 1963.

Levin, Samuel. "Marx vs. Malthus," Papers of the Michigan
    Academy of Arts and Letters, XXII (1937), 243-58.

Lux, André. "Evolution et Contradictions dans la Pensée de
    Malthus," Population (Paris), XXIII (November-December
    1968), 1091-1106.

Marcuse, Herbert. Soviet Marxism. Vintage edition. New
    York: Random House, 1961.

Marx, Karl. Capital, Vol. I. London: George Allen &
    Unwin, 1928.

_____. Critique of the Gotha Program. New York: Inter-
    national Publishers, 1938.

_____. Letters to Dr. Kugelman. New York: Inter-
    national Publishers, 1934.

Marx, Karl and Friedrich Engels. Werke. 1 Aufl. 41 vols.
    Berlin: Dietz Verlag, 1956-71.

Mattelart, Armand. Geopolitique du contrôle des naissances.
    Paris: Editions Universitaires, 1967.

Mauldin, W. Parker. "Fertility Control in Communist
    Countries: Policy and Practice," in Population Trends
    in Eastern Europe, the USSR, and Mainland China. New
    York: Milbank, Memorial Fund, 1960, pp. 179-223.

Mayer, Jean and H. Andre Van H. Mayer. "Birth Control and
    Population Policy in the Socialist World," Harvard
    Medical Alumni Bulletin, XLI (Spring 1967), 2-7.

Meek, Ronald L., ed. Marx and Engels on Malthus. London:
    Lawrence and Wishart, 1953.

Mertens, Clément, S.J. "Le Marxisme et les problèmes de
    population," Vie Economique et Sociale (Antwerp),
    XXXIII (May 1962), 201-17.

266

Murray, Robert F. "The Ethical and Moral Values of Black
    Americans and Population Policy," Documentary Study
    prepared for the Commission on Population Growth and
    the American Future. Hastings-on-Hudson, N.Y.:
    Institute of Society, Ethics and the Life Sciences,
    1971.

Neuhaus, Richard. In Defense of People; Ecology and the
    Seduction of Radicalism. New York: Macmillan Co.,
    1971.

Orleans, Leo. A. "Evidence from Chinese Medical Journals on
    Current Population Policy," The China Quarterly, XL
    (October-December 1969), 137-46.

Pei-Gang, Tchang, Mao Gang and Hou Tchiang-Tse. "La Loi
    de population en régime socialiste et le problème de
    la population en Chine," Etudes Economiques: Cahiers
    Mensuels d'Economie Socialiste (Paris), Nos. 114-115
    (1959), 18-69.

Petersen, William. "The Malthus-Godwin Debate, Then and
    Now," Demography, VIII (February 1971), 13-26.

_____. The Politics of Population. Garden City,
    N.Y.: Doubleday and Company, 1964.

Piotrow, Phyllis T., ed. Population and Family Planning in
    the People's Republic of China. The Victor-Borgstrom
    Fund and the Population Crisis Committee, 1970.

Plotnick, Alan R. "Malthus, Marx and Mao," Challenge, XII
    (June 1964), 9-12.

Podyachikh, Pyotr. "Population and Progress," Current
    Digest of the Soviet Press, XVIII (March 23, 1966),
    10-11.

Popov, A. "The Present Day Malthusians -- Apologists for
    Colonialism and a 'Positions of Strength' Policy,"
    International Affairs, XXXI (October 1956), 56-66.

Population Council. "Governmental Policy Statements on Popu-
    lation: An Inventory," Reports on Population/Family
    Planning, No. 3 (February 1970), 1-20.

Progressive Labor Party. "ZPG: A Fascist Movement!"
    pamphlet distributed by the Progressive Labor Party,
    1970. No copyright.

Quessel, Don Ludwig, "Karl Kautsky als Bevölkerungstheoreti-
    ker," Die Neue Zeit, XXIX (January 20, 1911), 551-65.

Ridgeway, James. The Politics of Ecology. New York: E. P.
    Dutton and Co., 1970.

Sauvy, Alfred. Fertility and Survival: Population Problems
    from Malthus to Mao-Tse-Tung. New York: Collier
    Books, 1963.

Sauvy, Alfred. General Theory of Population. New York: Basic Books, 1969.

_____. Malthus et les deux Marx: le problème de la faim et de la guerre dans le monde. Paris: Editions Denoel, 1963.

_____. "Les Marxistes et le malthusianisme," Cahiers Internationaux de Sociologie (Paris), XLI (1966), 1-14.

Smith, Kenneth. The Malthusian Controversy. London: Routledge & Kegan Paul, 1951.

Solo, Robert A. Economic Organizations and Social Systems. New York: Bobbs-Merril, 1967.

Somerville, John. The Philosophy of Marxism; An Exposition. New York: Random House, 1967.

Stycos, J. M. "Opinions of Latin American Intellectuals on Population Problems and Birth Control," Annals of the American Academy of Political And Social Science, CCCLX (July 1965), 11-26.

_____. "Some Directions for Research on Fertility Control," The Milbank Memorial Fund Quarterly, XXXVI (April 1958), 126-48.

_____. "Some Minority Opinions on Birth Control: Blacks, Women's Liberation, and the New Left," Documentary Study prepared for the Commission on Population Growth and the American Future. Hastings-on-Hudson, N.Y.: Institute of Society, Ethics and the Life Sciences, 1971.

Szabady, Egon, ed. World Views of Population Problems. Budapest: Akadémiai Kiadó, 1968.

Tucker, Robert. The Marxian Revolutionary Idea. New York: W. W. Norton, 1969.

Urlanis, Boris, et al. "Is There a Population Problem? Views Differ," Current Digest of the Soviet Press, XVII (January 19, 1966), 11-15.

Weissman, Steve. "Why the Population Bomb is a Rockefeller Baby," Ramparts, VIII (May 1970), 42-47.

Wertheim, W. F. "Recent Trends in China's Population Policy," Science and Society, XXX (Spring 1966), 129-35.

Yette, Samuel F. The Choice: The Issue of Black Survival in America. New York: G. P. Putnam's Sons, 1971.

I. *Contract Theory and Distributive Justice*

Adams, Robert M. "Must God Create the Best?" Philosophical Review, LXXXI (July 1972), 317-32.

Aristotle. Ethica Nicomachea and Politica in The Basic Works of Aristotle, ed. Richard McKeon. New York: Random House, 1941.

Baier, Kurt. The Moral Point of View. Abridged edition. New York: Random House, 1965.

Barry, Brian. "On Social Justice," The Oxford Review, No. 5 (Trinity Term, 1967), 29-52.

Bedau, Hugo A., ed. Justice and Equality. Englewood Cliffs, N.J.: Prentice-Hall, 1971.

Berlin, Sir Isaiah. "Two Concepts of Liberty," in Political Philosophy. Oxford: The University Press, 1967, pp. 141-52.

Bird, Otto. The Idea of Justice. New York: Frederick A. Praeger, 1967.

Brandt, Richard B., ed. Social Justice. Englewood Cliffs, N.J.: Prentice-Hall, 1962.

_____, ed. Value and Obligation. New York: Harcourt Brace and World, 1961.

Brock, Dan. "Contractualism, Utilitarianism and Social Inequalities," Social Theory and Practice, I (Spring 1971), 33-43.

Buchanan, James and Gordon Tullock, The Calculus of Consent. Ann Arbor: University of Michigan Press, 1962.

Callahan, Daniel. "What Obligations Do We Have to Future Generations," The American Ecclesiastical Review, CLXIV (April 1971), 265-80.

Care, Norman. "Contractualism and Moral Criticism," The Review of Metaphysics, XXIII (1969), 85-101.

Clauser, K. Danner. "The Sanctity of Life: Analysis of a Concept," Manuscript in possession of this writer.

Cunningham, R. L. "Justice: Efficiency or Fairness," The Personalist, LII (1971), 253-81.

Del Vecchio, Giorgo. Justice; An Historical and Philosophical Essay. Edinburgh: The University Press, 1952.

Dyck, Arthur. "Referent-Models of Loving: A Philosophical and Theological Analysis of Love in Ethical Theory and Moral Practice," Harvard Theological Review LXI (October 1968), 525-45.

Emmett, Dorothy. "Justice," Proceedings of the Aristotelian Society, supp. vol. XLIII (1969), pp. 123-40.

Firth, Roderick. "Ethical Absolutism and the Ideal Observer," Philosophy and Phenomenological Research, XII (March 1952), 317-45.

Foot, Phillipa. Theories of Ethics. Oxford: The University Press, 1967.

Frankel, Charles. "Justice and Rationality," in Philosophy, Science and Method, eds. Sidney Morgenbesser, Patrick Suppes, and Morton White. New York: St. Martin's Press, 1969, pp. 400-14.

Frankena, William. Ethics. Englewood Cliffs, N.J.: Prentice-Hall, 1963.

Friedrich, Carl J. and John W. Chapman, eds. Justice, Nomos VI. New York: Atherton Press, 1963.

Gert, Bernard. "Coercion and Freedom," in Coercion, Nomos XIV, eds. J. Roland Pennock and John W. Chapman. Chicago-New York: Aldine-Atherton, 1972, pp. 30-48.

_____. The Moral Rules. New York: Harper & Row, 1970.

Gewirth, Alan. "The Justification of Egalitarian Justice," American Philosophical Quarterly, VIII (October 1971), 331-41.

Golding, Martin P. "Ethical Issues in Biological Engineering," UCLA Law Review, XV (February 1968), 457-63.

_____. "What Is Our Obligation to Future Generations?" Working Paper of the Institute of Society, Ethics and the Life Sciences, Hastings-on-Hudson, N.Y., 1971.

Gough, J. W. The Social Contract. 2nd ed. Oxford: The Clarendon Press, 1965.

Grice, G. B. The Grounds of Moral Judgment. Cambridge, Eng.: The University Press, 1967.

Hardie, W. F. R. "The Final Good in Aristotle's Ethics," Philosophy, XL (1965), 277-95.

Hare, R. M. Freedom and Reason. New York: Oxford University Press, 1965.

_____. The Language of Morals. New York: Oxford University Press, 1964.

Harsanyi, John C. "Cardinal Utility in Welfare Economics and in the Theory of Risk Taking," Journal of Political Economy, LXI (1953), 434-35.

_____. "Cardinal Welfare, Individualistic Ethics, and Interpersonal Comparisons of Utility," Journal of Political Economy, LXIII (August 1955), 309-21.

_____. "Ethics in Terms of Hypothetical Imperatives," Mind, LXVII (July 1958), 305-16.

Hempel, Carl J. "Rational Action," Proceedings of the American Philosophical Association, 1961-62, pp. 5-23.

270

Hobbes, Thomas. Leviathan in The English Philosophers from Bacon to Mill, ed. Edwin A. Burtt. New York: The Modern Library, 1939.

von Humboldt, Wilhelm. The Limits of State Action, ed. J. W. Burrow. Cambridge, Eng.: The University Press, 1969.

Hume, David. "Of the Original Contract," in Hume's Moral and Political Philosophy, ed. Henry D. Aiken. New York: Hafner Publishing Co., 1948.

_____. A Treatise of Human Nature, eds. T. H. Green and T. H. Grose. 2 vols. London: Longmans, Green and Co., 1886.

Kant, Immanuel. Critique of Practical Reason. 1788. Library of Liberal Arts edition. Indianapolis: Bobbs-Merrill, 1959.

_____. Foundations of the Metaphysics of Morals. 1785. Library of Liberal Arts edition. Indianapolis: Bobbs-Merrill, 1959.

_____. Kant's Political Writings, ed. Hans Reiss, Cambridge, Eng.: The University Press, 1970.

_____. Lectures on Ethics. 1785-90. Torchbook edition. New York: Harper & Row, 1963.

_____. The Metaphysical Elements of Justice. 1797. Library of Liberal Arts edition. Indianapolis: Bobbs-Merrill, 1965.

_____. Perpetual Peace. 1795. Library of Liberal Arts Edition. Indianapolis: Bobbs-Merrill, 1957.

Kohlberg, Lawrence. "The Child as Moral Philosopher," Psychology Today, II (September 1968), 25-30.

_____. "The Development of Children's Orientation to a Moral Order: 1, Sequence in the Development of Moral Thought," Vita Humana, VI (1963), 11-33.

Lessnoff, Michael. "John Rawls' Theory of Justice," Political Studies, XIX (1971), 65-80.

Locke, John. An Essay Concerning the True Original Extent and End of Government (Second Treatise of Government) in The English Philosophers from Bacon to Mill, ed. Edwin Burtt. New York: The Modern Library, 1939.

Lyons, David. The Forms and Limits of Utilitarianism. Oxford: The Clarendon Press, 1965.

Lyons, David, Michael Teitelman and John Rawls, "Symposium: A Theory of Justice by John Rawls," The Journal of Philosophy, LXIX (October 5, 1972), 535-57.

Mill, John Stuart. Utilitarianism and On Liberty in The English Philosophers from Bacon to Mill, ed. Edwin A. Burtt. New York: The Modern Library, 1939.

Moore, G. E. Principia Ethica. Cambridge, Eng.: The
     University Press, 1903.

Nozick, Robert. "Coercion," in Philosophy, Science and
     Method, eds. Sidney Morgenbesser, Patrick Suppes, and
     Morton White. New York: St. Martin's Press, 1969,
     pp. 440-72.

Olafson, Frederick A., ed. Justice and Social Policy.
     Englewood Cliffs, N.J.: Prentice-Hall, 1961.

Olson, Mancur. The Logic of Collective Action: Public Goods
     and the Theory of Groups. Cambridge, Mass.: Harvard
     University Press, 1965, 1968.

Pennock, J. Roland and John W. Chapman, eds. Equality.
     Nomos 9. New York: Atherton Press, 1967.

Perelman, Ch. The Idea of Justice and the Problem of Argu-
     ment. London: Routledge & Kegan Paul, 1963.

_____. Justice. New York: Random House, 1967.

Piaget, Jean. The Moral Judgment of the Child. London:
     Kegan Paul, Trench, Trubner, 1932.

Rawls, John. Chapters on Justice, 1964-1965. Unpublished
     MS in the possession of this writer used in Philosophy
     171, Harvard University, Fall Semester, 1966.

_____. "Constitutional Liberty and the Concept of
     Justice," in Justice. Nomos Vol. 6, eds. Carl J.
     Friedrich and John Chapman. New York: Atherton Press,
     1963, pp. 98-125.

_____. "Distributive Justice," in Philosophy, Politics,
     and Society, eds. Peter Laslett and W. G. Runciman.
     3rd series. Oxford: Basil Blackwell, 1969, pp. 58-82.

_____. "Distributive Justice: Some Addenda," Natural
     Law Forum, XIII (1968), 51-71.

_____. "Justice as Fairness," Journal of Philosophy,
     LIV (1957), 653-62.

_____. "Justice as Fairness," Philosophical Review,
     LXVII (1958), 164-94.

_____. Justice as Fairness. 1967. Unpublished MS in
     the possession of this writer used in Philosophy 171,
     Harvard University, Fall Semester, 1967.

_____. Justice as Fairness. 1969. Unpublished MS in
     the possession of this writer used in Philosophy 171,
     Harvard University, Fall Semester, 1969.

_____. "The Justification of Civil Disobedience,"
     in Civil Disobedience: Theory and Practice, ed. Hugo
     A. Bedau. New York: Pegasus, 1969, pp. 240-55.

272

Rawls, John. "Legal Obligation and the Duty of Fair Play," in Law and Philosophy, ed. Sidney Hook. New York: New York University Press, 1964, pp. 3-18.

_____. "Outline of a Decision Procedure for Ethics," Philosophical Review, LX (1951), 177-97.

_____. "The Sense of Justice," Philosophical Review, LXII (1963), 281-305.

_____. A Theory of Justice. Cambridge, Mass.: The Belknap Press of Harvard University Press, 1971.

_____. "Two Concepts of Rules," Philosophical Review, LXIV (1955), 3-32.

Rescher, Nicholas. Distributive Justice; A Constructive Critique of Utilitarian Theory. Indianapolis: Bobbs-Merrill Company, 1966.

_____. Introduction to Value Theory. Englewood Cliffs, N.J.: Prentice-Hall, 1969.

Reynolds, Charles. "A Proposal for Understanding the Place of Reason in Christian Ethics," Journal of Religion, L (1970), 155-68.

Richards, David A. J. A Theory of Reasons for Action. Oxford: The Clarendon Press, 1971.

Rousseau, Jean Jacques. The Social Contract. Chicago: Henry Regnery Company, 1954.

Selby-Bigge, L. A., ed. British Moralists. 2 vols. New York: Dover Publications, 1965.

Sen, A. K. Collective Choice and Social Welfare. San Francisco: Holden-Day, 1970.

Sidgwick, Henry. The Methods of Ethics (1907). 7th ed. New York: Dover Publications, 1966.

Singer, Marcus G. Generalization in Ethics. New York: Alfred A. Knopf, 1961.

Wagner, Walter C. "Future Morality," The Futurist, October 1971, 197-99.

Williams, Bernard A. O. "The Idea of Equality," in Philosophy, Politics, and Society, eds. Peter Laslett and W. G. Runciman. 2nd series. Oxford: Basil Blackwell, 1962, pp. 110-31.

Wolff, Robert Paul. "Reflections on Game Theory and the Nature of Value," Ethics, LXXII (April 1961), 171-79.

_____. "A Refutation of Rawls' Theorem on Justice," The Journal of Philosophy, LXIII (March 31, 1966), 179-90.

Young, Michael. The Rise of Meritocracy. London: Thames
     and Hudson, 1958.

J. *Natural Law Theory*

Adams, James Luther. "The Law of Nature in Greco-Roman
     Thought," Journal of Religion, XXV (1945), 97-118.

_____. "The Law of Nature: Some General
     Considerations," Journal of Religion, XXV (1945),
     88-96.

Anscombe, G. E. I. and P. T. Geach. Three Philosophers.
     Oxford: The University Press, 1961.

Armstrong, Ross. Primary and Secondary Precepts in Thomistic
     Natural Law Theory. The Hague: Martinus Nijhoff, 1966.

Beis, R. H. "Contraception and the Logical Structure of
     the Thomist Natural Law Theory," Ethics, LXXV (July
     1965), 277-84.

Bourke, Vernon J. Ethics: A Textbook in Moral Philosophy.
     New York: Macmillan Co., 1958.

_____. "Natural Law, Thomism -- and Professor
     Nielsen," Natural Law Forum, V (1960), 112-19.

Carlyle, R. W. and A. J. Carlyle. A History of Medieval
     Political Theory in the West. 6 vols. Edinburgh:
     Blackwood and Sons, 1903-36.

Chroust, Anton-Hermann. "The Philosophy of Law from St.
     Augustine to St. Thomas Aquinas," The New Scholasti-
     cism, XX (1946), 26-71.

Cochrane, Charles N. Christianity and Classical Culture.
     Oxford: The Clarendon Press, 1940.

D'Entreves, A. P. Natural Law; An Historical Survey.
     Torchbook edition. New York: Harper & Row, 1965.

Farrell, Walter. The Natural Moral Law According to St.
     Thomas and Suarez. Ditchling, England: St. Dominic's
     Press, 1930.

_____. "Sources of St. Thomas' Concept of Natural
     Law," The Thomist, XX (1957), 237-94.

Flückiger, Felix. Geschichte des Naturrechts. Zolliken-
     Zürich: Evangelischer Verlag, 1954.

Fuchs, Joseph, S.J. Natural Law; A Theological Investigation.
     New York: Sheed and Ward, 1965.

Gierke, Otto. Natural Law and the Theory of Society. Trans.
     Ernest Barker. Cambridge, Eng.: The University
     Press, 1934.

274

Gilson, Etienne. _Moral Values and the Moral Life; The System of St. Thomas Aquinas._ St. Louis, Mo.: B. Herder Book Co., 1941.

Grotius, Hugo. _Hugonis Grotii De jure belli ac pacis libri tres_, ed. J. B. Scott. 2 vols. Classics of International Law edition. Washington, D.C.: Carnegie Institution, 1913-25.

Lottin, Odon. _Le droit naturel chez Saint Thomas et ses prédécesseurs. Ephemerides Theologicae Lovanienses_, 1925-26.

Maritain, Jacques. _Man and the State._ Chicago: University of Chicago Press, 1951.

_____. _The Rights of Man and Natural Law._ New York: Charles Scribner's Sons, 1943.

Niebuhr, Reinhold. _Man's Nature and His Communities._ New York: Charles Scribner's Sons, 1965.

_____. _The Nature and Destiny of Man._ 2 vols. New York: Charles Scribner's Sons, 1941.

Nielsen, Kai. "An Examination of the Thomistic Theory of Natural Moral Law," _Natural Law Forum_, V (1960), 112-19.

Rommen, Heinrich. _The Natural Law._ St. Louis, Mo.: B. Herder Book Co., 1947.

Suarez, Francisco de. _Selections from Three Works_, Vol. II, ed. J. B. Scott. Classics of International Law edition. Oxford: The Clarendon Press, 1944.

Thomas Aquinas, Saint. _Summa contra Gentiles._ Fathers of the English Dominican Province edition. 5 vols. London: Burns, Oates and Washbourne, 1923-29.

_____. _Summa Theologica._ Fathers of the English Dominican Province edition. 21 vols. London: R. and T. Washbourne, 1912-25.

Tonneau, Jean. "The Teaching of the Thomist Tract on Law," _The Thomist_, XX (1957), 11-88.

Troeltsch, Ernst. _The Social Teachings of the Christian Churches._ 2 vols. New York: Harper and Brothers, 1960.

Ulpian. _The Institutes of Gaius and Rules of Ulpian._ Edinburgh: T. and T. Clark, 1904.

Vanderpol, A. _La Doctrine scholastique du droit de guerre._ Paris: A. Pedone, 1919.

Worland, Stephen. _Scholasticism and Welfare Economics._ Notre Dame: University of Notre Dame Press, 1967.

275

K. *Population Policy*

Ball, William R. "Population Control, Civic and Constitutional
Concerns," in Religion and the Public Order, Vol. 4,
ed. Donald Giannella. Ithaca: Cornell University
Press, 1968, pp. 128-69.

Berelson, Bernard. "Beyond Family Planning," Studies in
Family Planning, No. 38, February 1969, 1-16; also,
Science, CLXIII (February 7, 1969), 533-43.

_____. "National Family Planning Programs: A
Guide," Studies in Family Planning, No. 5 (December
1964), 1-12.

Blake, Judith. "Population Policy for Americans: Is the
Government Being Misled?" Science, CLXIV (May 2, 1969),
522-29.

Boulding, Kenneth. The Meaning of the Twentieth Century. New
York: Harper & Row, 1964.

Brown, Peter and Eunice Corfman. "An Historical Analysis of
Some Moral-Political Values as These Bear on Population
Control and Distribution," Documentary Study prepared
for the Commission on Population Growth and the American
Future. Hastings-on-Hudson, New York: Institute of
Society, Ethics and the Life Sciences, 1971.

Bumpass, L. and C. Westoff, "The Perfect Contraceptive Population," Science, CLXIX (September 18, 1970), 1177-82.

Callahan, Daniel. Ethics and Population Limitation. New
York: The Population Council, 1971. A somewhat shorter
version of this appears in Science, CLXXV (February 4,
1972), 477-86.

Cowles, Raymond B. "The Non-Baby Bonus," The Meaning of
Wilderness to Science, ed. David Brower. Sierra Club,
1960.

Crowe, Beryl L. "The Tragedy of the Commons Revisited,"
Science, CLXVI (November 28, 1969), 11-3-07.

Davis, Kingsley. "The Nature and Purpose of Population
Policy," in California's Twenty Million, eds. Kingsley
Davis and Frederick G. Styles. Population Monograph
Series, No. 10. Berkeley, California: Institute of
International Studies, University of California, 1971,
pp. 3-29.

_____. "Population Policy: Will Current Programs
Succeed?" Science, CLVIII (November 10, 1967), 730-39.

Day, Alice Taylor. "Population Control and Personal Freedom:
Are They Compatible?" The Humanist (November-December
1968), 7-10.

276

Demeny, Paul. "The Economics of Government Payments to Limit
    Population: A Comment," Economic Development and
    Cultural Change, IX (July 1961), 641-44.

Djerassi, Carl. "Birth Control after 1984: A Realistic
    Appraisal of Future Contraceptive Developments," in
    Are Our Descendants Doomed, eds. Harrison Brown and
    Edward Hutchings, Jr. New York: The Viking Press,
    1972, pp. 122-63.

_____. "Contraception 1984: Putting Something in
    the Water Supply," Family Planning Perspectives, II
    (June 1970), 29.

Dyck, Arthur. "Population Policy and Ethical Acceptability,"
    in National Academy of Sciences, Rapid Population
    Growth; Consequences and Policy Implications. Balti-
    more: Johns Hopkins Press, 1971, pp. 618-38.

_____. "Procreative Rights and Population Policy,"
    MS in the possession of this writer to be published in
    a forthcoming volume edited by Leon Kass and Daniel
    Callahan, Human Rights and Population Policy. Yale
    University Press.

_____. "Questions for the Global Conscience,"
    Psychology Today, II (September 1968), 38-42.

_____. "Religious Views and Population Policy in
    the United States," Documentary Study prepared for the
    Commission on Population Growth and the American
    Future. Hastings-on-Hudson, New York: Institute of
    Society, Ethics and the Life Sciences, 1971.

Eldridge, Hope T. "Population: Population Policies,"
    International Encyclopedia of the Social Sciences.
    New York: Macmillan and The Free Press, 1968. Vol.
    XII, pp. 381-88.

Elliot, Robin, Lynn C. Landman, Richard Lincoln and Theodore
    Tsuruoka. "U.S. Population Growth and Family Planning:
    A Review of the Literature," Family Planning Perspec-
    tives, II (October 1970), i-xvi.

Enke, Stephen. "The Economics of Government Payments to
    Limit Population," Economic Development and Cultural
    Change, VIII (July 1960), 339-48.

_____. "Government Bonuses for Smaller Families,"
    Population Review, IV (1960), 48-49.

Fagley, Richard M. "A Protestant View of Population Control,"
    Law and Contemporary Problems, XXV (Summer 1960),
    470-49.

Finnigan, Oliver D. III, and T. H. Sun. "Planning, Starting,
    and Operating an Educational Incentives Project,"
    Studies in Family Planning, III (January 1972), 1-7.

Golding, Martin P., Donald P. Warwick, Robert M. Veatch and
    Peter G. Brown. "Population and Four American Values,"
    Documentary Study prepared for the Commission on Popu-
    lation Growth and the American Future. Hastings-on-
    Hudson, New York: Institute of Society, Ethics, and
    the Life Sciences, 1971.

Harvard Law Review. Note. "Legal Analysis and Population
    Control: The Problem of Coercion," Harvard Law Review,
    LXXXIV (June 1971), 1856-1911.

Johnson, President Lyndon B. "Message to Congress on
    Domestic Health and Education," March 1, 1966.

Kangas, Lenni. "Integrated Incentives for Fertility Control,"
    Science, CLXIX (1969), 1278-84.

Ketchel, Melvin M. "Fertility Control Agents as a Possible
    Solution to the World Population Problem," Perspectives
    in Biology and Medicine, XI (Summer 1968), 687-703.

Krishnakumar, S. "Kerala's Pioneering Experiment in Massive
    Vasectomy Camps," Studies in Family Planning, III
    (August 1972), 177-85.

Meier, Richard L. Modern Science and the Human Fertility
    Problem. New York: John Wiley & Sons, 1959.

Murray, Robert. "Some Aspects of Population Policy from the
    Perspective of the Population Geneticist," Documentary
    Study prepared for the Commission on Population Growth
    and the American Future. Hastings-on-Hudson, New York:
    Institute of Society, Ethics and the Life Sciences,
    1971.

Nixon, Richard. "Message from the President of the United
    States Relative to Population Growth," H. R. Doc. No.
    139, 91st Congress, 1st Session 3 (1969).

Packwood, Robert. "S. 3632, 91st Congress, 2nd Session (1970).
    A Bill . . . to Limit the Number of Personal Exemptions
    Allowable for Children of a Taxpayer Who Are Born After
    1972."

Pohlman, Edward. Incentives and Compensations in Birth
    Planning. Chapel Hill, North Carolina: Carolina
    Population Center, 1971.

Potter, Ralph B. "Coercion and Population Policy," MS in
    possession of this writer, to be published in a forth-
    coming volume edited by Daniel Callahan and Leon Kass,
    Human Rights and Population Policy. Yale University
    Press.

Ridker, Ronald G. "Desired Family Size and the Efficacy of
    Current Family Programs," Population Studies, XXIII
    (1969), 279-84.

_____. "Savings Accounts for Family Planning:
    An Illustration from the Tea Estates of India," Studies
    in Family Planning, II (1971), 241-48.

Ridker, Ronald G. "Synopsis of a Proposal for a Family
    Planning Bond," Studies in Family Planning, No. 43
    (1969), 11-16.

Rogers, Everett M. "Incentives in the Diffusion of Family
    Planning Innovations," Studies in Family Planning, II
    (December 1971), 241-48.

Samuel, T. "The Strengthening of the Motivation for Family
    Limitation in India," The Journal of Family Welfare,
    XIII (1966), 11-12.

Simon, Julian L. "The Role of Bonuses and Persuasive Propa-
    ganda in the Reduction of Birth Rates," Economic
    Development and Cultural Change, XVI (September 1968),
    404-11.

Smith, M. Brewster. "Ethical Implications of Population
    Policies: A Psychologist's View," The American
    Psychologist, XXVII (January 1972), 31-36.

Sollitto, M. S. and Stephen Viederman. "The Business Commun-
    ity and Population Policy," Documentary Study prepared
    for the Commission on Population Growth and the Ameri-
    can Future. Hastings-on-Hudson, New York: Institute
    of Society, Ethics and the Life Sciences, 1971.

Spengler, Joseph J. "Population Problem: In Search of a
    Solution," Science, CLXVI (December 5, 1969), 1234-38.

Taylor, Howard C. Jr., and Bernard Berelson. "Comprehensive
    Family Planning Based on Maternal/Child Health Servi-
    ces: A Feasibility Study for a World Program,"
    Studies in Family Planning, II (February 1971), 21-54.

Thakor, V. H., and Vonod M. Patel. "The Gujarat State
    Massive Vasectomy Campaign," Studies in Family Planning,
    III (August 1972), 186-92.

Veatch, Robert M. "An Ethical Analysis of Population Policy
    Proposals," Documentary Study prepared for the Com-
    mission on Population Growth and the American Future.
    Hastings-on-Hudson, New York: Institute of Society,
    Ethics and the Life Sciences, 1971.

_____. "A Proposal for Taxing Childbearing: Can
    It Be Just?" Working Paper of the Institute of Society,
    Ethics and the Life Sciences. Hastings-on-Hudson,
    New York, 1971.

Williamson, John. "Welfare Policy and Population Policy:
    A Conflict in Goals?" Urban and Social Change Review,
    IV (Fall 1970), 21-23.

Wishik, Samuel. "Population Programs and Policy," Villanova
    Law Review, XV (Summer 1970), 808-17.